BOUNTY™

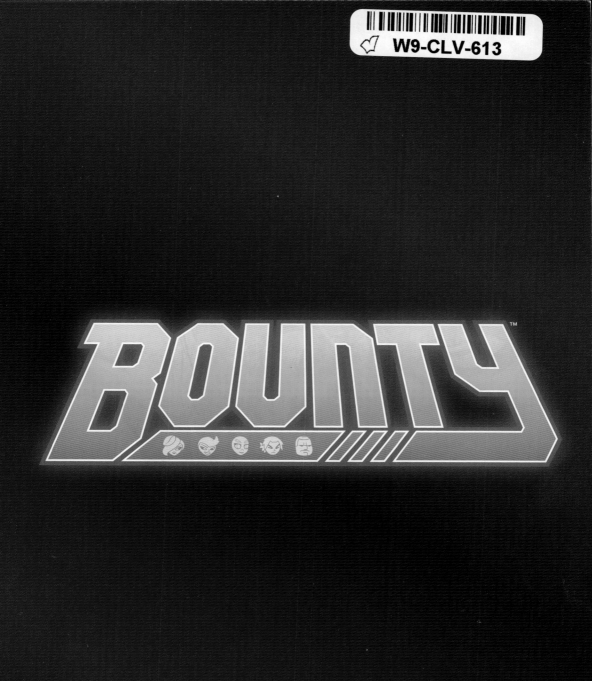

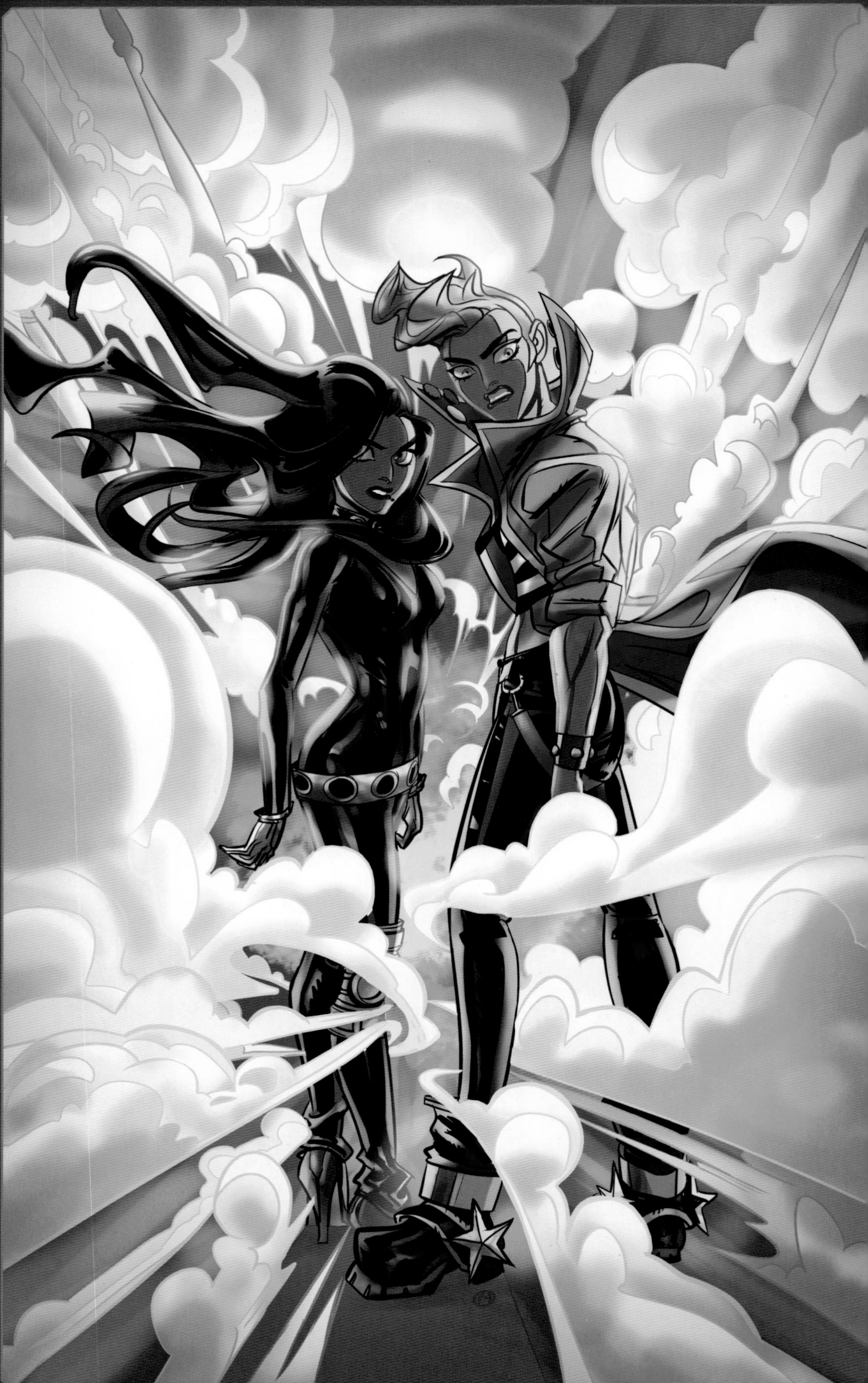

STORY
KURTIS WIEBE

ART
MINDY LEE

COLORS
LEONARDO OLEA

LETTERS
NATE PIEKOS OF BLAMBOT®

COVER ART AND CHAPTER BREAKS
MINDY LEE WITH **ANDY COTNAM**
AND **LEONARDO OLEA**

DARK HORSE BOOKS

PRESIDENT AND PUBLISHER
MIKE RICHARDSON

EDITOR
DANIEL CHABON

ASSISTANT EDITOR
CARDNER CLARK

DESIGNER
JIMMY PRESLER

DIGITAL ART TECHNICIAN
CHRISTINA McKENZIE

Neil Hankerson Executive Vice President · Tom Weddle Chief Financial Officer · Randy Stradley
Vice President of Publishing · Matt Parkinson Vice President of Marketing · David Scroggy
Vice President of Product Development · Dale LaFountain Vice President of Information
Technology · Cara Niece Vice President of Production and Scheduling · Nick McWhorter Vice
President of Media Licensing · Mark Bernardi Vice President of Digital and Book Trade Sales
· Ken Lizzi General Counsel · Dave Marshall Editor in Chief · Davey Estrada Editorial Director ·
Scott Allie Executive Senior Editor · Chris Warner Senior Books Editor · Cary Grazzini Director
of Specialty Projects · Lia Ribacchi Art Director · Vanessa Todd Director of Print Purchasing ·
Matt Dryer Director of Digital Art and Prepress · Sarah Robertson Director of Product Sales ·
Michael Gombos Director of International Publishing and Licensing

Published by Dark Horse Books

A division of Dark Horse Comics, Inc.
10956 SE Main Street, Milwaukie, OR 97222

First edition: March 2017
ISBN 978-1-50670-044-1

Library of Congress Cataloging-in-Publication Data

Names: Wiebe, Kurtis J., 1979- author. | Lee, Mindy, artist. | Olea,
     Leonardo, colorist, artist. | Piekos, Nate, letterer. | Cotnam, Andy,
     artist.
Title: Bounty / story, Kurtis Wiebe ; art, Mindy Lee ; colors, Leonardo Olea
     ; letters, Nate Piekos of Blambot ; cover art and chapter breaks, Mindy
     Lee, with Andy Cotnam and Leonardo Olea.
Description: First edition. | Milwaukie, OR : Dark Horse Books, 2017- | v. 1.
     "This volume collects the Dark Horse Comics series Bounty #1-#5"
Identifiers: LCCN 2016038574 | ISBN 9781506700441 (paperback)
Subjects: | BISAC: COMICS & GRAPHIC NOVELS / Science Fiction. | COMICS &
     GRAPHIC NOVELS / Fantasy. | COMICS & GRAPHIC NOVELS / General.
Classification: LCC PN6728.B6417 W54 2017 | DDC 741.5/973--dc23
LC record available at https://lccn.loc.gov/2016038574

1 3 5 7 9 10 8 6 4 2
Printed in China

International Licensing: (503) 905-2377 | Comic Shop Locator Service: (888) 266-4226

This volume collects the Dark Horse Comics series *Bounty* #1-#5.

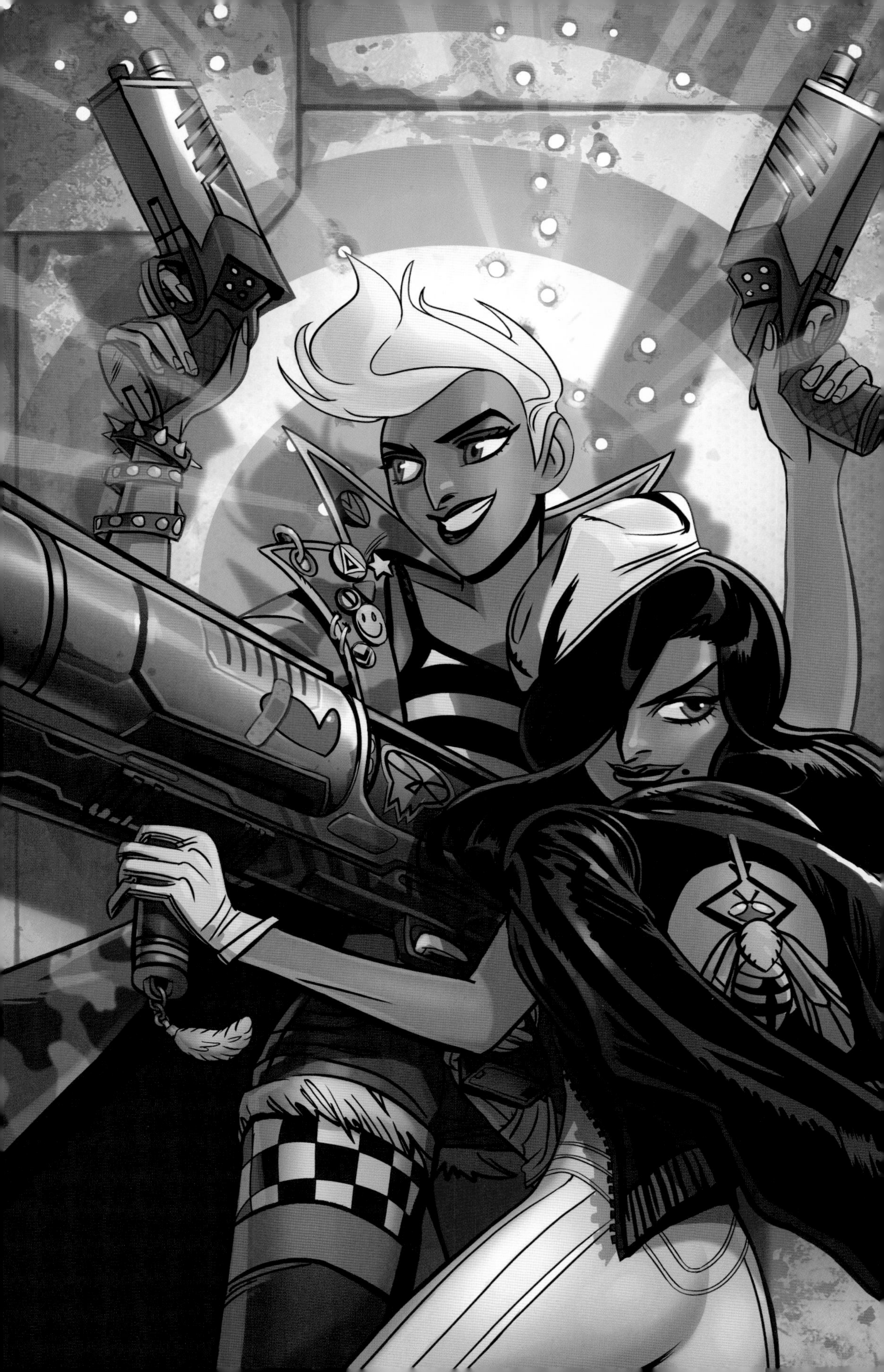

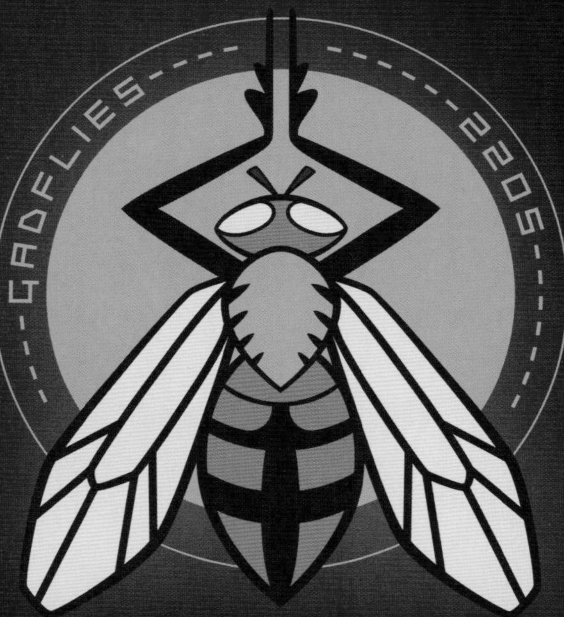
GADFLIES
2205

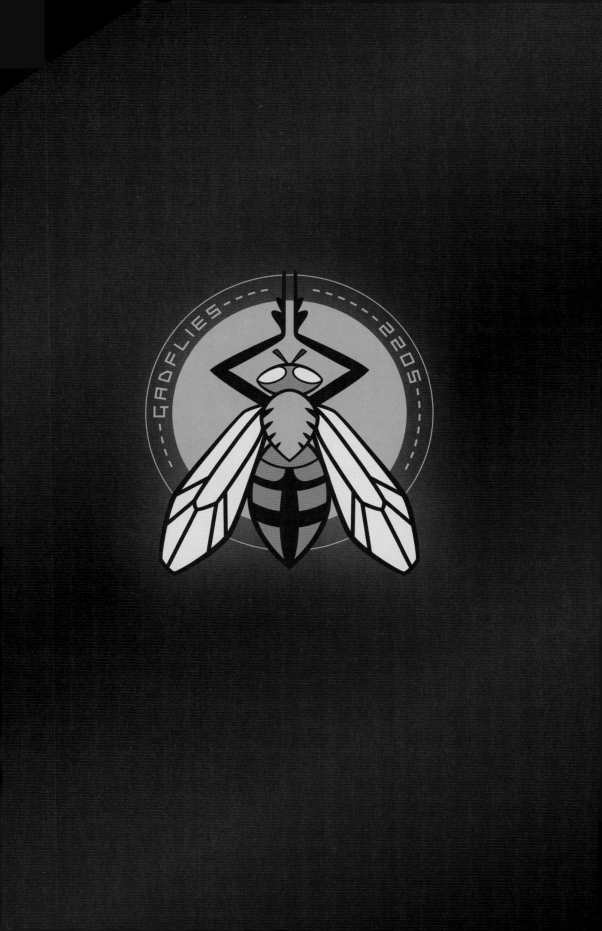

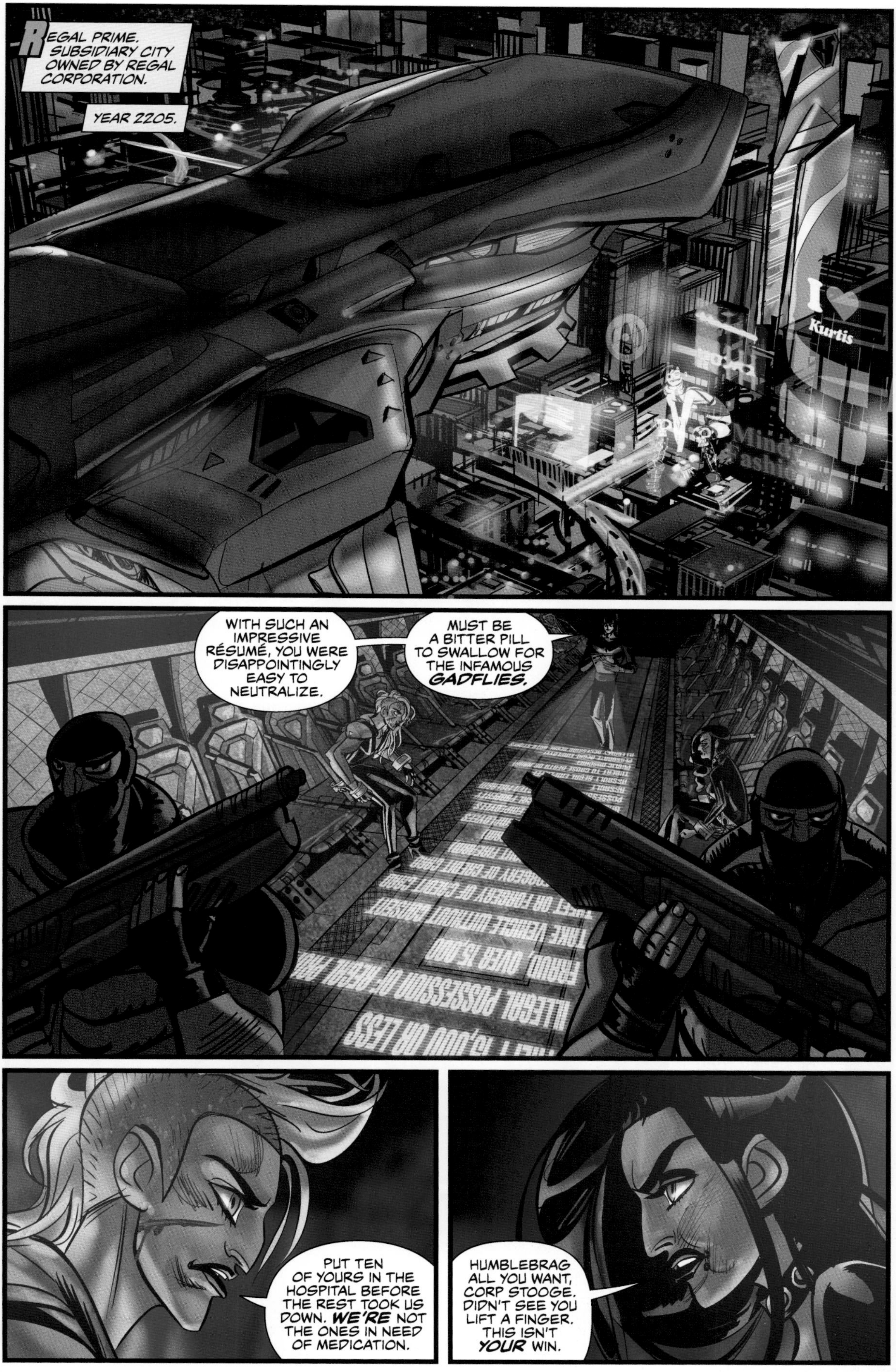
REGAL PRIME. SUBSIDIARY CITY OWNED BY REGAL CORPORATION.
YEAR 2205.
Kurtis
WITH SUCH AN IMPRESSIVE RÉSUMÉ, YOU WERE DISAPPOINTINGLY EASY TO NEUTRALIZE.
MUST BE A BITTER PILL TO SWALLOW FOR THE INFAMOUS *GADFLIES.*
PUT TEN OF YOURS IN THE HOSPITAL BEFORE THE REST TOOK US DOWN. *WE'RE* NOT THE ONES IN NEED OF MEDICATION.
HUMBLEBRAG ALL YOU WANT, CORP STOOGE. DIDN'T SEE YOU LIFT A FINGER. THIS ISN'T *YOUR* WIN.

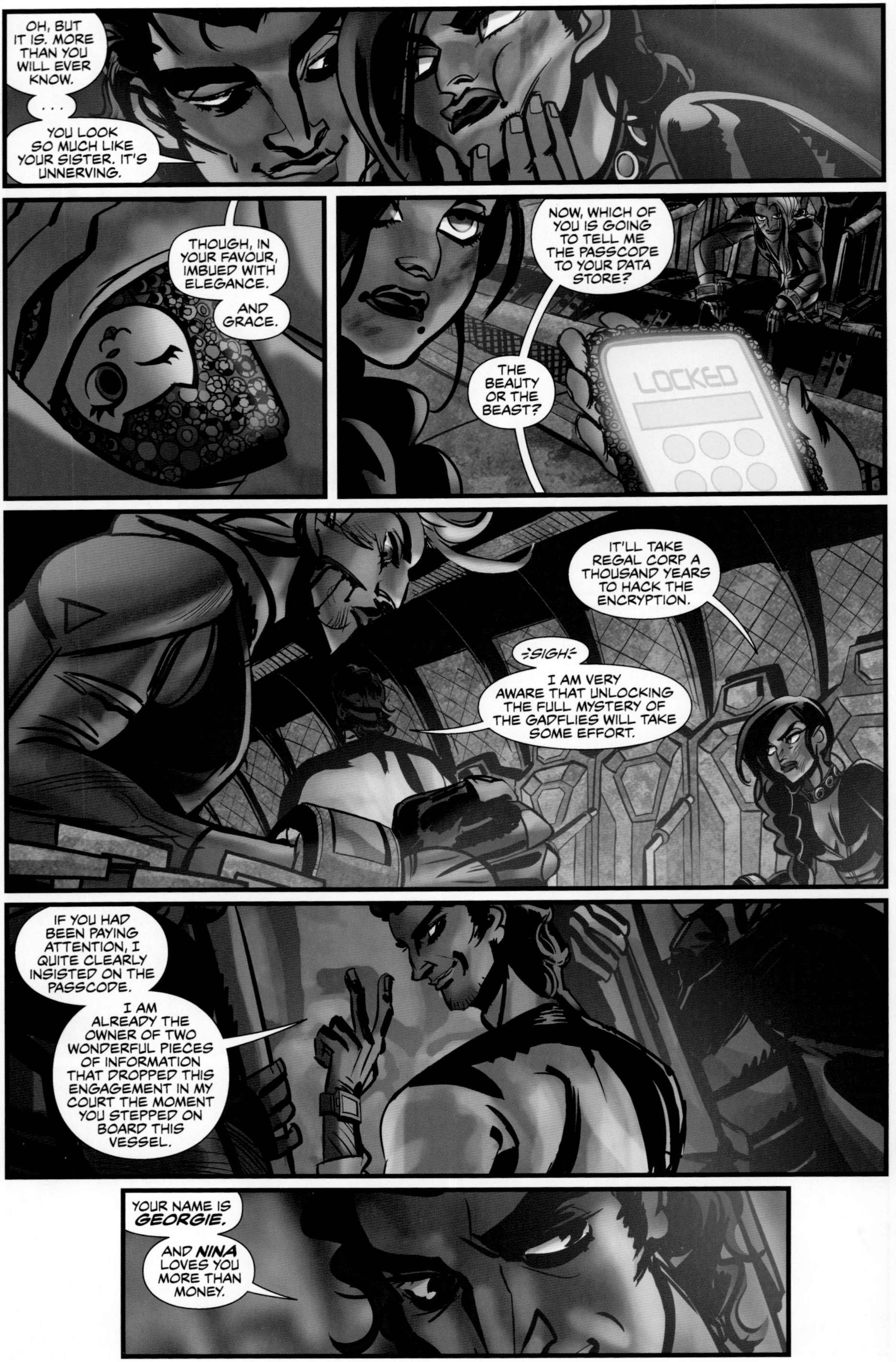
OH, BUT IT IS. MORE THAN YOU WILL EVER KNOW.
. . .
YOU LOOK SO MUCH LIKE YOUR SISTER. IT'S UNNERVING.
THOUGH, IN YOUR FAVOUR, IMBUED WITH ELEGANCE.
AND GRACE.
NOW, WHICH OF YOU IS GOING TO TELL ME THE PASSCODE TO YOUR DATA STORE?
THE BEAUTY OR THE BEAST?
LOCKED
IT'LL TAKE REGAL CORP A THOUSAND YEARS TO HACK THE ENCRYPTION.
SIGH
I AM VERY AWARE THAT UNLOCKING THE FULL MYSTERY OF THE GADFLIES WILL TAKE SOME EFFORT.
IF YOU HAD BEEN PAYING ATTENTION, I QUITE CLEARLY INSISTED ON THE PASSCODE.
I AM ALREADY THE OWNER OF TWO WONDERFUL PIECES OF INFORMATION THAT DROPPED THIS ENGAGEMENT IN MY COURT THE MOMENT YOU STEPPED ON BOARD THIS VESSEL.
YOUR NAME IS GEORGIE.
AND NINA LOVES YOU MORE THAN MONEY.

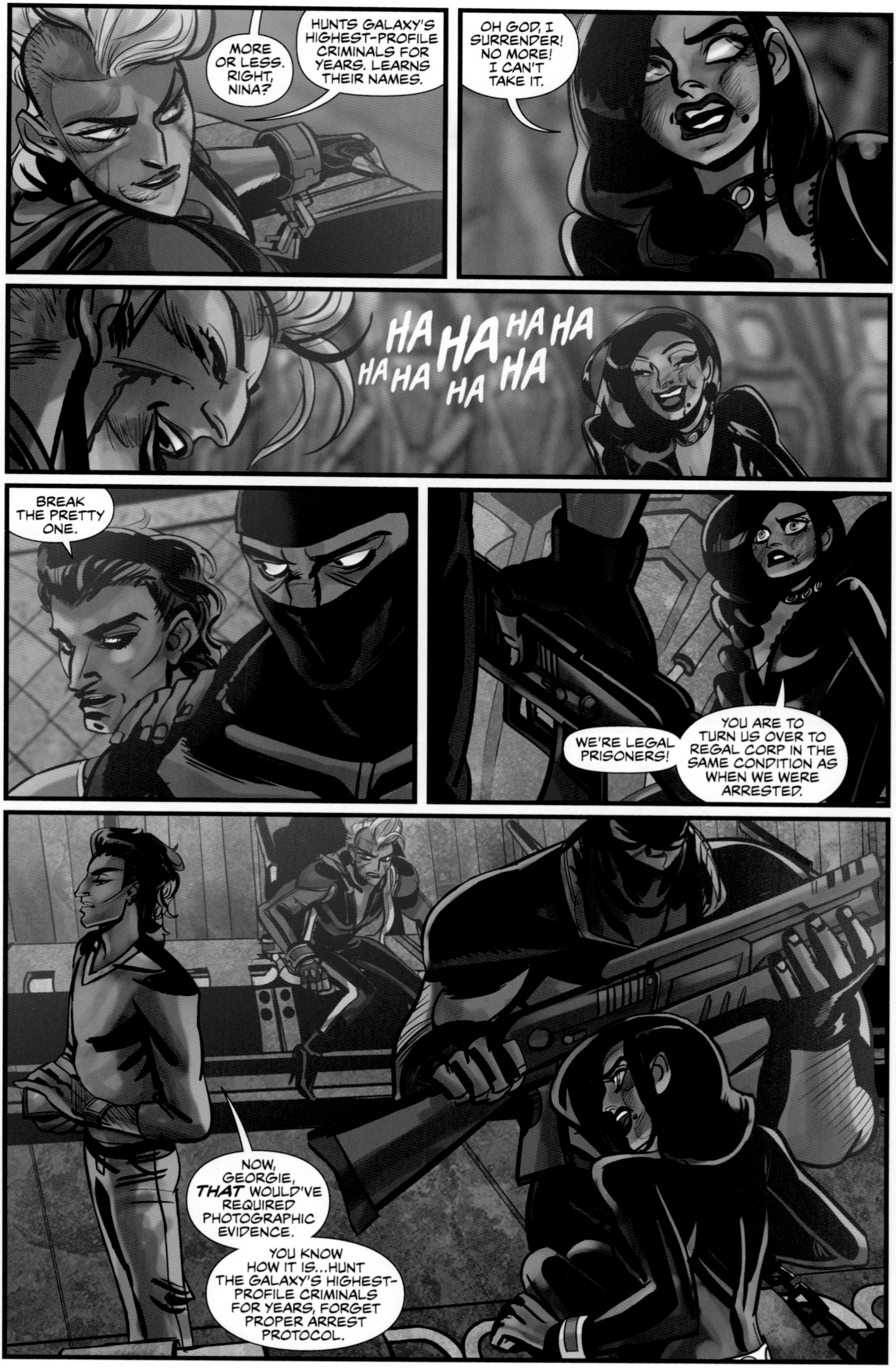
MORE OR LESS. RIGHT, NINA?
HUNTS GALAXY'S HIGHEST-PROFILE CRIMINALS FOR YEARS. LEARNS THEIR NAMES.
OH GOD, I SURRENDER! NO MORE! I CAN'T TAKE IT.
HA HA HA HA HA HA HA HA HA
BREAK THE PRETTY ONE.
WE'RE LEGAL PRISONERS!
YOU ARE TO TURN US OVER TO REGAL CORP IN THE SAME CONDITION AS WHEN WE WERE ARRESTED.
NOW, GEORGIE, THAT WOULD'VE REQUIRED PHOTOGRAPHIC EVIDENCE.
YOU KNOW HOW IT IS...HUNT THE GALAXY'S HIGHEST-PROFILE CRIMINALS FOR YEARS, FORGET PROPER ARREST PROTOCOL.

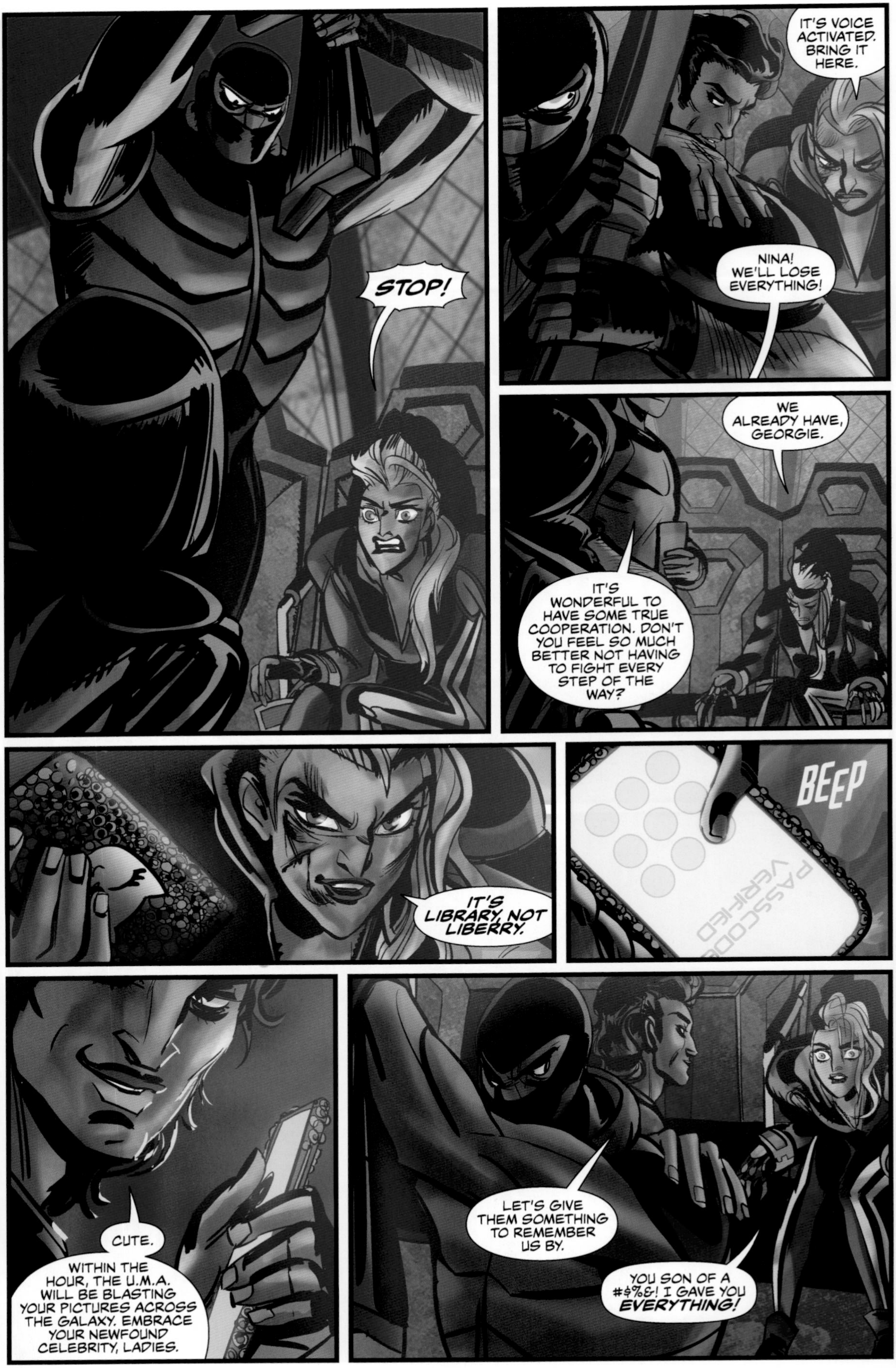
STOP!
IT'S VOICE ACTIVATED. BRING IT HERE.
NINA! WE'LL LOSE EVERYTHING!
WE ALREADY HAVE, GEORGIE.
IT'S WONDERFUL TO HAVE SOME TRUE COOPERATION. DON'T YOU FEEL SO MUCH BETTER NOT HAVING TO FIGHT EVERY STEP OF THE WAY?
IT'S LIBRARY, NOT LIBERRY.
BEEP
PASSCODE VERIFIED
CUTE.
WITHIN THE HOUR, THE U.M.A. WILL BE BLASTING YOUR PICTURES ACROSS THE GALAXY. EMBRACE YOUR NEWFOUND CELEBRITY, LADIES.
LET'S GIVE THEM SOMETHING TO REMEMBER US BY.
YOU SON OF A #$%&! I GAVE YOU EVERYTHING!

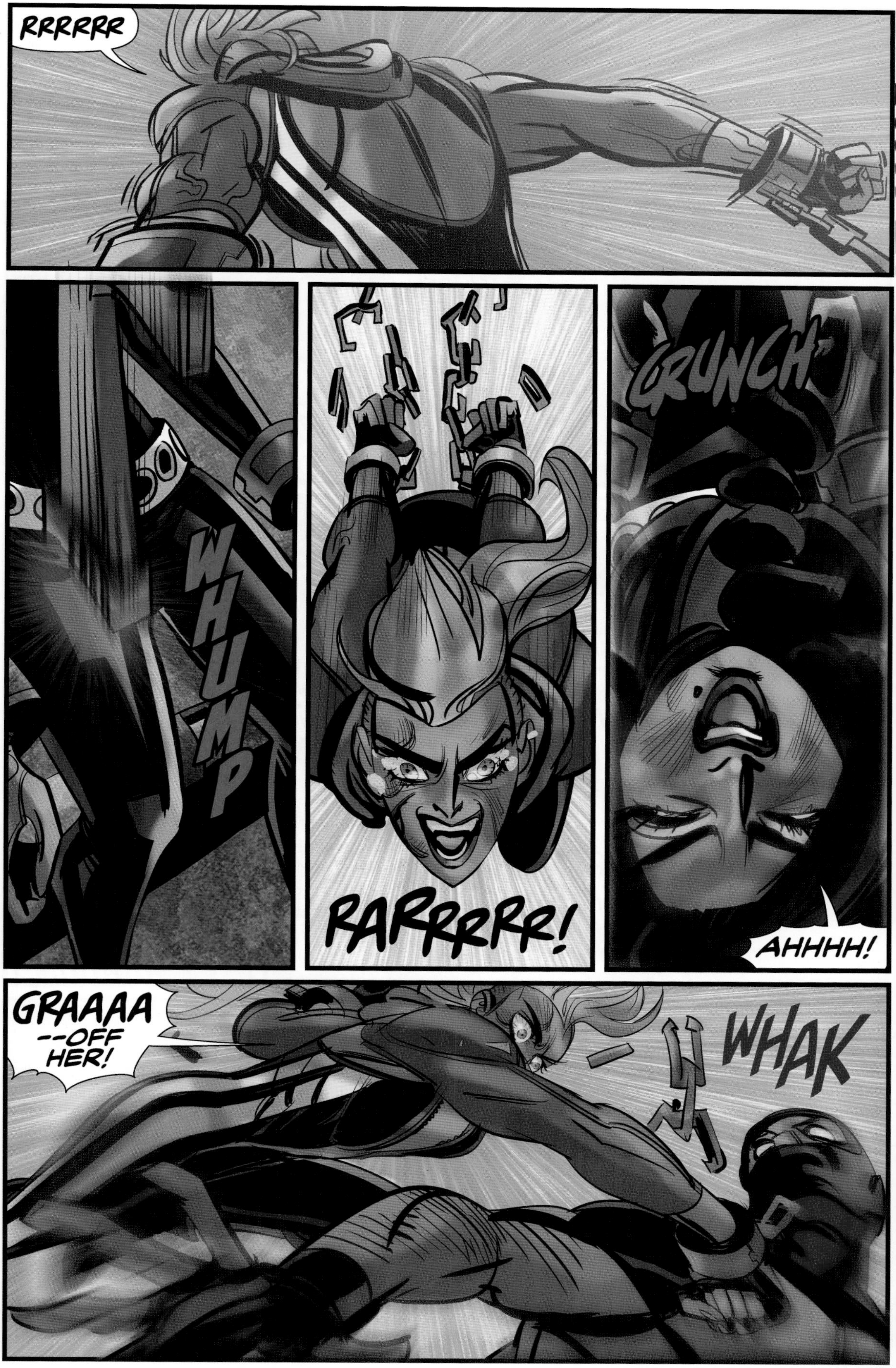
RRRRRR
WHUMP
RARRRRR!
GRUNCH
AHHHH!
GRAAAA --OFF HER!
WHAK

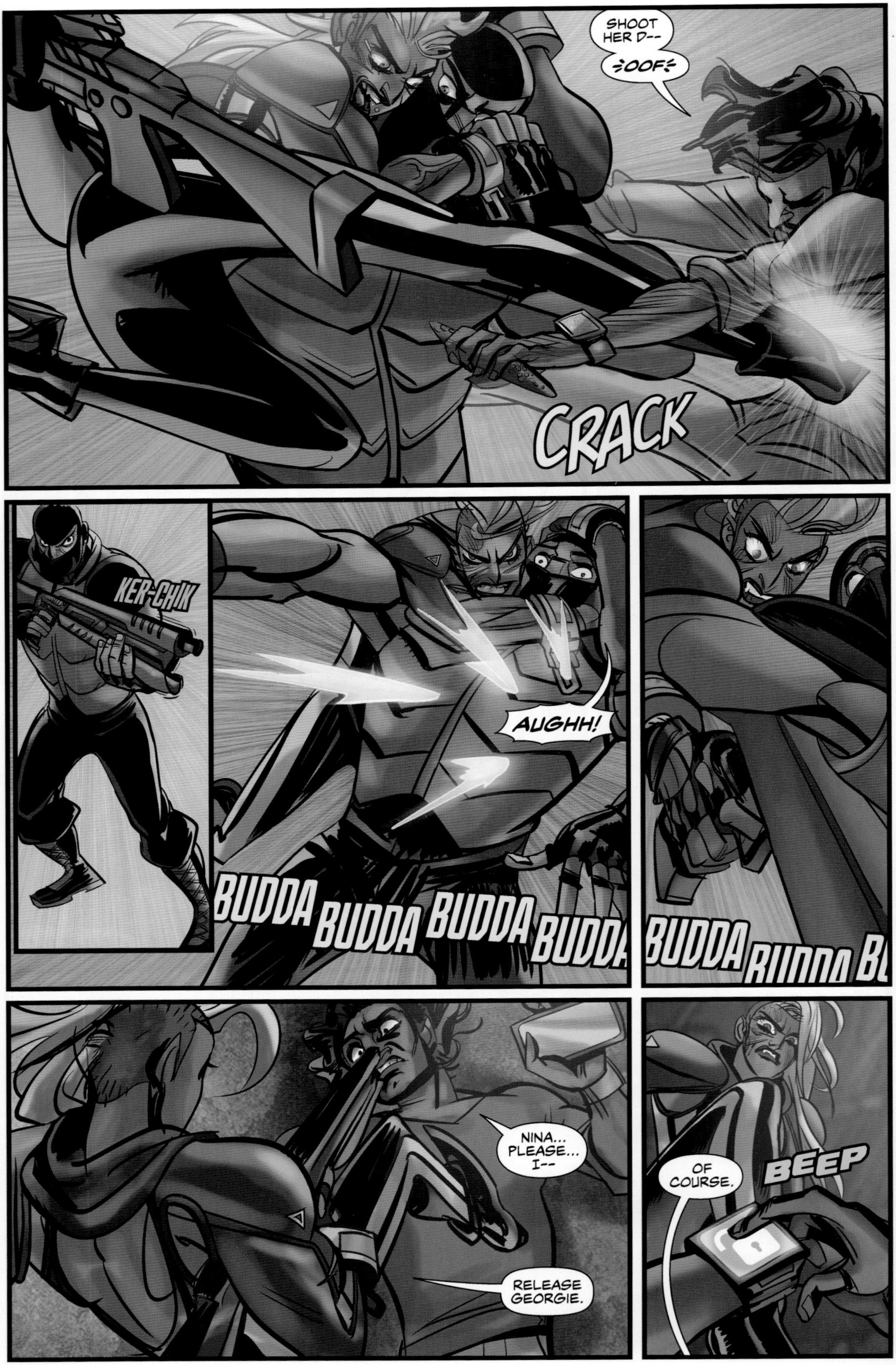
SHOOT HER D--
OOF
CRACK
KER-CHIK
AUGHH!
BUDDA BUDDA BUDDA BUDDA
BUDDA
NINA... PLEASE... I--
RELEASE GEORGIE.
OF COURSE.
BEEP

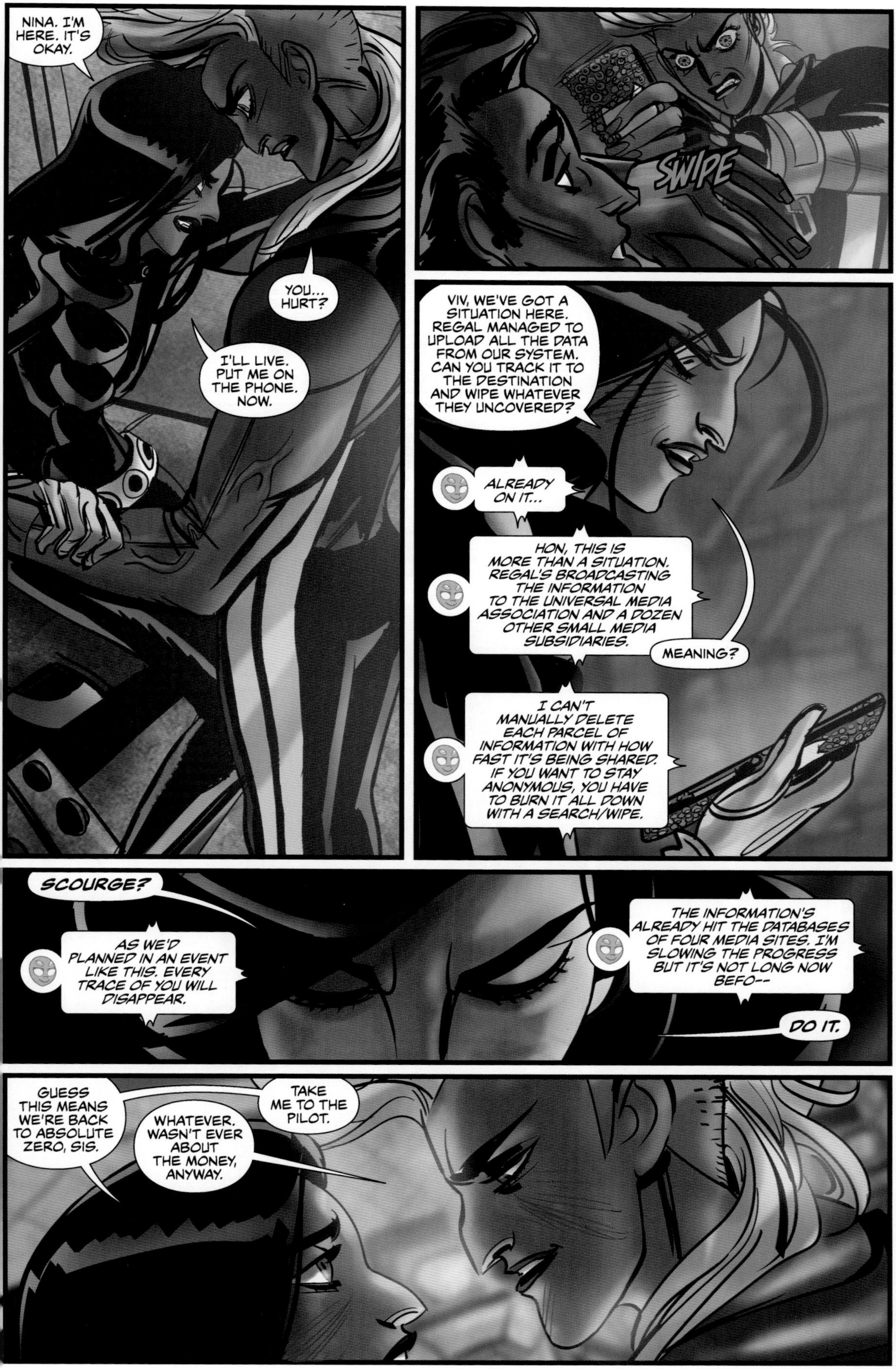
NINA. I'M HERE. IT'S OKAY.
YOU... HURT?
I'LL LIVE. PUT ME ON THE PHONE. NOW.
SWIPE
VIV, WE'VE GOT A SITUATION HERE. REGAL MANAGED TO UPLOAD ALL THE DATA FROM OUR SYSTEM. CAN YOU TRACK IT TO THE DESTINATION AND WIPE WHATEVER THEY UNCOVERED?
ALREADY ON IT...
HON, THIS IS MORE THAN A SITUATION. REGAL'S BROADCASTING THE INFORMATION TO THE UNIVERSAL MEDIA ASSOCIATION AND A DOZEN OTHER SMALL MEDIA SUBSIDIARIES.
MEANING?
I CAN'T MANUALLY DELETE EACH PARCEL OF INFORMATION WITH HOW FAST IT'S BEING SHARED. IF YOU WANT TO STAY ANONYMOUS, YOU HAVE TO BURN IT ALL DOWN WITH A SEARCH/WIPE.
SCOURGE?
AS WE'D PLANNED IN AN EVENT LIKE THIS. EVERY TRACE OF YOU WILL DISAPPEAR.
THE INFORMATION'S ALREADY HIT THE DATABASES OF FOUR MEDIA SITES. I'M SLOWING THE PROGRESS BUT IT'S NOT LONG NOW BEFO--
DO IT.
GUESS THIS MEANS WE'RE BACK TO ABSOLUTE ZERO, SIS.
TAKE ME TO THE PILOT.
WHATEVER. WASN'T EVER ABOUT THE MONEY, ANYWAY.

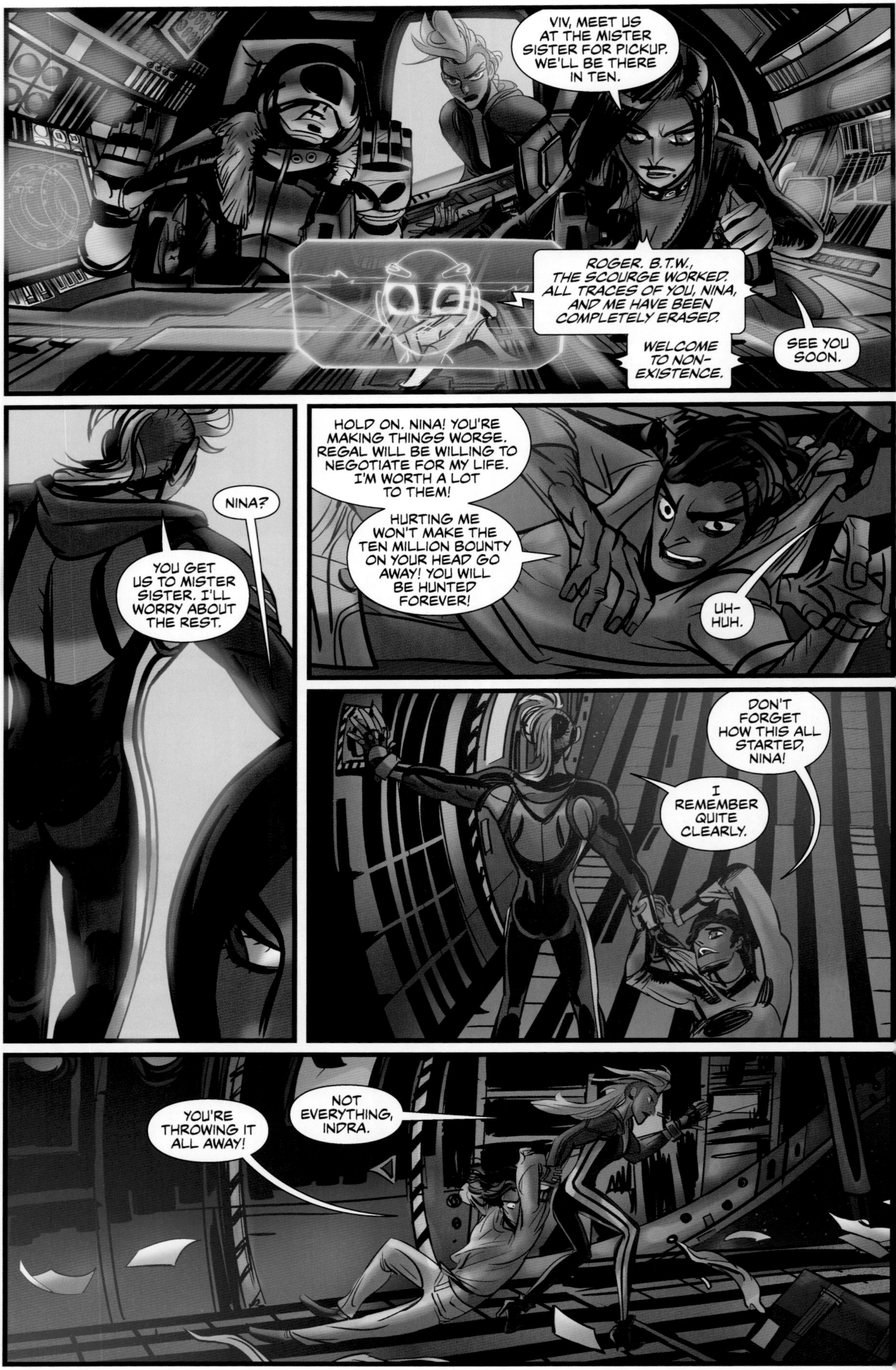
VIV, MEET US AT THE MISTER SISTER FOR PICKUP. WE'LL BE THERE IN TEN.
ROGER. B.T.W., THE SCOURGE WORKED. ALL TRACES OF YOU, NINA, AND ME HAVE BEEN COMPLETELY ERASED.
WELCOME TO NON-EXISTENCE.
SEE YOU SOON.
NINA?
YOU GET US TO MISTER SISTER. I'LL WORRY ABOUT THE REST.
HOLD ON. NINA! YOU'RE MAKING THINGS WORSE. REGAL WILL BE WILLING TO NEGOTIATE FOR MY LIFE. I'M WORTH A LOT TO THEM!
HURTING ME WON'T MAKE THE TEN MILLION BOUNTY ON YOUR HEAD GO AWAY! YOU WILL BE HUNTED FOREVER!
UH-HUH.
DON'T FORGET HOW THIS ALL STARTED, NINA!
I REMEMBER QUITE CLEARLY.
YOU'RE THROWING IT ALL AWAY!
NOT EVERYTHING, INDRA.

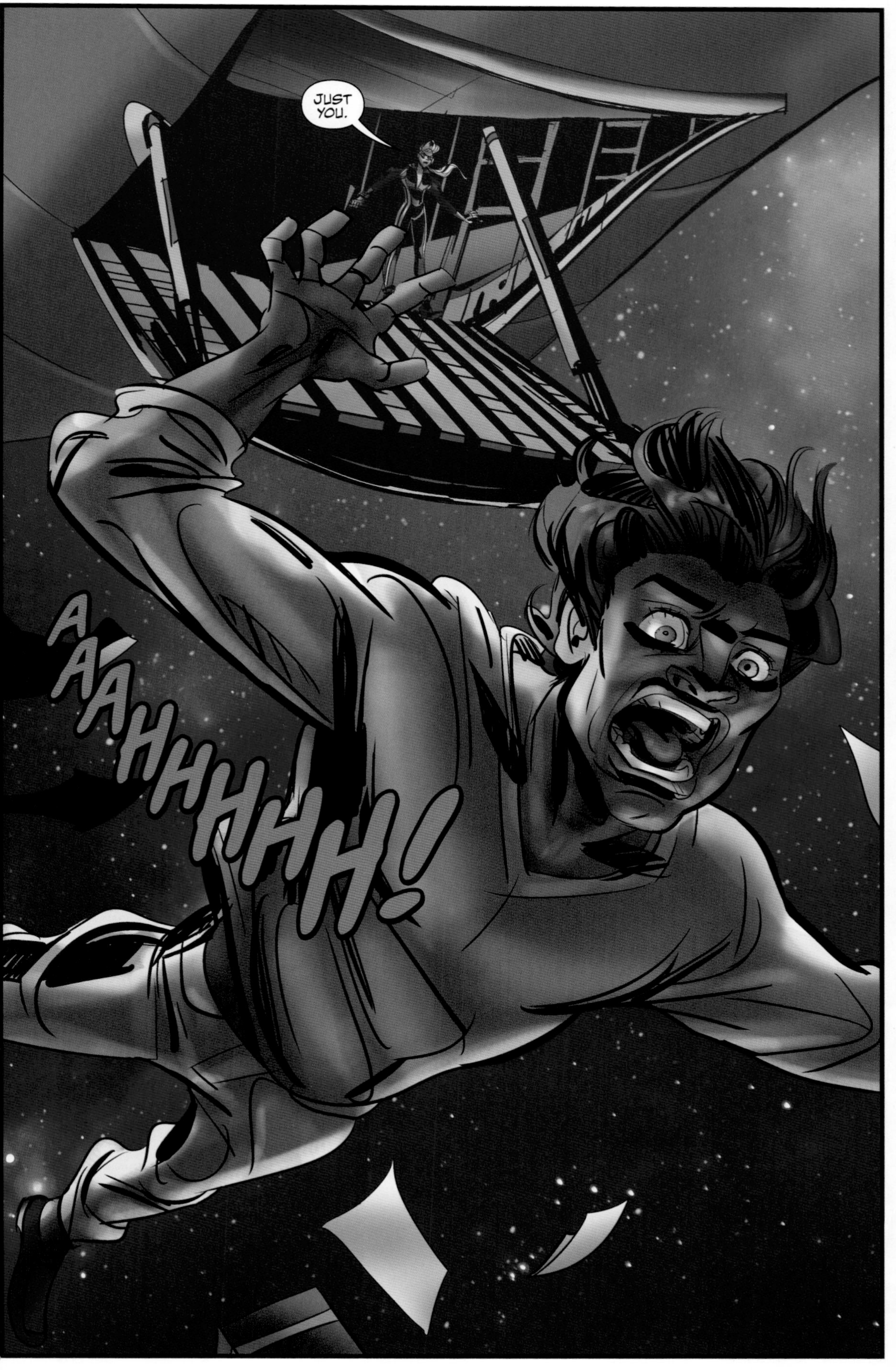
JUST YOU.
AAAHHHHHH!

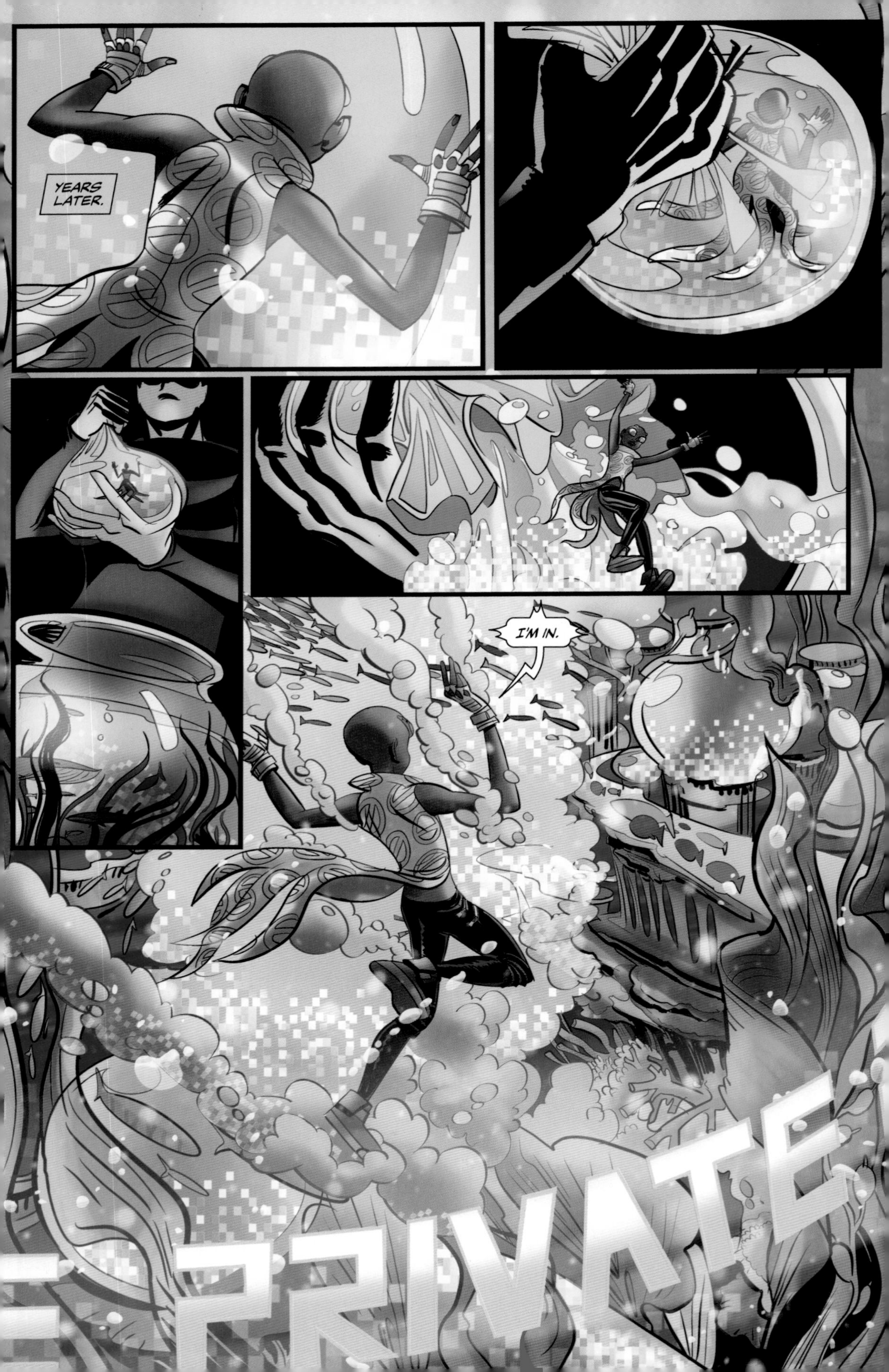
YEARS LATER.
I'M IN.
PRIVATE

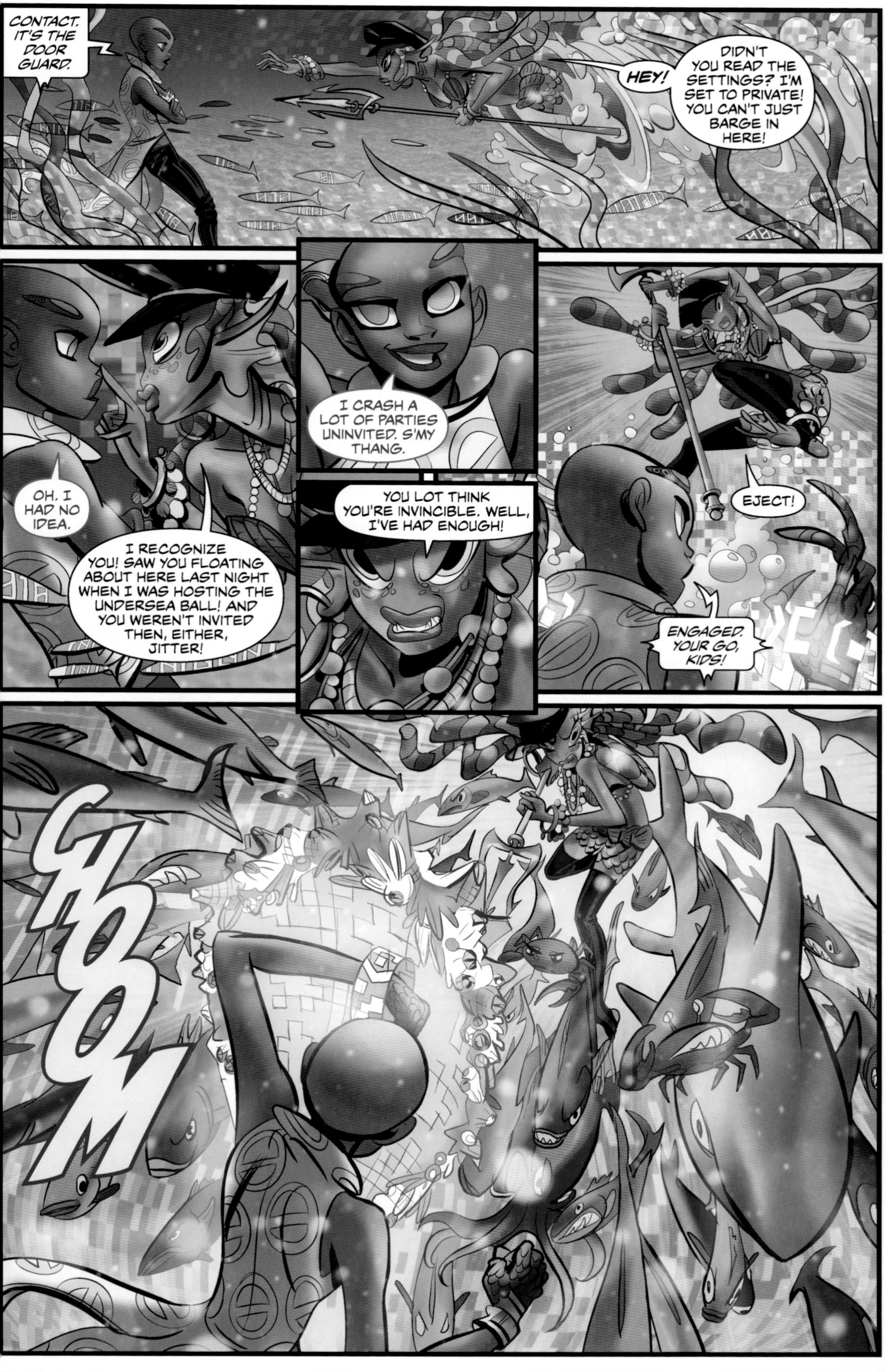
CONTACT. IT'S THE DOOR GUARD.
HEY!
DIDN'T YOU READ THE SETTINGS? I'M SET TO PRIVATE! YOU CAN'T JUST BARGE IN HERE!
OH. I HAD NO IDEA.
I RECOGNIZE YOU! SAW YOU FLOATING ABOUT HERE LAST NIGHT WHEN I WAS HOSTING THE UNDERSEA BALL! AND YOU WEREN'T INVITED THEN, EITHER, JITTER!
I CRASH A LOT OF PARTIES UNINVITED. S'MY THANG.
YOU LOT THINK YOU'RE INVINCIBLE. WELL, I'VE HAD ENOUGH!
EJECT!
ENGAGED. YOUR GO, KIDS!
CHOOM

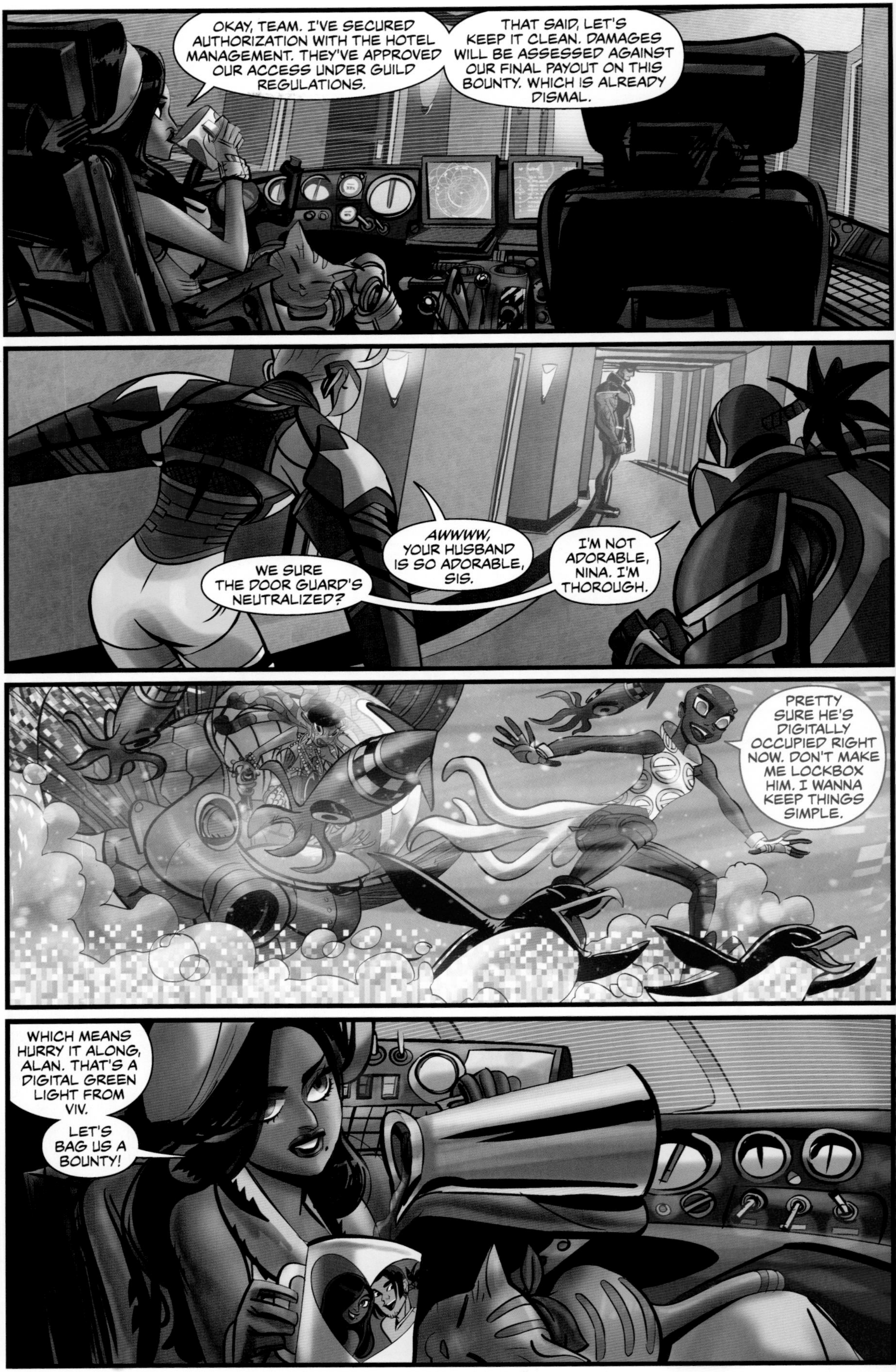
OKAY, TEAM. I'VE SECURED AUTHORIZATION WITH THE HOTEL MANAGEMENT. THEY'VE APPROVED OUR ACCESS UNDER GUILD REGULATIONS.
THAT SAID, LET'S KEEP IT CLEAN. DAMAGES WILL BE ASSESSED AGAINST OUR FINAL PAYOUT ON THIS BOUNTY. WHICH IS ALREADY DISMAL.
WE SURE THE DOOR GUARD'S NEUTRALIZED?
AWWWW, YOUR HUSBAND IS SO ADORABLE, SIS.
I'M NOT ADORABLE, NINA. I'M THOROUGH.
PRETTY SURE HE'S DIGITALLY OCCUPIED RIGHT NOW. DON'T MAKE ME LOCKBOX HIM. I WANNA KEEP THINGS SIMPLE.
WHICH MEANS HURRY IT ALONG, ALAN. THAT'S A DIGITAL GREEN LIGHT FROM VIV.
LET'S BAG US A BOUNTY!

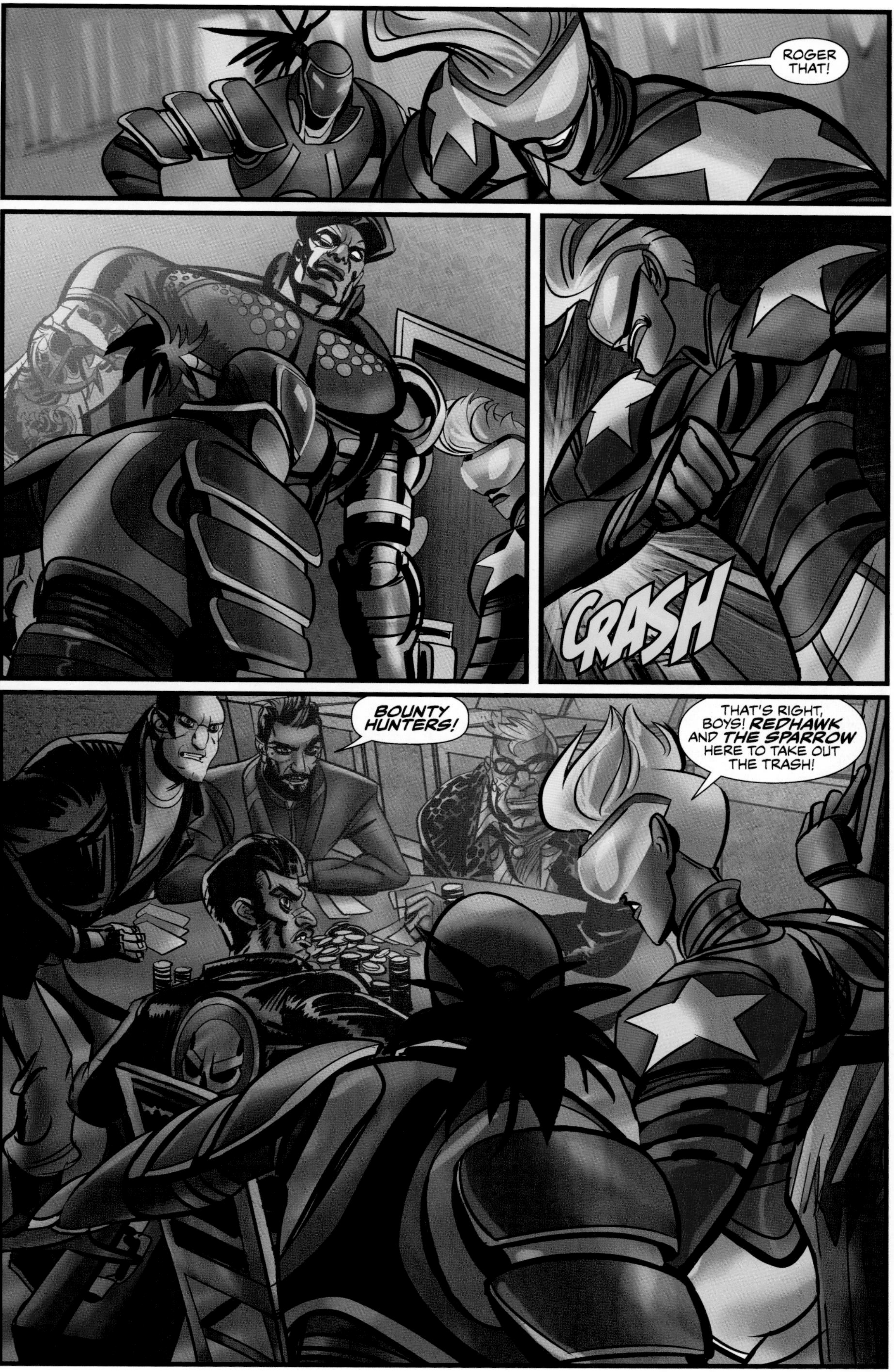
ROGER THAT!
CRASH
BOUNTY HUNTERS!
THAT'S RIGHT, BOYS! REDHAWK AND THE SPARROW HERE TO TAKE OUT THE TRASH!

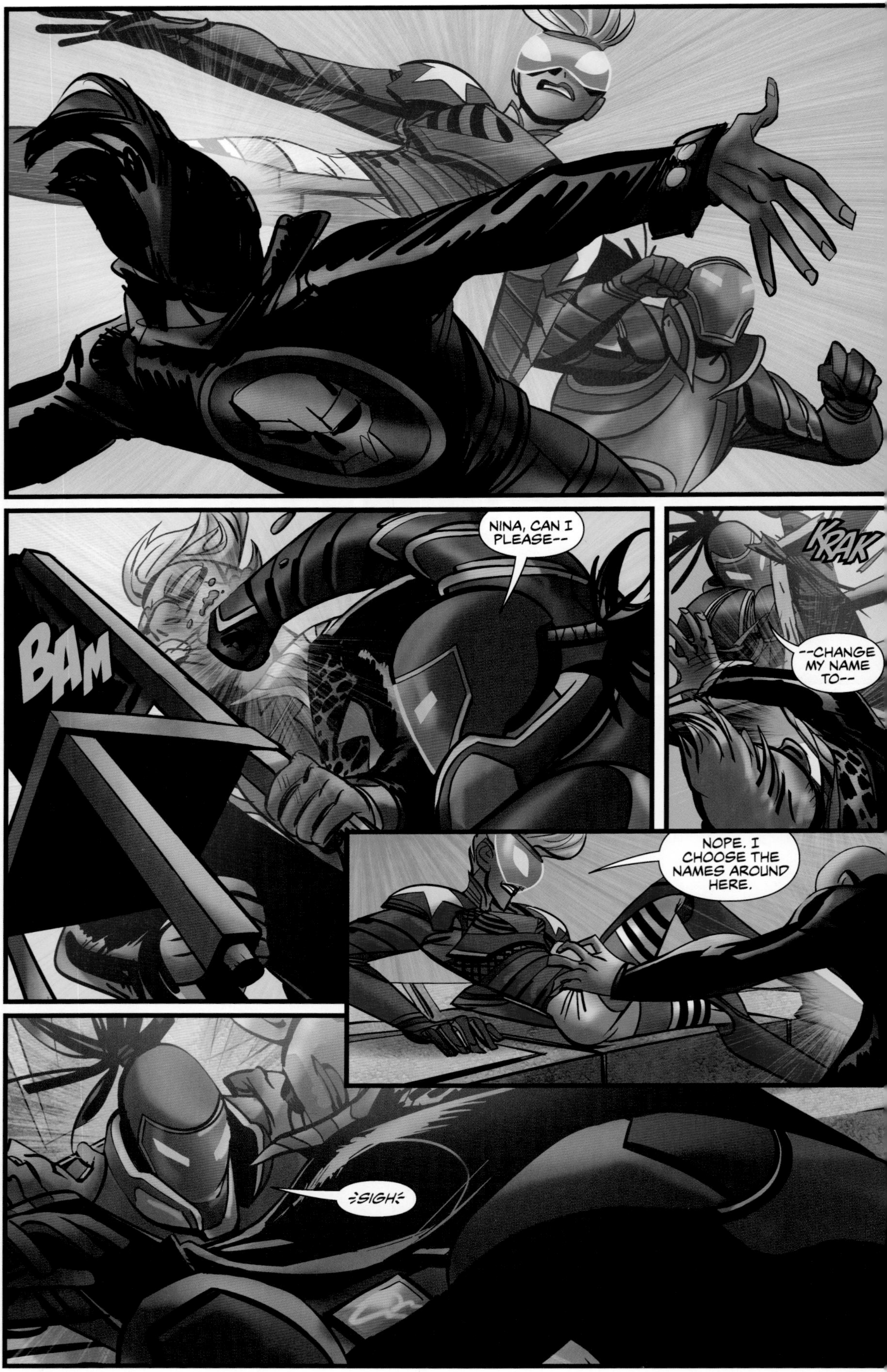
NINA, CAN I PLEASE--
BAM
KRAK
--CHANGE MY NAME TO--
NOPE. I CHOOSE THE NAMES AROUND HERE.
SIGH

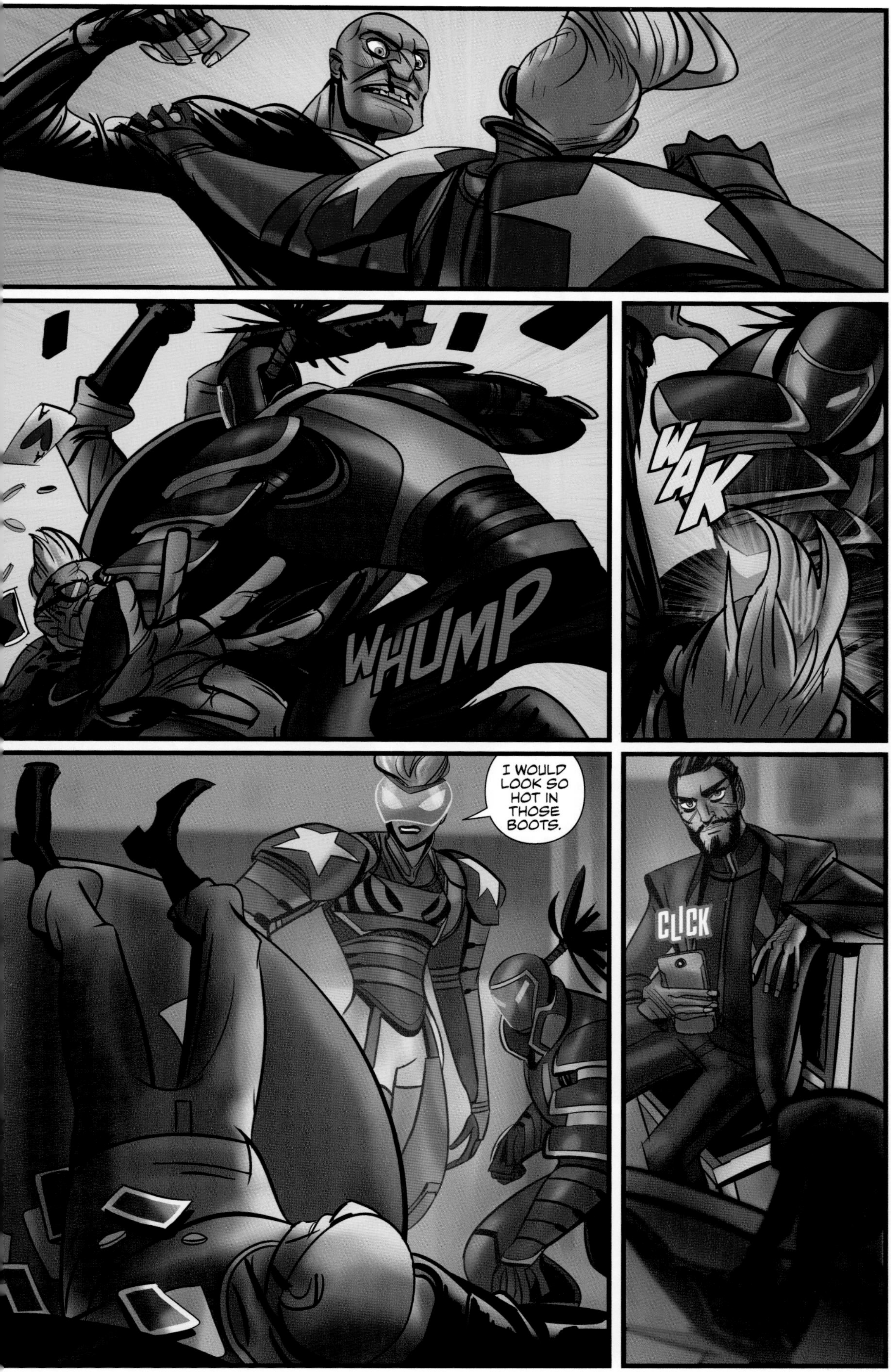
WHUMP
WAK
I WOULD LOOK SO HOT IN THOSE BOOTS.
CLICK

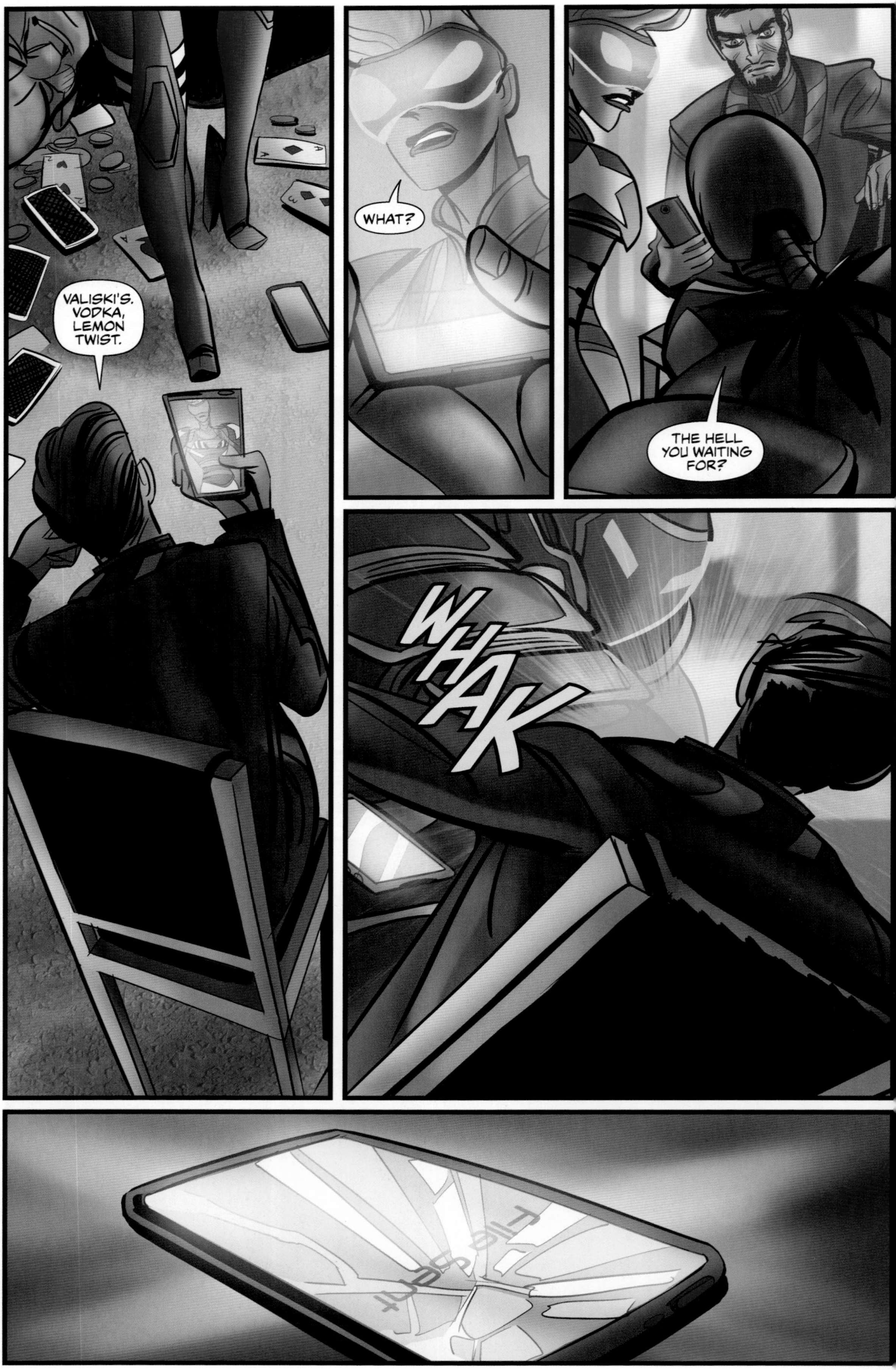
VALISKI'S. VODKA, LEMON TWIST.
WHAT?
THE HELL YOU WAITING FOR?
WHAK

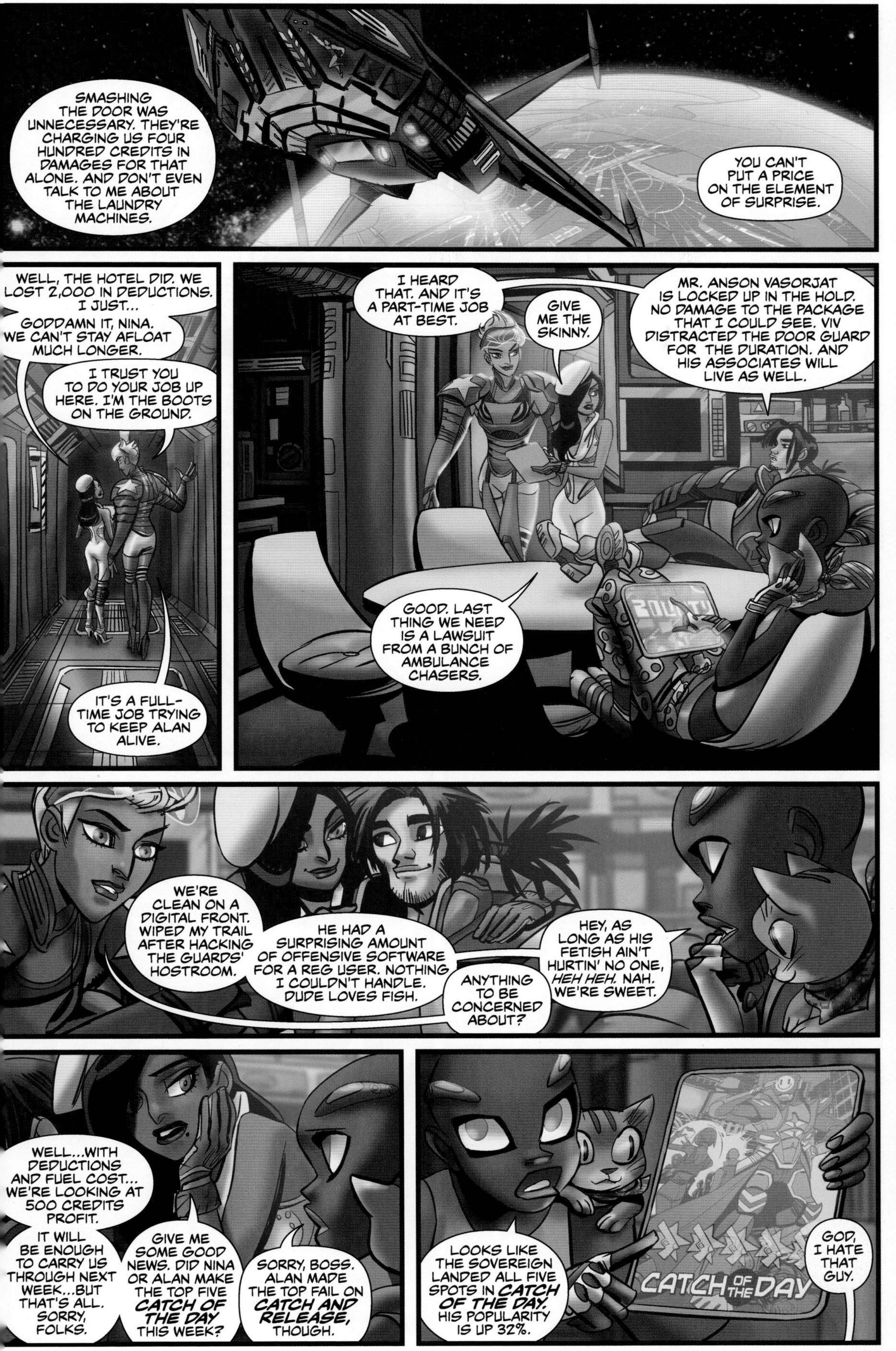
SMASHING THE DOOR WAS UNNECESSARY. THEY'RE CHARGING US FOUR HUNDRED CREDITS IN DAMAGES FOR THAT ALONE. AND DON'T EVEN TALK TO ME ABOUT THE LAUNDRY MACHINES.
YOU CAN'T PUT A PRICE ON THE ELEMENT OF SURPRISE.
WELL, THE HOTEL DID. WE LOST 2,000 IN DEDUCTIONS. I JUST...
GODDAMN IT, NINA. WE CAN'T STAY AFLOAT MUCH LONGER.
I TRUST YOU TO DO YOUR JOB UP HERE. I'M THE BOOTS ON THE GROUND.
IT'S A FULL-TIME JOB TRYING TO KEEP ALAN ALIVE.
I HEARD THAT. AND IT'S A PART-TIME JOB AT BEST.
GIVE ME THE SKINNY.
MR. ANSON VASORJAT IS LOCKED UP IN THE HOLD. NO DAMAGE TO THE PACKAGE THAT I COULD SEE. VIV DISTRACTED THE DOOR GUARD FOR THE DURATION. AND HIS ASSOCIATES WILL LIVE AS WELL.
GOOD. LAST THING WE NEED IS A LAWSUIT FROM A BUNCH OF AMBULANCE CHASERS.
WE'RE CLEAN ON A DIGITAL FRONT. WIPED MY TRAIL AFTER HACKING THE GUARDS' HOSTROOM.
HE HAD A SURPRISING AMOUNT OF OFFENSIVE SOFTWARE FOR A REG USER. NOTHING I COULDN'T HANDLE. DUDE LOVES FISH.
ANYTHING TO BE CONCERNED ABOUT?
HEY, AS LONG AS HIS FETISH AIN'T HURTIN' NO ONE, *HEH HEH.* NAH. WE'RE SWEET.
WELL...WITH DEDUCTIONS AND FUEL COST... WE'RE LOOKING AT 500 CREDITS PROFIT.
IT WILL BE ENOUGH TO CARRY US THROUGH NEXT WEEK...BUT THAT'S ALL. SORRY, FOLKS.
GIVE ME SOME GOOD NEWS. DID NINA OR ALAN MAKE THE TOP FIVE *CATCH OF THE DAY* THIS WEEK?
SORRY, BOSS. ALAN MADE THE TOP FAIL ON *CATCH AND RELEASE,* THOUGH.
LOOKS LIKE THE SOVEREIGN LANDED ALL FIVE SPOTS IN *CATCH OF THE DAY.* HIS POPULARITY IS UP 32%.
CATCH OF THE DAY
GOD, I HATE THAT GUY.

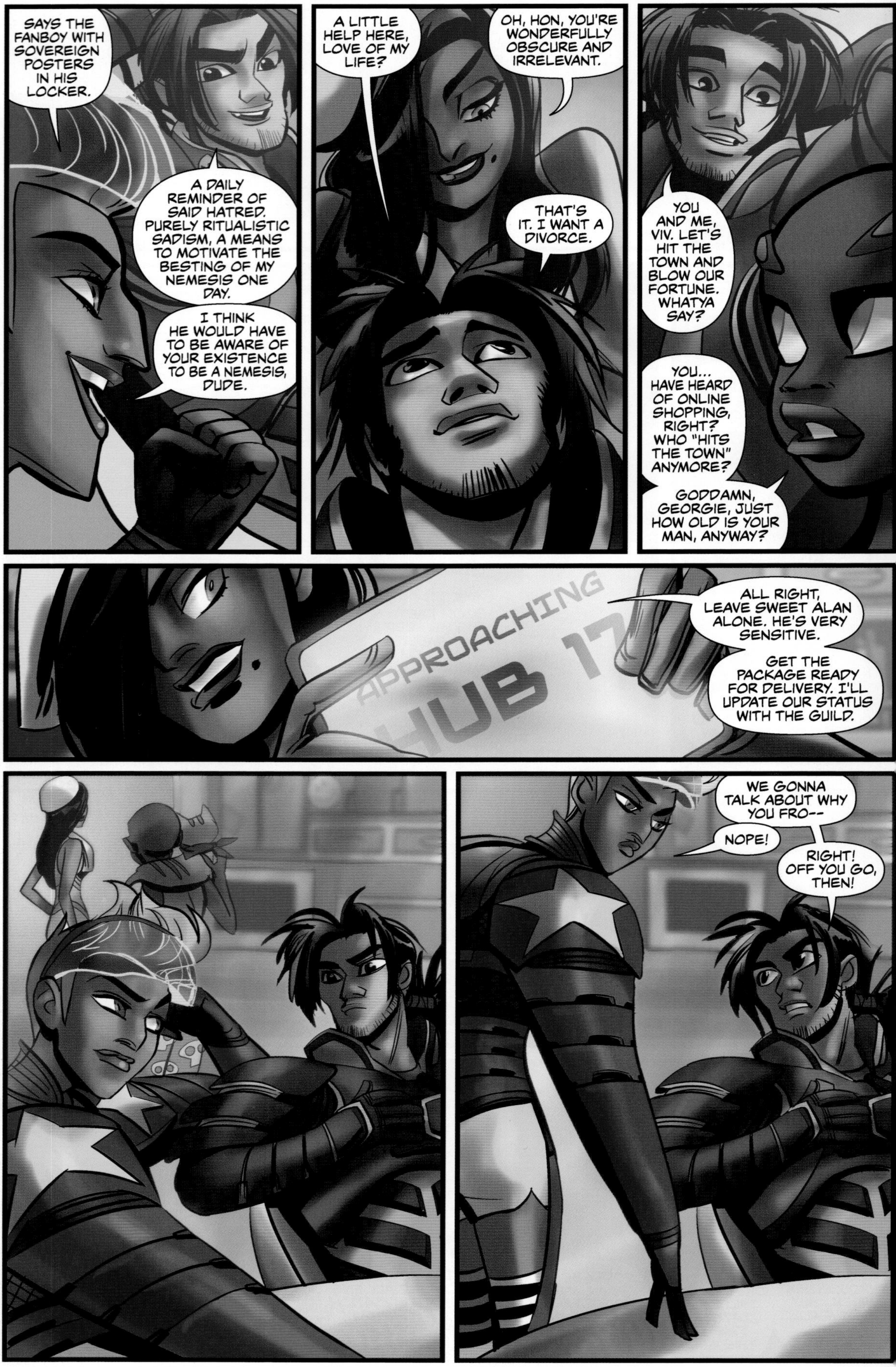
SAYS THE FANBOY WITH SOVEREIGN POSTERS IN HIS LOCKER.
A DAILY REMINDER OF SAID HATRED. PURELY RITUALISTIC SADISM, A MEANS TO MOTIVATE THE BESTING OF MY NEMESIS ONE DAY.
I THINK HE WOULD HAVE TO BE AWARE OF YOUR EXISTENCE TO BE A NEMESIS, DUDE.
A LITTLE HELP HERE, LOVE OF MY LIFE?
OH, HON, YOU'RE WONDERFULLY OBSCURE AND IRRELEVANT.
THAT'S IT. I WANT A DIVORCE.
YOU AND ME, VIV. LET'S HIT THE TOWN AND BLOW OUR FORTUNE. WHATYA SAY?
YOU... HAVE HEARD OF ONLINE SHOPPING, RIGHT? WHO "HITS THE TOWN" ANYMORE?
GODDAMN, GEORGIE, JUST HOW OLD IS YOUR MAN, ANYWAY?
APPROACHING HUB 17
ALL RIGHT, LEAVE SWEET ALAN ALONE. HE'S VERY SENSITIVE.
GET THE PACKAGE READY FOR DELIVERY. I'LL UPDATE OUR STATUS WITH THE GUILD.
WE GONNA TALK ABOUT WHY YOU FRO--
NOPE!
RIGHT! OFF YOU GO, THEN!

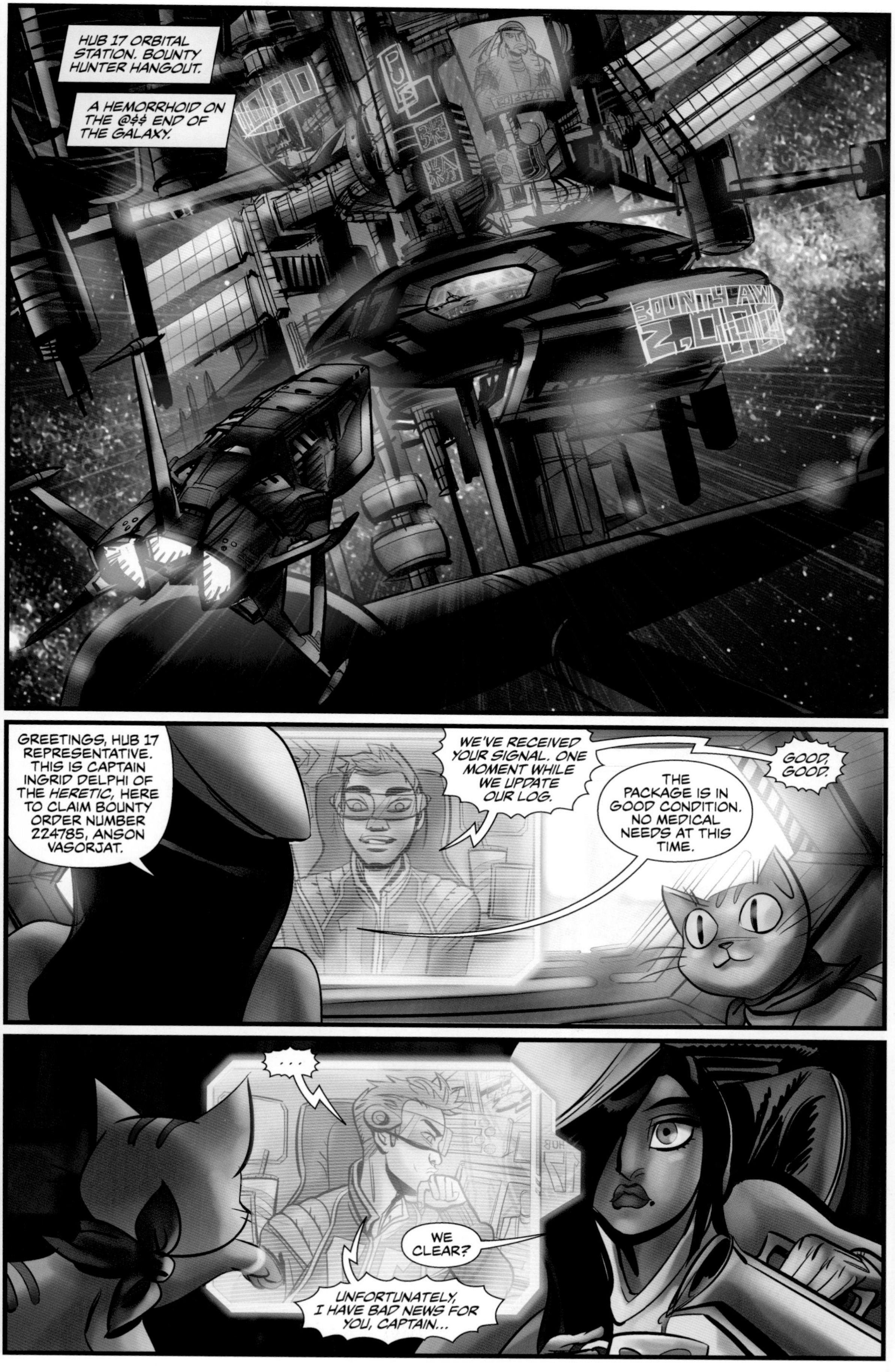
HUB 17 ORBITAL STATION. BOUNTY HUNTER HANGOUT.
A HEMORRHOID ON THE @$$ END OF THE GALAXY.
GREETINGS, HUB 17 REPRESENTATIVE. THIS IS CAPTAIN INGRID DELPHI OF THE *HERETIC*, HERE TO CLAIM BOUNTY ORDER NUMBER 224785, ANSON VASORJAT.
WE'VE RECEIVED YOUR SIGNAL. ONE MOMENT WHILE WE UPDATE OUR LOG.
GOOD, GOOD.
THE PACKAGE IS IN GOOD CONDITION. NO MEDICAL NEEDS AT THIS TIME.
...
WE CLEAR?
UNFORTUNATELY, I HAVE BAD NEWS FOR YOU, CAPTAIN...

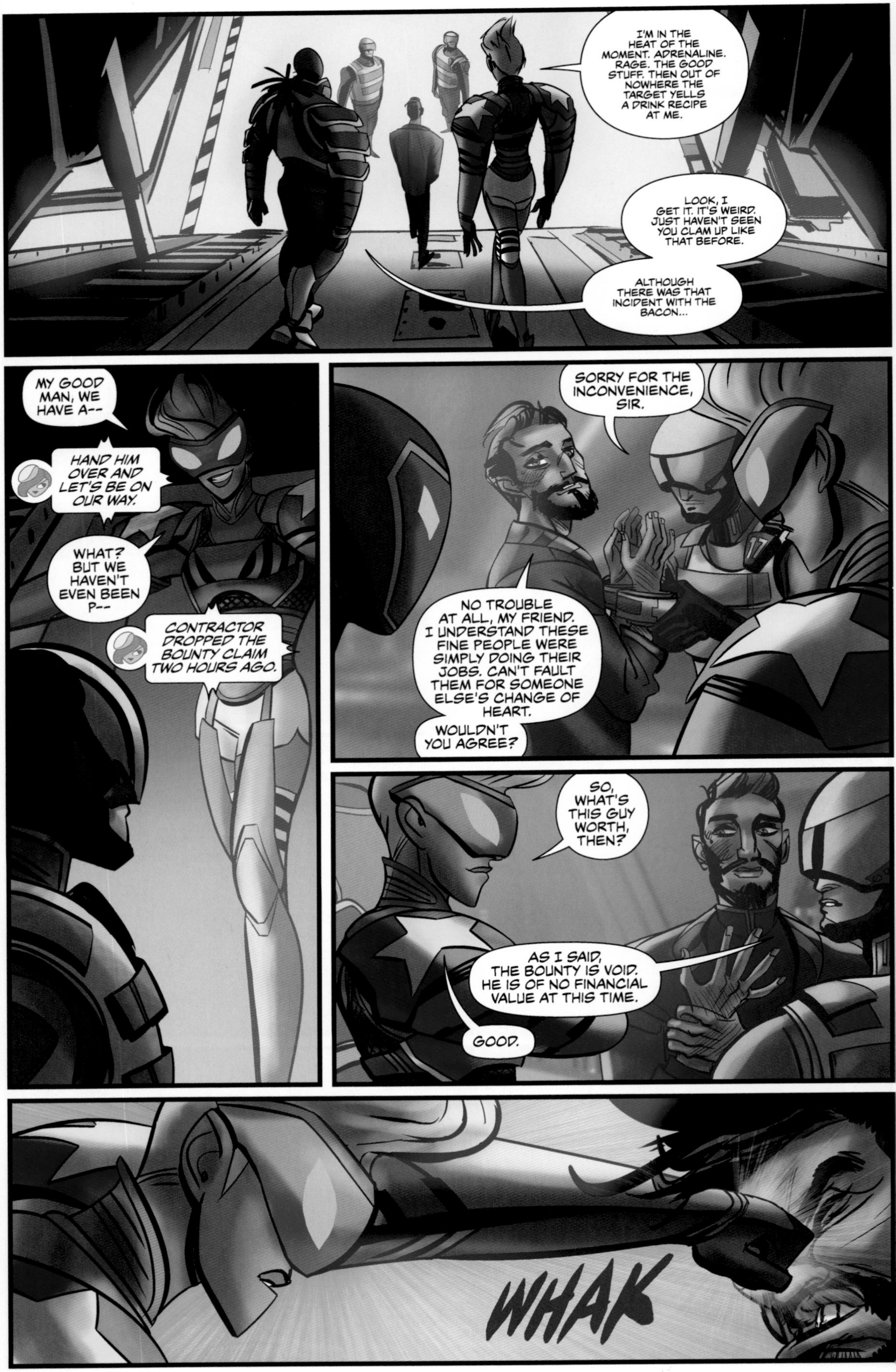
I'M IN THE HEAT OF THE MOMENT. ADRENALINE. RAGE. THE GOOD STUFF. THEN OUT OF NOWHERE THE TARGET YELLS A DRINK RECIPE AT ME.
LOOK, I GET IT. IT'S WEIRD. JUST HAVEN'T SEEN YOU CLAM UP LIKE THAT BEFORE.
ALTHOUGH THERE WAS THAT INCIDENT WITH THE BACON...
MY GOOD MAN, WE HAVE A--
HAND HIM OVER AND LET'S BE ON OUR WAY.
WHAT? BUT WE HAVEN'T EVEN BEEN P--
CONTRACTOR DROPPED THE BOUNTY CLAIM TWO HOURS AGO.
SORRY FOR THE INCONVENIENCE, SIR.
NO TROUBLE AT ALL, MY FRIEND. I UNDERSTAND THESE FINE PEOPLE WERE SIMPLY DOING THEIR JOBS. CAN'T FAULT THEM FOR SOMEONE ELSE'S CHANGE OF HEART.
WOULDN'T YOU AGREE?
SO, WHAT'S THIS GUY WORTH, THEN?
AS I SAID, THE BOUNTY IS VOID. HE IS OF NO FINANCIAL VALUE AT THIS TIME.
GOOD.
WHAK

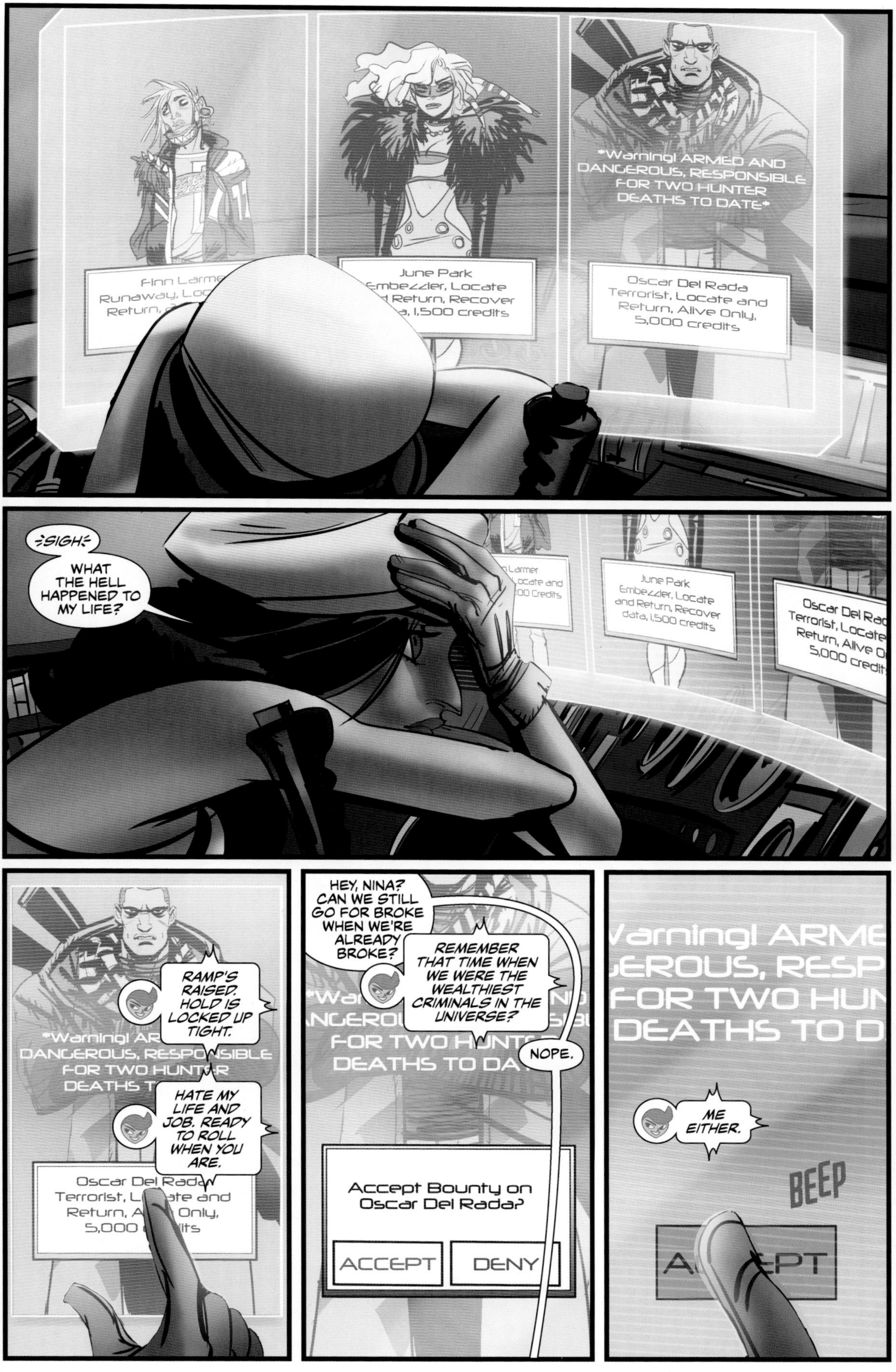

Warning! ARMED AND DANGEROUS, RESPONSIBLE FOR TWO HUNTER DEATHS TO DATE
June Park Embezzler, Locate and Return, Recover data, 1,500 credits
Oscar Del Rada Terrorist, Locate and Return, Alive Only, 5,000 credits
SIGH
WHAT THE HELL HAPPENED TO MY LIFE?
June Park Embezzler, Locate and Return, Recover data, 1,500 credits
RAMP'S RAISED. HOLD IS LOCKED UP TIGHT.
HATE MY LIFE AND JOB. READY TO ROLL WHEN YOU ARE.
HEY, NINA? CAN WE STILL GO FOR BROKE WHEN WE'RE ALREADY BROKE?
REMEMBER THAT TIME WHEN WE WERE THE WEALTHIEST CRIMINALS IN THE UNIVERSE?
NOPE.
Accept Bounty on Oscar Del Rada?
ACCEPT
DENY
ME EITHER.
BEEP

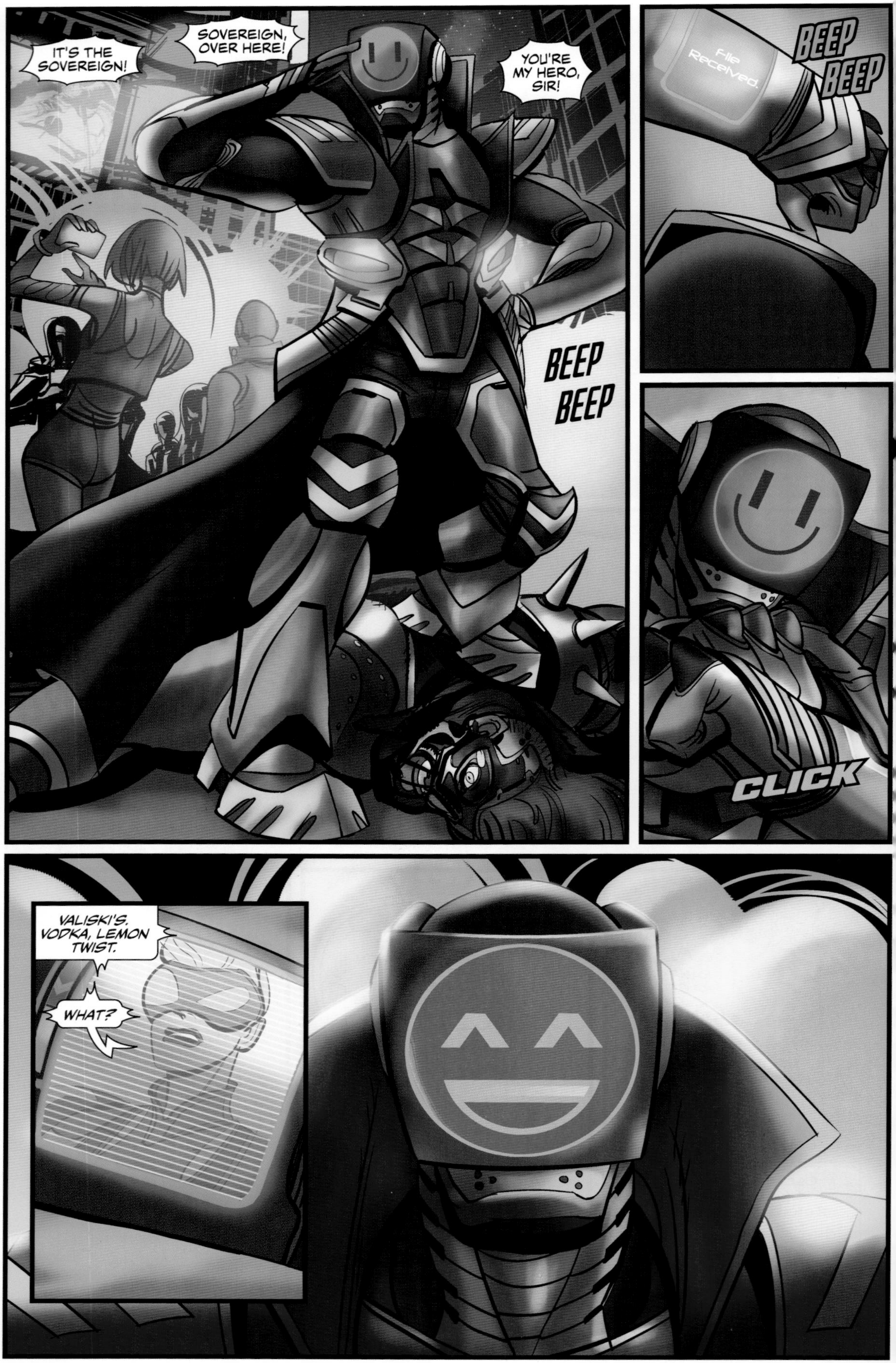

IT'S THE SOVEREIGN!
SOVEREIGN, OVER HERE!
YOU'RE MY HERO, SIR!
BEEP BEEP
File Received.
BEEP BEEP
CLICK
VALISKI'S. VODKA, LEMON TWIST.
WHAT?

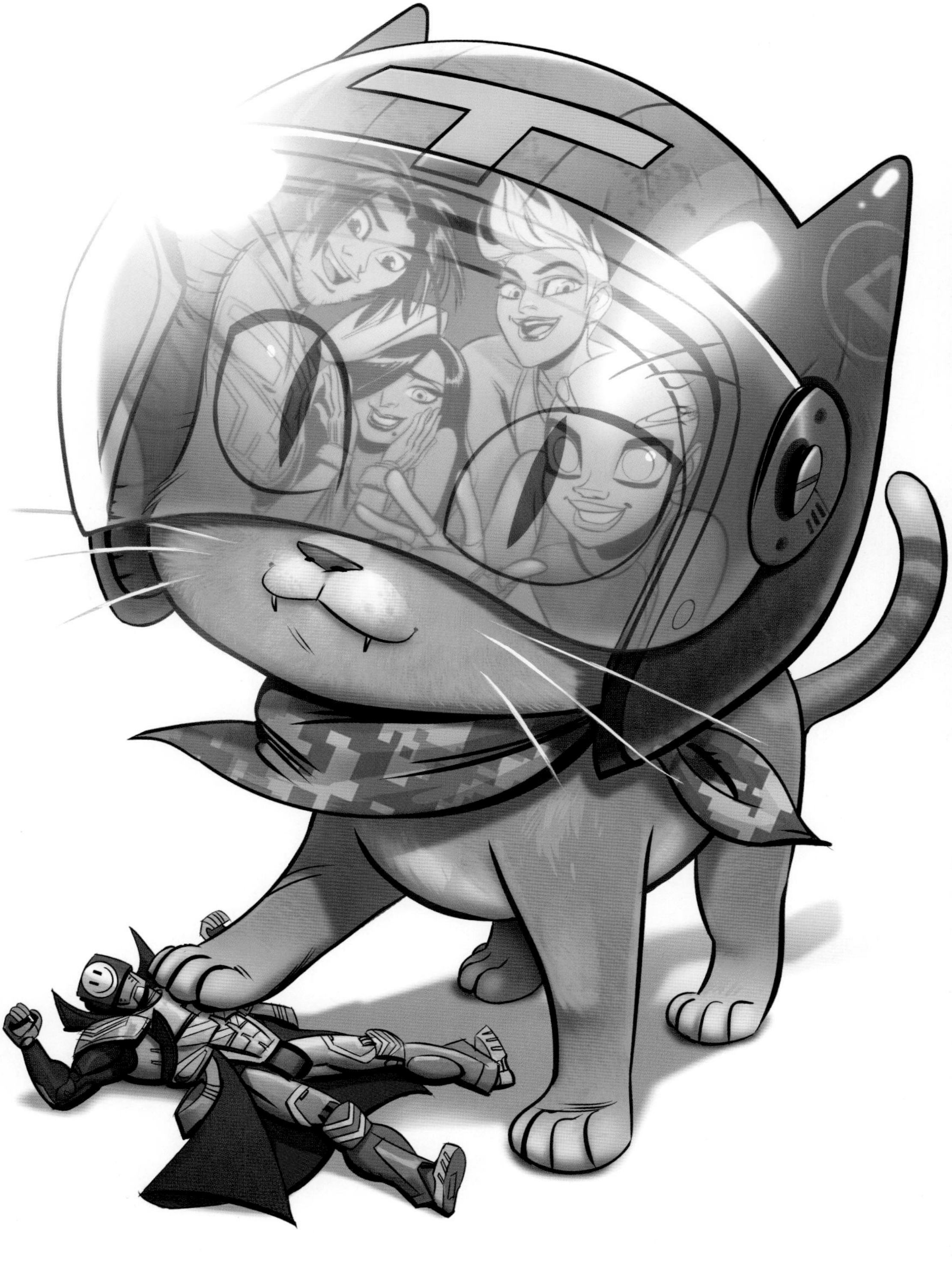

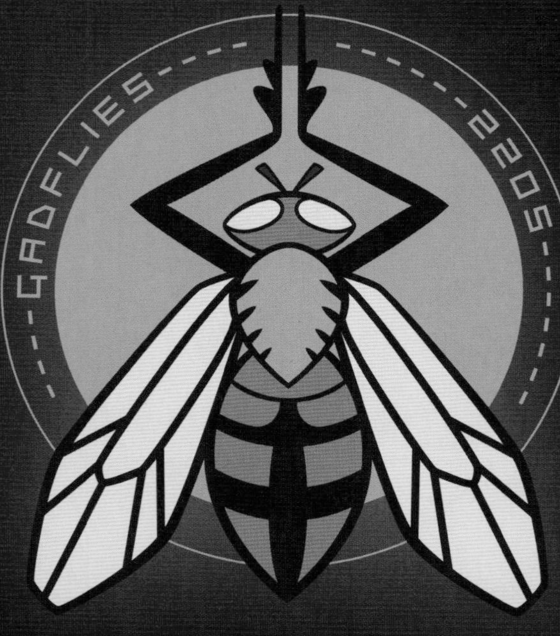
GADFLIES
2205

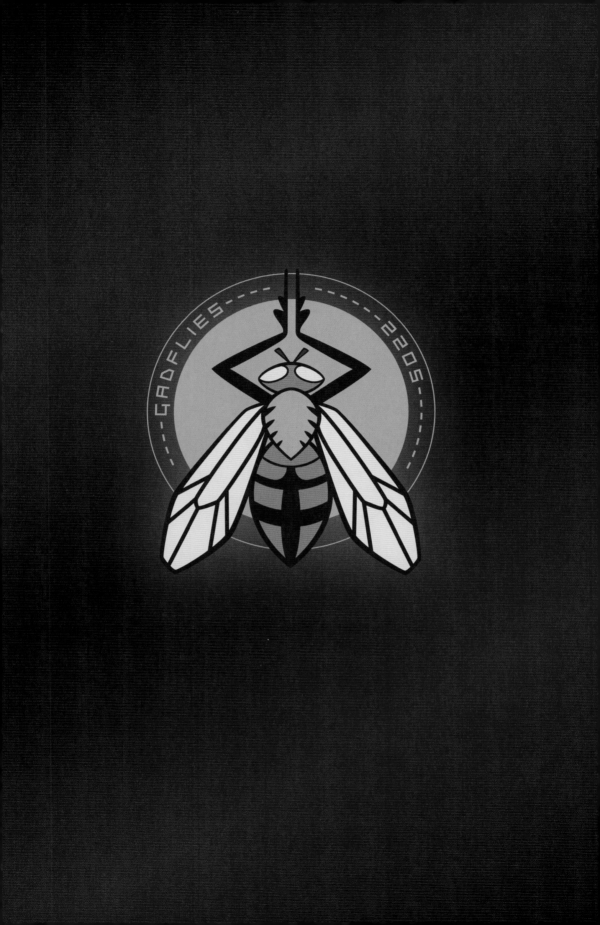

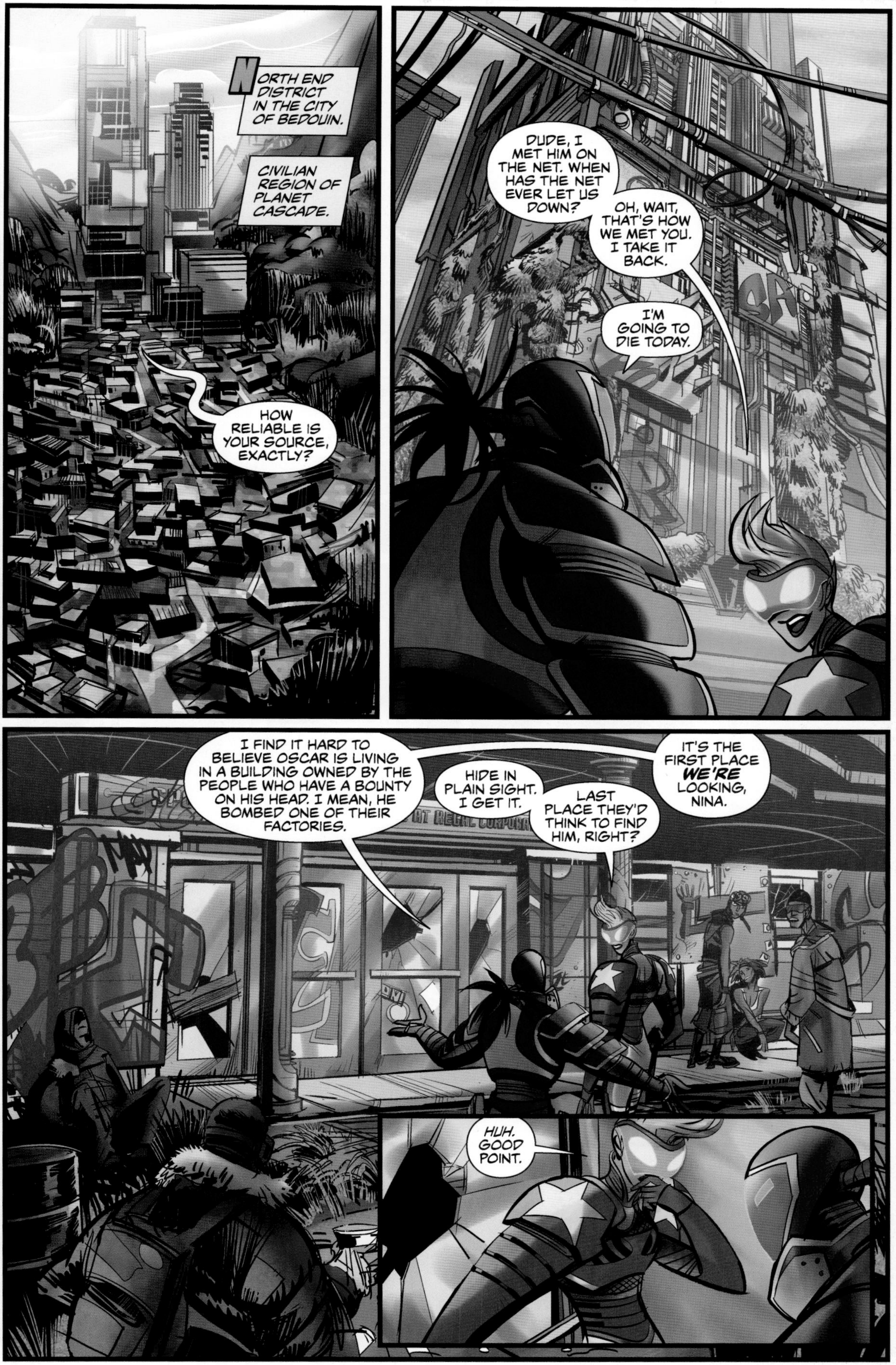
NORTH END DISTRICT IN THE CITY OF BEDOUIN.
CIVILIAN REGION OF PLANET CASCADE.
HOW RELIABLE IS YOUR SOURCE, EXACTLY?
DUDE, I MET HIM ON THE NET. WHEN HAS THE NET EVER LET US DOWN?
OH, WAIT, THAT'S HOW WE MET YOU. I TAKE IT BACK.
I'M GOING TO DIE TODAY.
I FIND IT HARD TO BELIEVE OSCAR IS LIVING IN A BUILDING OWNED BY THE PEOPLE WHO HAVE A BOUNTY ON HIS HEAD. I MEAN, HE BOMBED ONE OF THEIR FACTORIES.
HIDE IN PLAIN SIGHT. I GET IT.
LAST PLACE THEY'D THINK TO FIND HIM, RIGHT?
IT'S THE FIRST PLACE ***WE'RE*** LOOKING, NINA.
HUH. GOOD POINT.

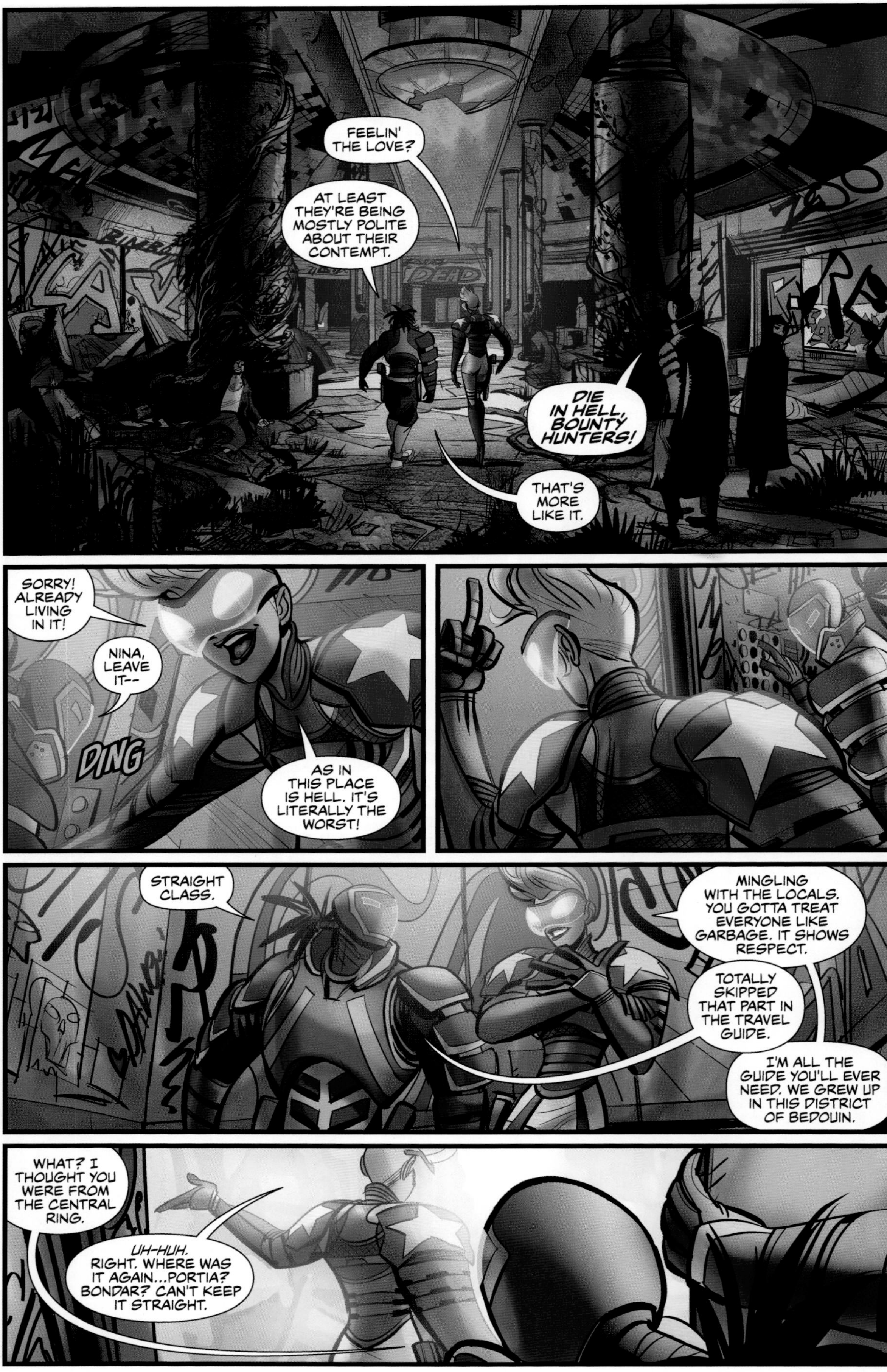
FEELIN' THE LOVE?
AT LEAST THEY'RE BEING MOSTLY POLITE ABOUT THEIR CONTEMPT.
DEAD
DIE IN HELL, BOUNTY HUNTERS!
THAT'S MORE LIKE IT.
SORRY! ALREADY LIVING IN IT!
NINA, LEAVE IT--
DING
AS IN THIS PLACE IS HELL. IT'S LITERALLY THE WORST!
STRAIGHT CLASS.
MINGLING WITH THE LOCALS. YOU GOTTA TREAT EVERYONE LIKE GARBAGE. IT SHOWS RESPECT.
TOTALLY SKIPPED THAT PART IN THE TRAVEL GUIDE.
I'M ALL THE GUIDE YOU'LL EVER NEED. WE GREW UP IN THIS DISTRICT OF BEDOUIN.
WHAT? I THOUGHT YOU WERE FROM THE CENTRAL RING.
UH-HUH. RIGHT. WHERE WAS IT AGAIN...PORTIA? BONDAR? CAN'T KEEP IT STRAIGHT.

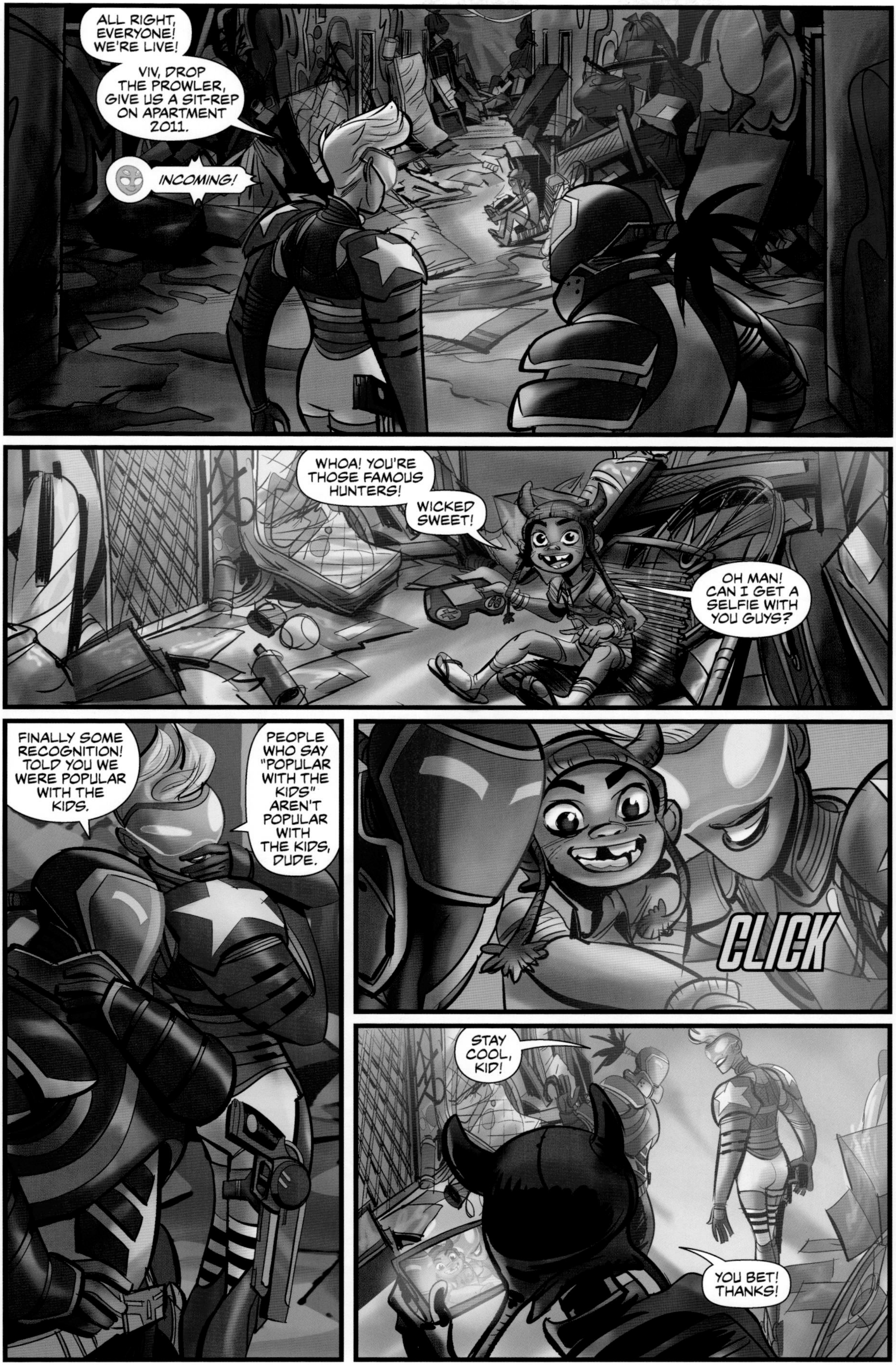
ALL RIGHT, EVERYONE! WE'RE LIVE!
VIV, DROP THE PROWLER, GIVE US A SIT-REP ON APARTMENT 2011.
INCOMING!
WHOA! YOU'RE THOSE FAMOUS HUNTERS!
WICKED SWEET!
OH MAN! CAN I GET A SELFIE WITH YOU GUYS?
FINALLY SOME RECOGNITION! TOLD YOU WE WERE POPULAR WITH THE KIDS.
PEOPLE WHO SAY "POPULAR WITH THE KIDS" AREN'T POPULAR WITH THE KIDS, DUDE.
CLICK
STAY COOL, KID!
YOU BET! THANKS!

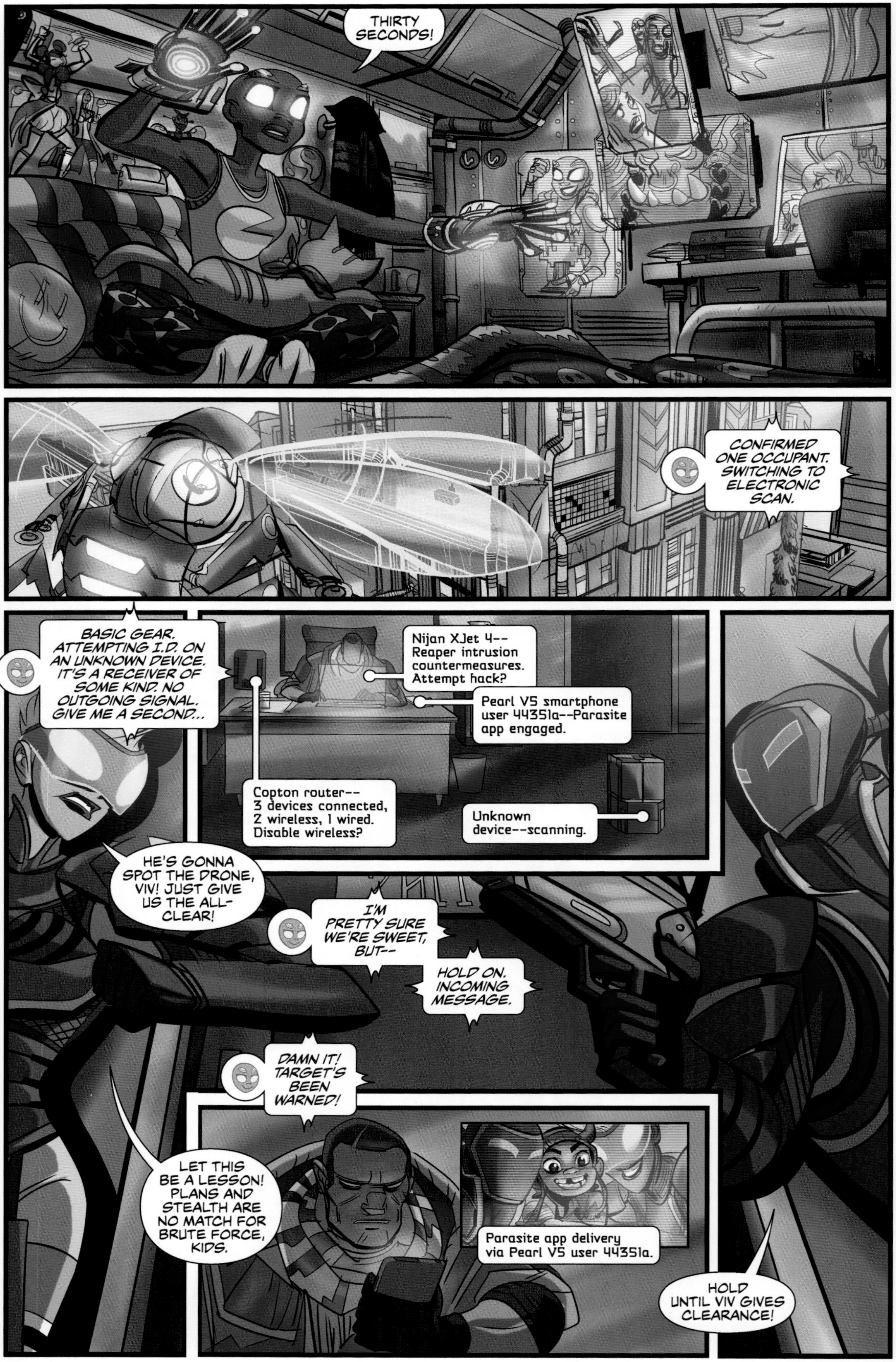
THIRTY SECONDS!
CONFIRMED ONE OCCUPANT. SWITCHING TO ELECTRONIC SCAN.
BASIC GEAR. ATTEMPTING I.D. ON AN UNKNOWN DEVICE. IT'S A RECEIVER OF SOME KIND. NO OUTGOING SIGNAL. GIVE ME A SECOND...
Nijan XJet 4--Reaper intrusion countermeasures. Attempt hack?
Pearl V5 smartphone user 44351a--Parasite app engaged.
Copton router--3 devices connected, 2 wireless, 1 wired. Disable wireless?
Unknown device--scanning.
HE'S GONNA SPOT THE DRONE, VIV! JUST GIVE US THE ALL-CLEAR!
I'M PRETTY SURE WE'RE SWEET, BUT--
HOLD ON. INCOMING MESSAGE.
DAMN IT! TARGET'S BEEN WARNED!
LET THIS BE A LESSON! PLANS AND STEALTH ARE NO MATCH FOR BRUTE FORCE, KIDS.
Parasite app delivery via Pearl V5 user 44351a.
HOLD UNTIL VIV GIVES CLEARANCE!

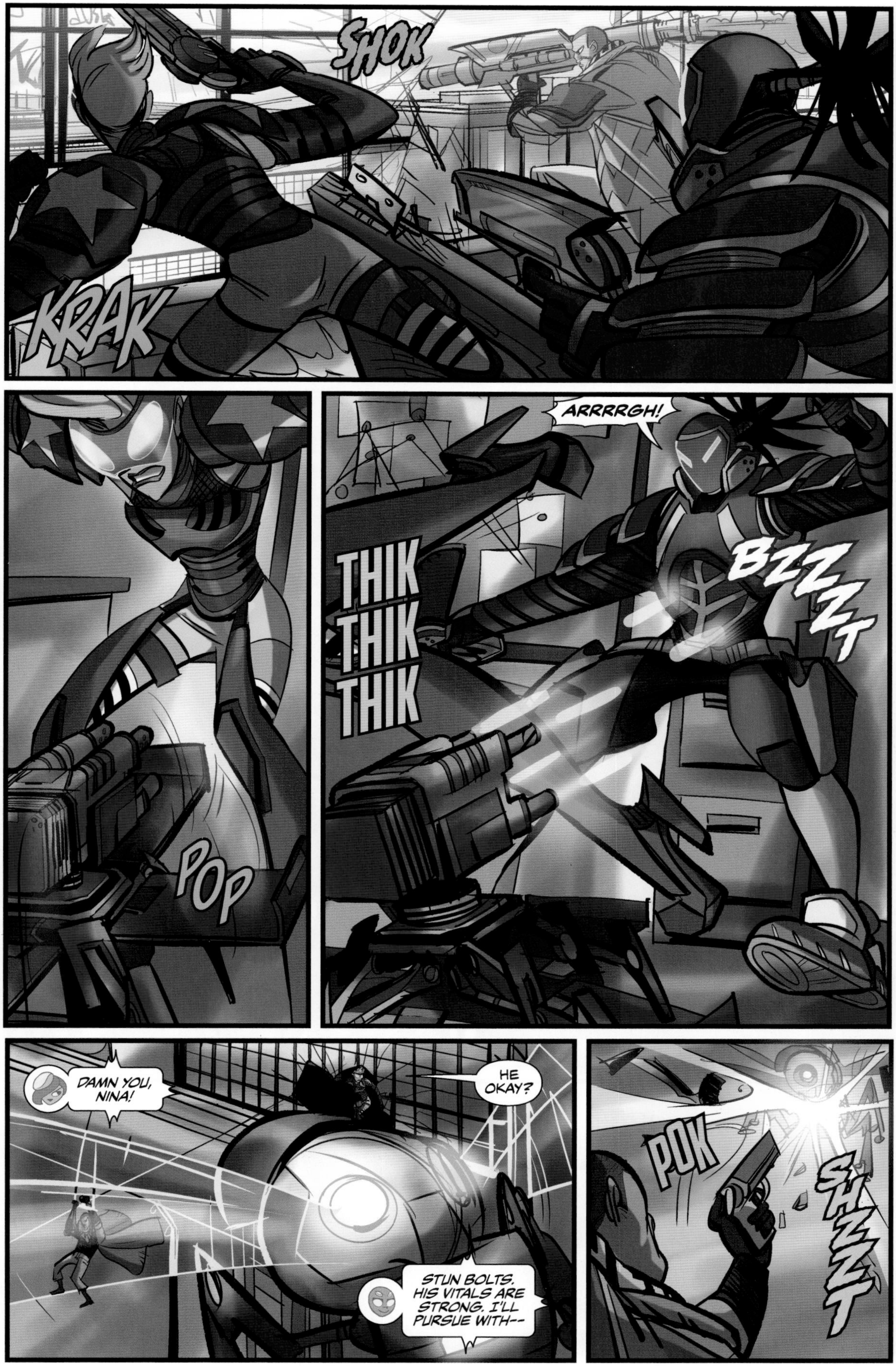
SHOK
KRAK
ARRRRGH!
THIK THIK THIK
BZZZZT
POP
DAMN YOU, NINA!
HE OKAY?
STUN BOLTS. HIS VITALS ARE STRONG. I'LL PURSUE WITH--
POK
SHZZZT

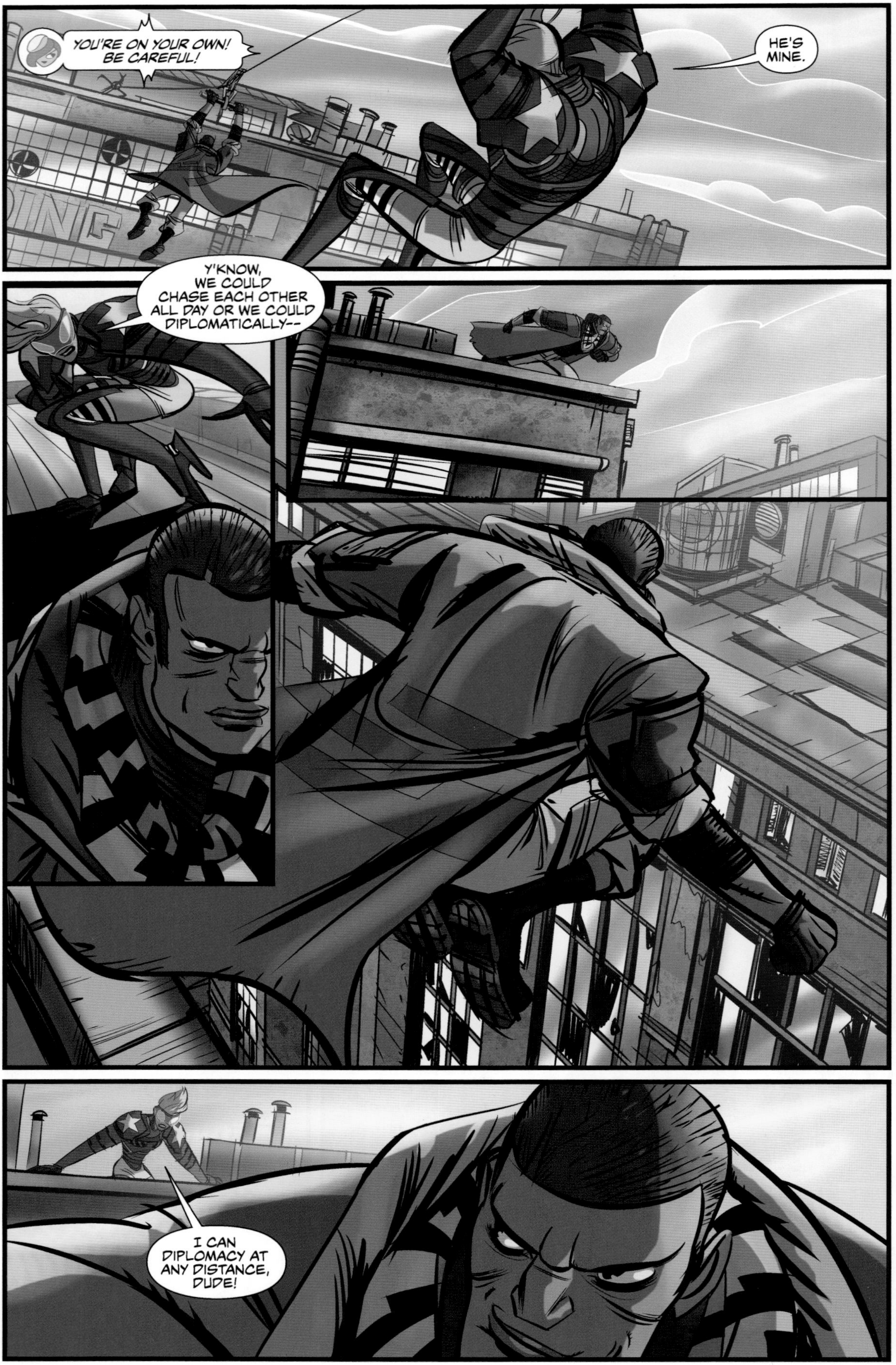
YOU'RE ON YOUR OWN! BE CAREFUL!
HE'S MINE.
Y'KNOW, WE COULD CHASE EACH OTHER ALL DAY OR WE COULD DIPLOMATICALLY--
I CAN DIPLOMACY AT ANY DISTANCE, DUDE!

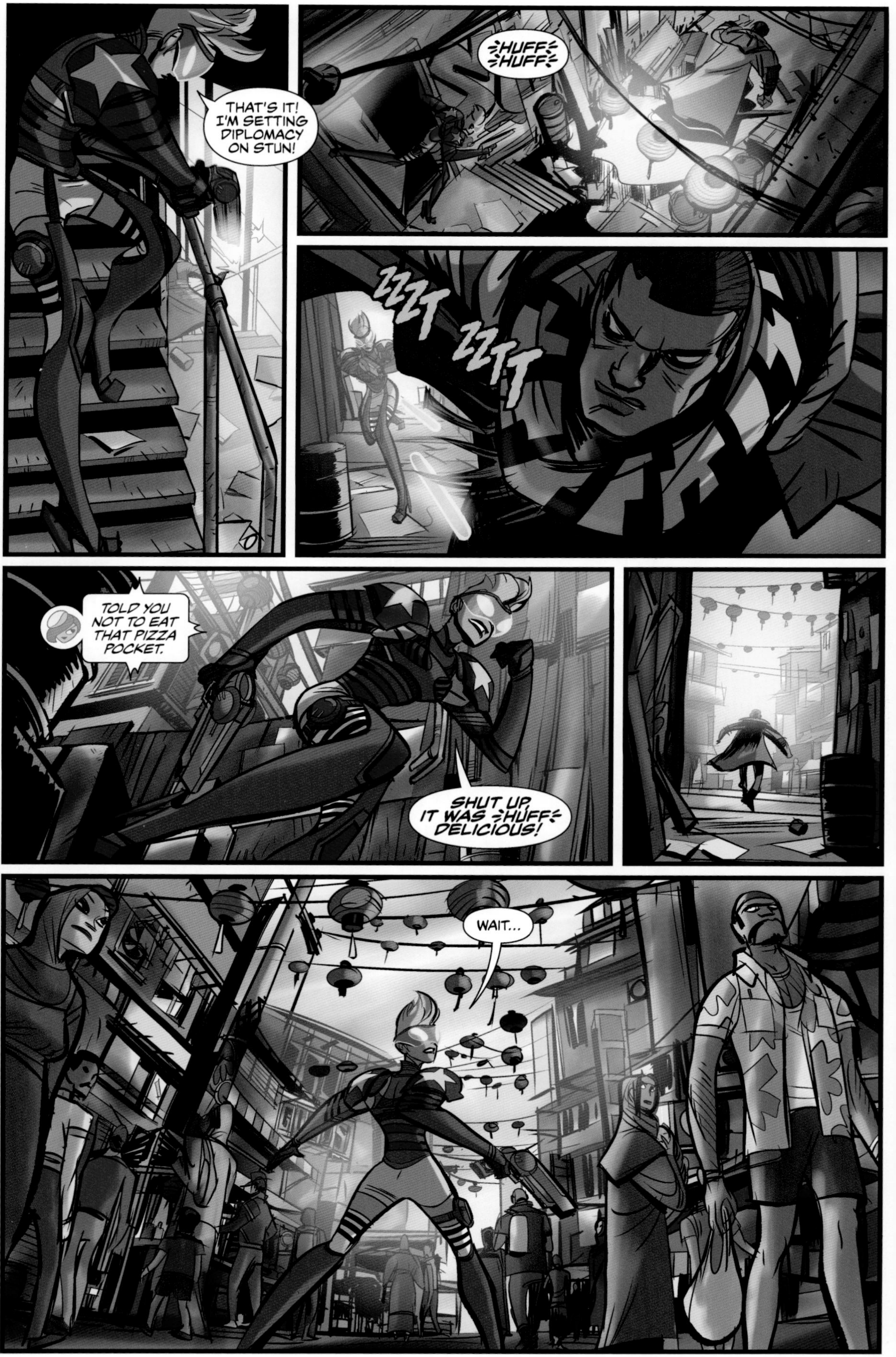
THAT'S IT! I'M SETTING DIPLOMACY ON STUN!
HUFF HUFF
ZZZT
ZZTT
TOLD YOU NOT TO EAT THAT PIZZA POCKET.
SHUT UP. IT WAS HUFF DELICIOUS!
WAIT...

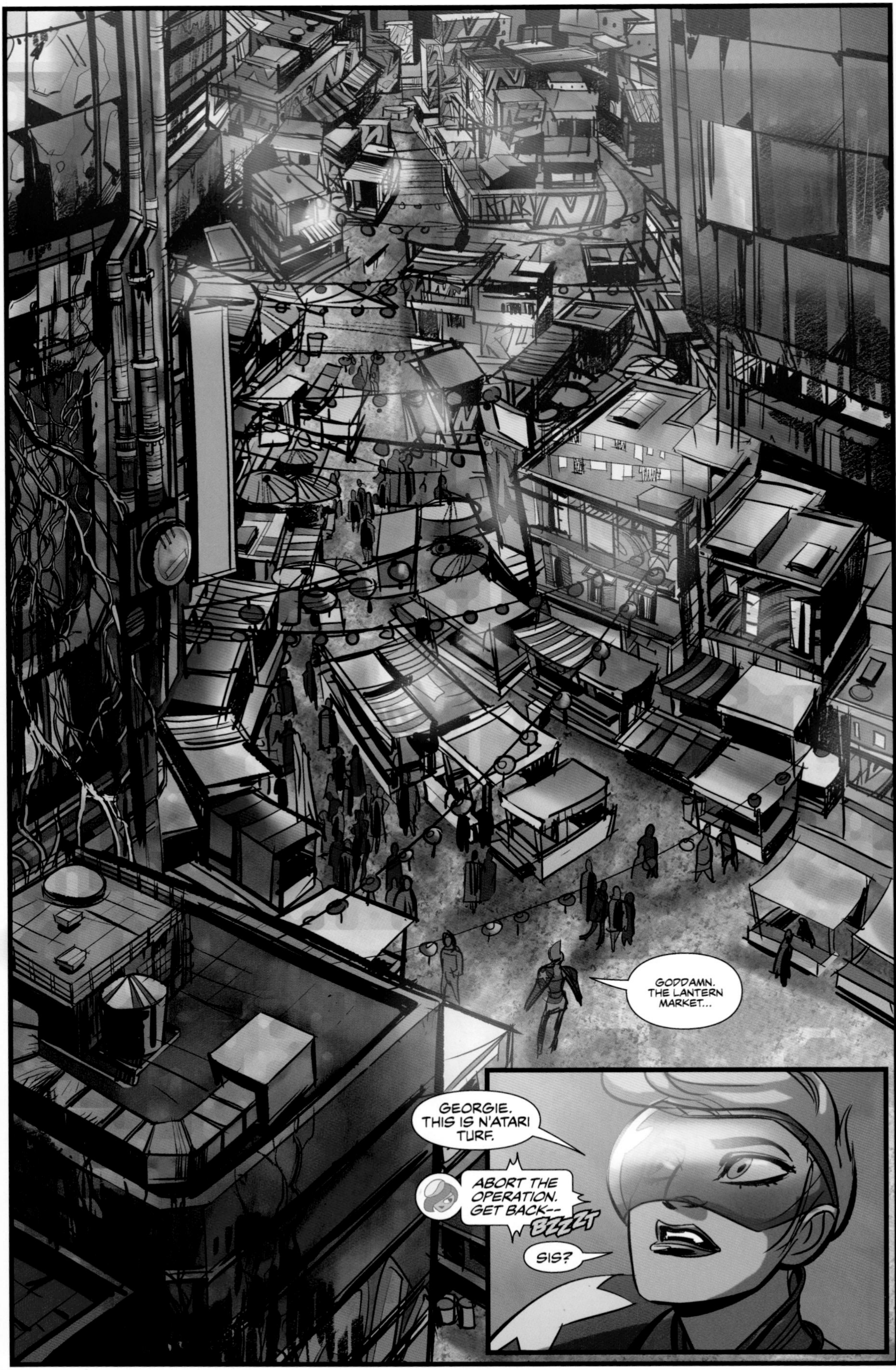
GODDAMN. THE LANTERN MARKET...
GEORGIE. THIS IS N'ATARI TURF.
ABORT THE OPERATION. GET BACK--
BZZZT
SIS?

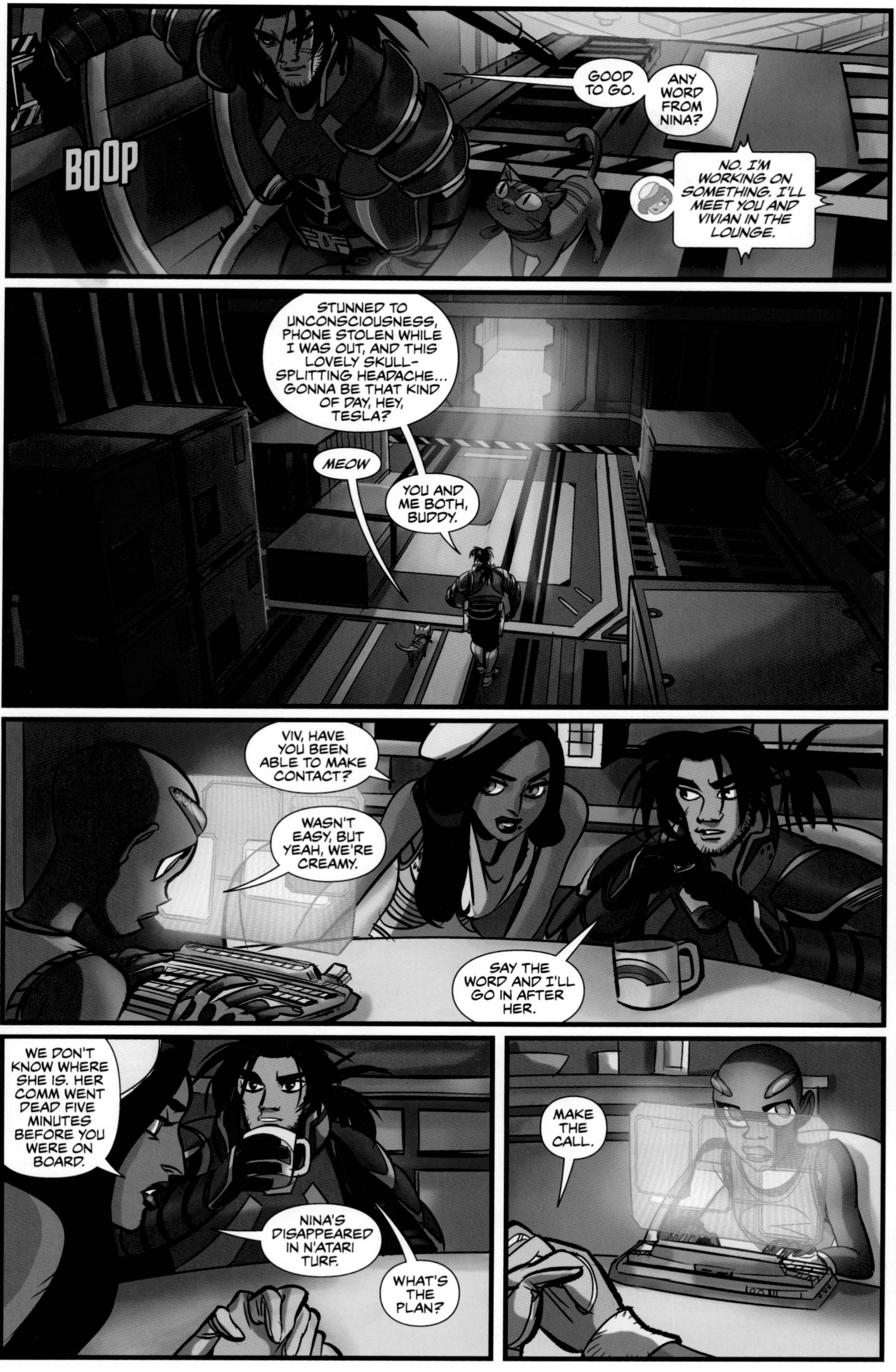
GOOD TO GO.
ANY WORD FROM NINA?
BOOP
NO. I'M WORKING ON SOMETHING. I'LL MEET YOU AND VIVIAN IN THE LOUNGE.
STUNNED TO UNCONSCIOUSNESS, PHONE STOLEN WHILE I WAS OUT, AND THIS LOVELY SKULL-SPLITTING HEADACHE... GONNA BE THAT KIND OF DAY, HEY, TESLA?
MEOW
YOU AND ME BOTH, BUDDY.
VIV, HAVE YOU BEEN ABLE TO MAKE CONTACT?
WASN'T EASY, BUT YEAH, WE'RE CREAMY.
SAY THE WORD AND I'LL GO IN AFTER HER.
WE DON'T KNOW WHERE SHE IS. HER COMM WENT DEAD FIVE MINUTES BEFORE YOU WERE ON BOARD.
NINA'S DISAPPEARED IN N'ATARI TURF.
WHAT'S THE PLAN?
MAKE THE CALL.

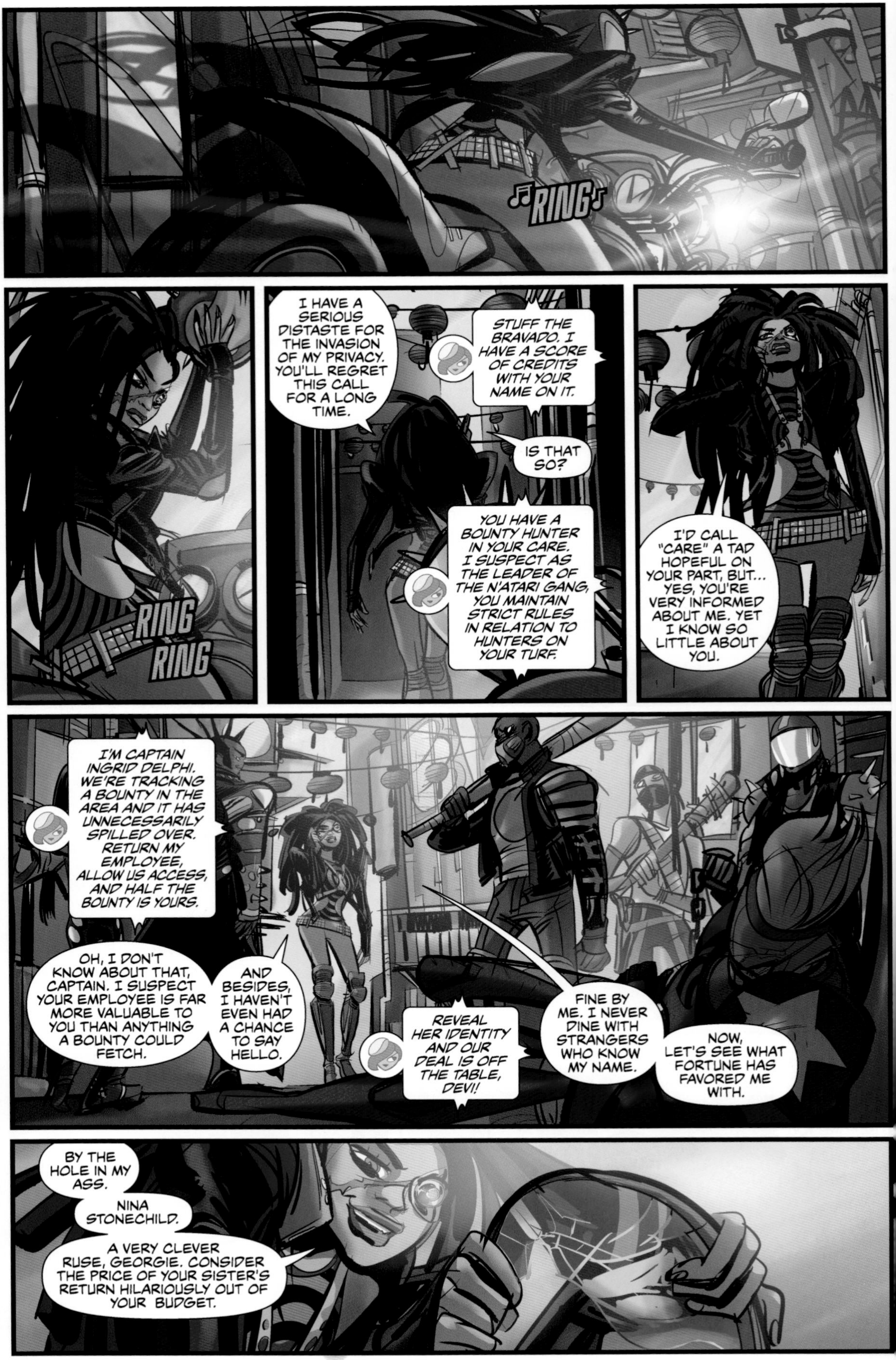
RING
RING
RING
I HAVE A SERIOUS DISTASTE FOR THE INVASION OF MY PRIVACY. YOU'LL REGRET THIS CALL FOR A LONG TIME.
STUFF THE BRAVADO. I HAVE A SCORE OF CREDITS WITH YOUR NAME ON IT.
IS THAT SO?
YOU HAVE A BOUNTY HUNTER IN YOUR CARE. I SUSPECT AS THE LEADER OF THE N'ATARI GANG, YOU MAINTAIN STRICT RULES IN RELATION TO HUNTERS ON YOUR TURF.
I'D CALL "CARE" A TAD HOPEFUL ON YOUR PART, BUT... YES, YOU'RE VERY INFORMED ABOUT ME. YET I KNOW SO LITTLE ABOUT YOU.
I'M CAPTAIN INGRID DELPHI. WE'RE TRACKING A BOUNTY IN THE AREA AND IT HAS UNNECESSARILY SPILLED OVER. RETURN MY EMPLOYEE, ALLOW US ACCESS, AND HALF THE BOUNTY IS YOURS.
OH, I DON'T KNOW ABOUT THAT, CAPTAIN. I SUSPECT YOUR EMPLOYEE IS FAR MORE VALUABLE TO YOU THAN ANYTHING A BOUNTY COULD FETCH.
AND BESIDES, I HAVEN'T EVEN HAD A CHANCE TO SAY HELLO.
REVEAL HER IDENTITY AND OUR DEAL IS OFF THE TABLE, DEVI!
FINE BY ME. I NEVER DINE WITH STRANGERS WHO KNOW MY NAME.
NOW, LET'S SEE WHAT FORTUNE HAS FAVORED ME WITH.
BY THE HOLE IN MY ASS.
NINA STONECHILD.
A VERY CLEVER RUSE, GEORGIE. CONSIDER THE PRICE OF YOUR SISTER'S RETURN HILARIOUSLY OUT OF YOUR BUDGET.

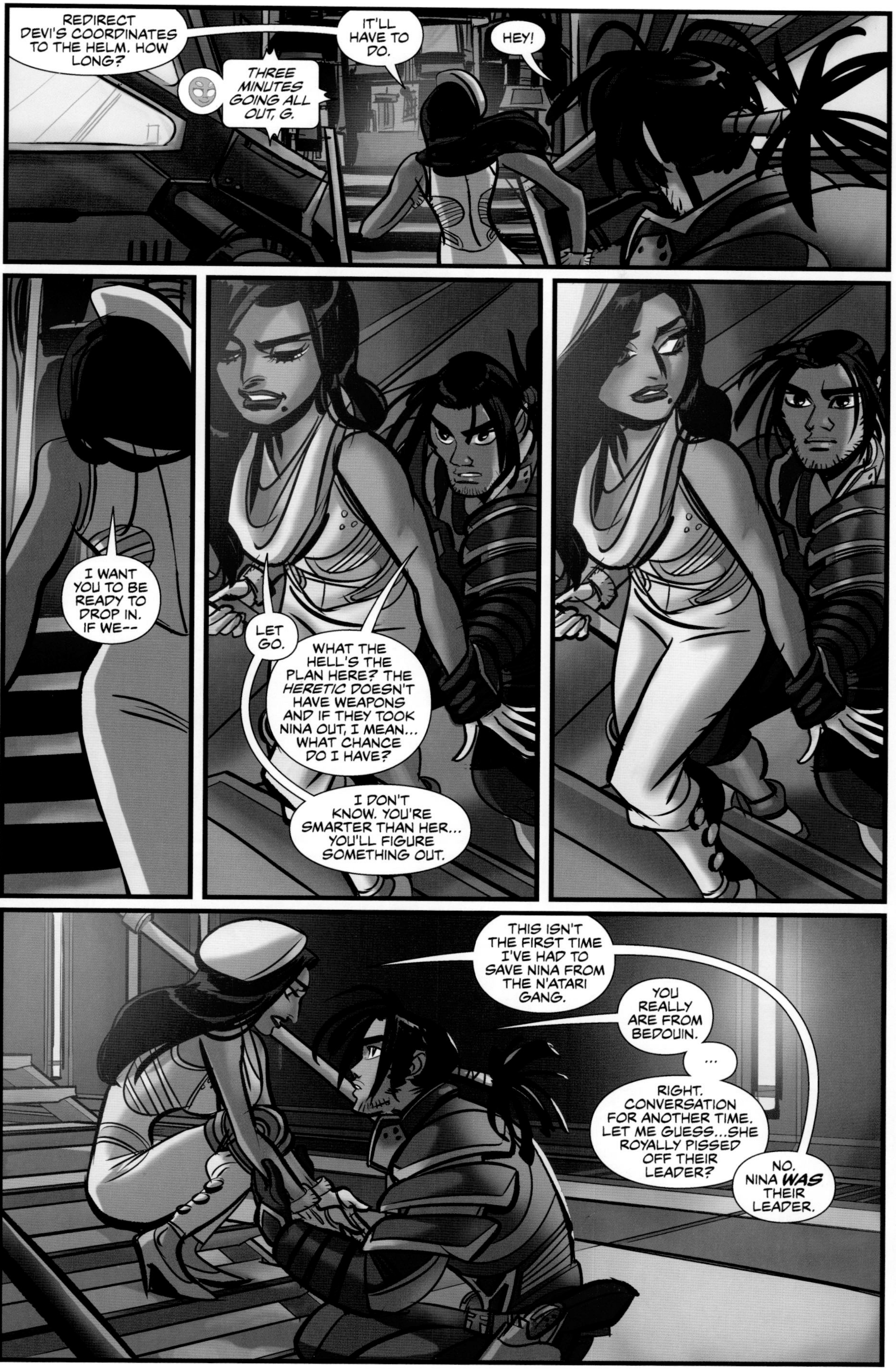
REDIRECT DEVI'S COORDINATES TO THE HELM. HOW LONG?
THREE MINUTES GOING ALL OUT, G.
IT'LL HAVE TO DO.
HEY!
I WANT YOU TO BE READY TO DROP IN. IF WE--
LET GO.
WHAT THE HELL'S THE PLAN HERE? THE *HERETIC* DOESN'T HAVE WEAPONS AND IF THEY TOOK NINA OUT, I MEAN... WHAT CHANCE DO I HAVE?
I DON'T KNOW. YOU'RE SMARTER THAN HER... YOU'LL FIGURE SOMETHING OUT.
THIS ISN'T THE FIRST TIME I'VE HAD TO SAVE NINA FROM THE N'ATARI GANG.
YOU REALLY ARE FROM BEDOUIN.
...
RIGHT. CONVERSATION FOR ANOTHER TIME. LET ME GUESS...SHE ROYALLY PISSED OFF THEIR LEADER?
NO. NINA **WAS** THEIR LEADER.

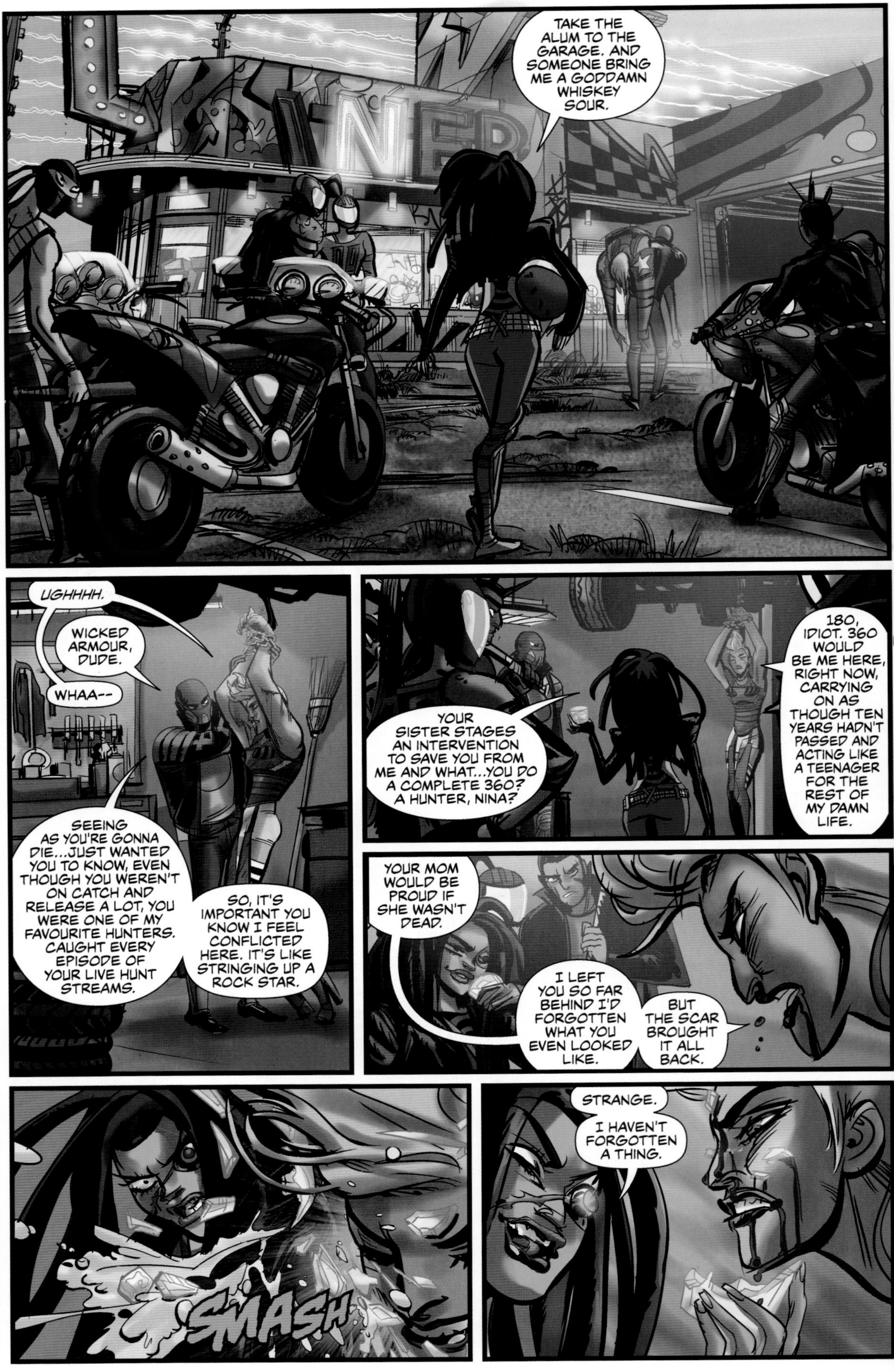

TAKE THE ALUM TO THE GARAGE. AND SOMEONE BRING ME A GODDAMN WHISKEY SOUR.
UGHHHH.
WICKED ARMOUR, DUDE.
WHAA--
SEEING AS YOU'RE GONNA DIE...JUST WANTED YOU TO KNOW, EVEN THOUGH YOU WEREN'T ON CATCH AND RELEASE A LOT, YOU WERE ONE OF MY FAVOURITE HUNTERS. CAUGHT EVERY EPISODE OF YOUR LIVE HUNT STREAMS.
SO, IT'S IMPORTANT YOU KNOW I FEEL CONFLICTED HERE. IT'S LIKE STRINGING UP A ROCK STAR.
YOUR SISTER STAGES AN INTERVENTION TO SAVE YOU FROM ME AND WHAT...YOU DO A COMPLETE 360? A HUNTER, NINA?
180, IDIOT. 360 WOULD BE ME HERE, RIGHT NOW, CARRYING ON AS THOUGH TEN YEARS HADN'T PASSED AND ACTING LIKE A TEENAGER FOR THE REST OF MY DAMN LIFE.
YOUR MOM WOULD BE PROUD IF SHE WASN'T DEAD.
I LEFT YOU SO FAR BEHIND I'D FORGOTTEN WHAT YOU EVEN LOOKED LIKE.
BUT THE SCAR BROUGHT IT ALL BACK.
SMASH
STRANGE.
I HAVEN'T FORGOTTEN A THING.

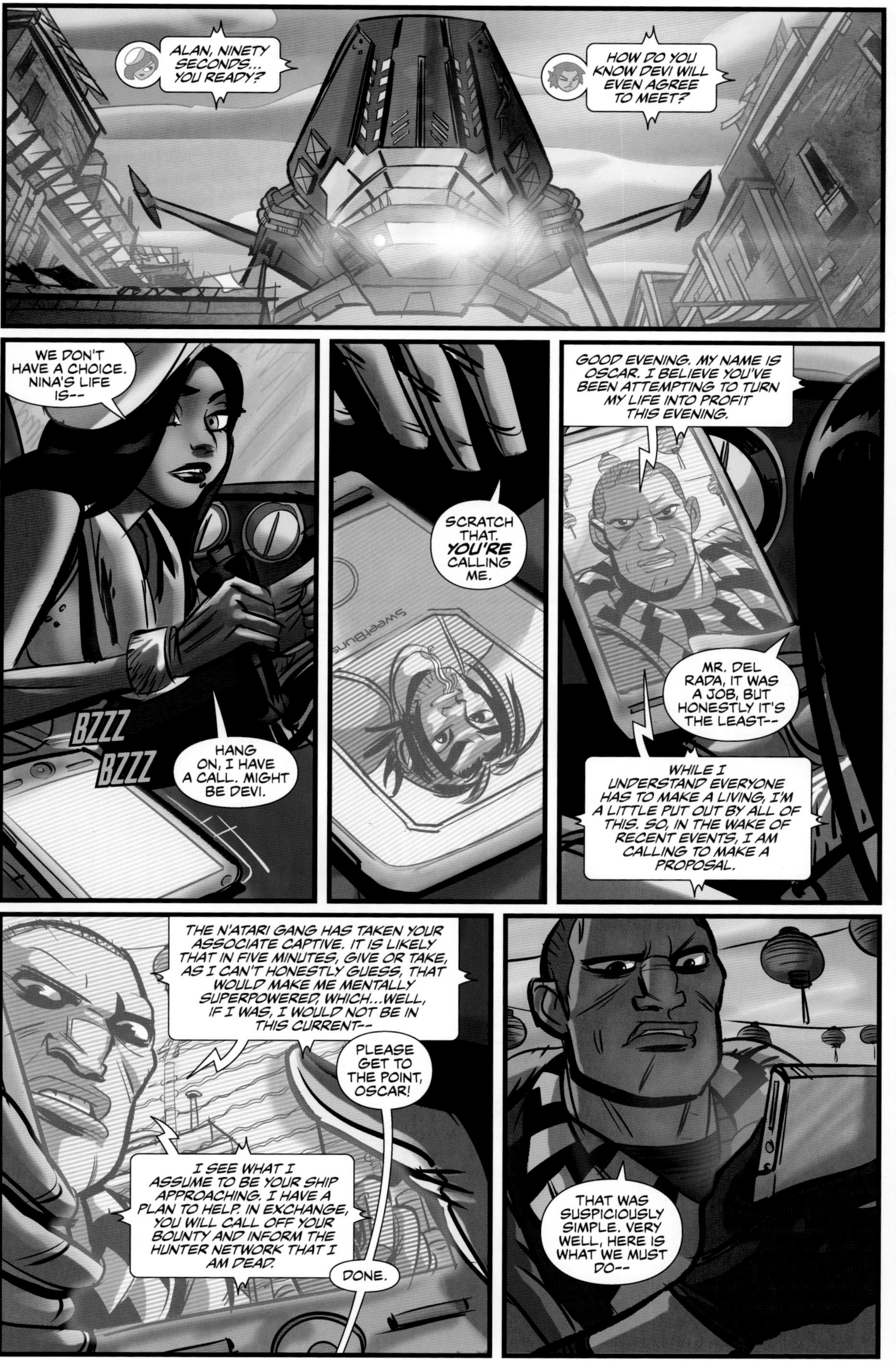
ALAN, NINETY SECONDS... YOU READY?
HOW DO YOU KNOW DEVI WILL EVEN AGREE TO MEET?
WE DON'T HAVE A CHOICE. NINA'S LIFE IS--
BZZZ BZZZ
HANG ON, I HAVE A CALL. MIGHT BE DEVI.
SCRATCH THAT. YOU'RE CALLING ME.
SweetBuns
GOOD EVENING. MY NAME IS OSCAR. I BELIEVE YOU'VE BEEN ATTEMPTING TO TURN MY LIFE INTO PROFIT THIS EVENING.
MR. DEL RADA, IT WAS A JOB, BUT HONESTLY IT'S THE LEAST--
WHILE I UNDERSTAND EVERYONE HAS TO MAKE A LIVING, I'M A LITTLE PUT OUT BY ALL OF THIS. SO, IN THE WAKE OF RECENT EVENTS, I AM CALLING TO MAKE A PROPOSAL.
THE N'ATARI GANG HAS TAKEN YOUR ASSOCIATE CAPTIVE. IT IS LIKELY THAT IN FIVE MINUTES, GIVE OR TAKE, AS I CAN'T HONESTLY GUESS, THAT WOULD MAKE ME MENTALLY SUPERPOWERED, WHICH...WELL, IF I WAS, I WOULD NOT BE IN THIS CURRENT--
PLEASE GET TO THE POINT, OSCAR!
I SEE WHAT I ASSUME TO BE YOUR SHIP APPROACHING. I HAVE A PLAN TO HELP. IN EXCHANGE, YOU WILL CALL OFF YOUR BOUNTY AND INFORM THE HUNTER NETWORK THAT I AM DEAD.
DONE.
THAT WAS SUSPICIOUSLY SIMPLE. VERY WELL, HERE IS WHAT WE MUST DO--

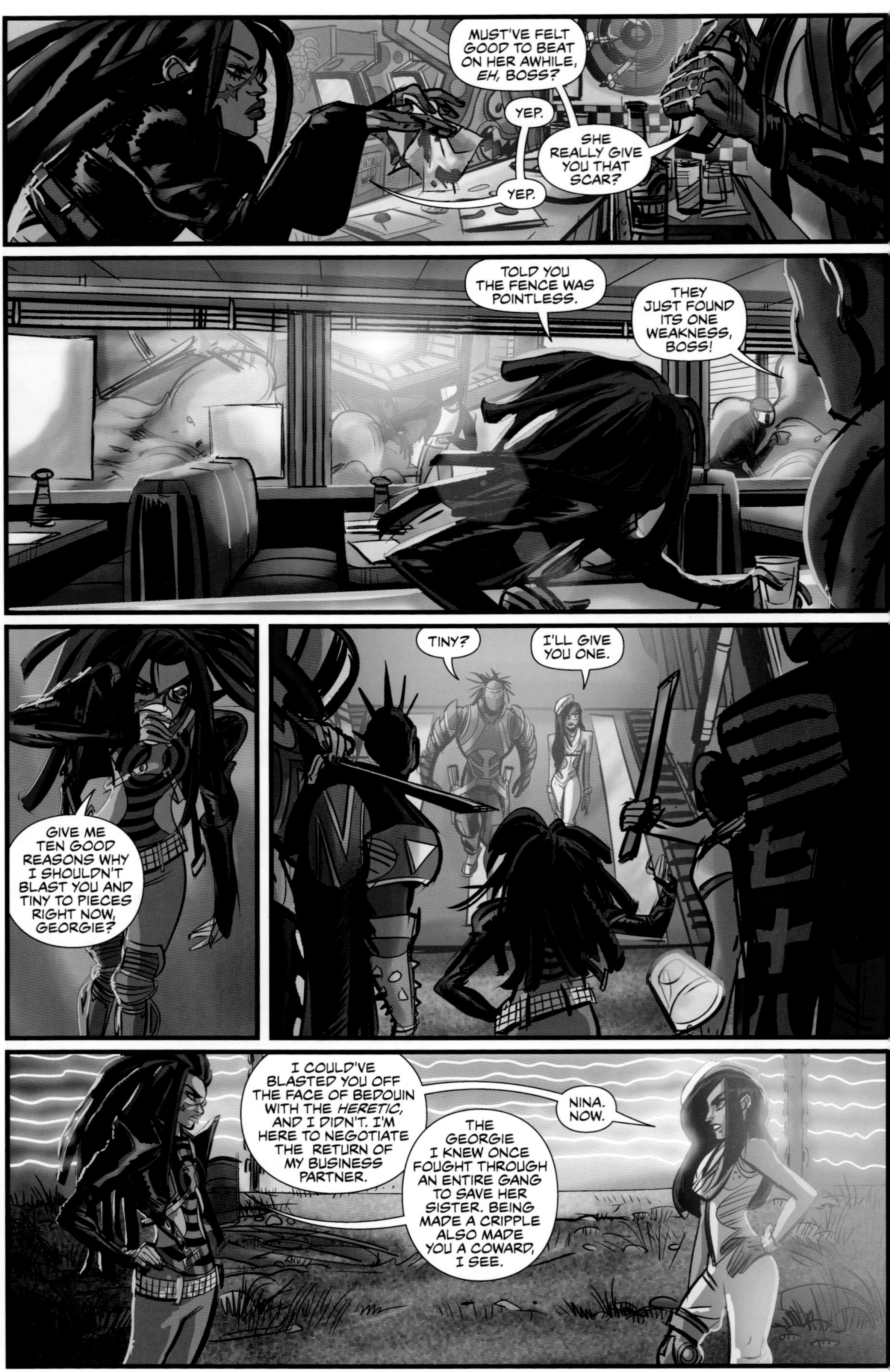
MUST'VE FELT GOOD TO BEAT ON HER AWHILE, *EH*, BOSS?
YEP.
SHE REALLY GIVE YOU THAT SCAR?
YEP.
TOLD YOU THE FENCE WAS POINTLESS.
THEY JUST FOUND ITS ONE WEAKNESS, BOSS!
GIVE ME TEN GOOD REASONS WHY I SHOULDN'T BLAST YOU AND TINY TO PIECES RIGHT NOW, GEORGIE?
TINY?
I'LL GIVE YOU ONE.
I COULD'VE BLASTED YOU OFF THE FACE OF BEDOUIN WITH THE *HERETIC*, AND I DIDN'T. I'M HERE TO NEGOTIATE THE RETURN OF MY BUSINESS PARTNER.
NINA. NOW.
THE GEORGIE I KNEW ONCE FOUGHT THROUGH AN ENTIRE GANG TO SAVE HER SISTER. BEING MADE A CRIPPLE ALSO MADE YOU A COWARD, I SEE.

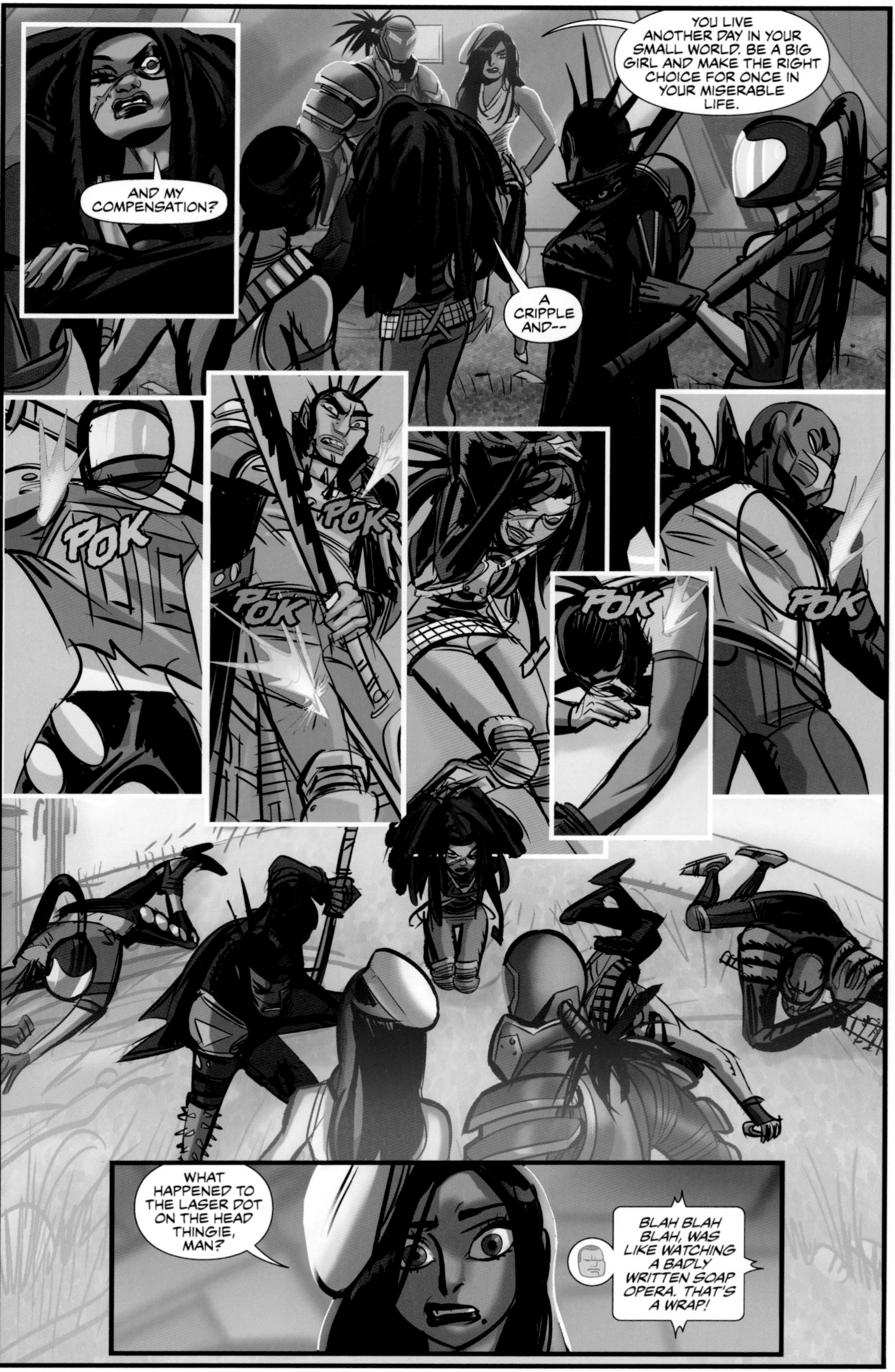
AND MY COMPENSATION?
YOU LIVE ANOTHER DAY IN YOUR SMALL WORLD. BE A BIG GIRL AND MAKE THE RIGHT CHOICE FOR ONCE IN YOUR MISERABLE LIFE.
A CRIPPLE AND--
POK
POK
POK
POK
POK
WHAT HAPPENED TO THE LASER DOT ON THE HEAD THINGIE, MAN?
BLAH BLAH BLAH, WAS LIKE WATCHING A BADLY WRITTEN SOAP OPERA. THAT'S A WRAP!

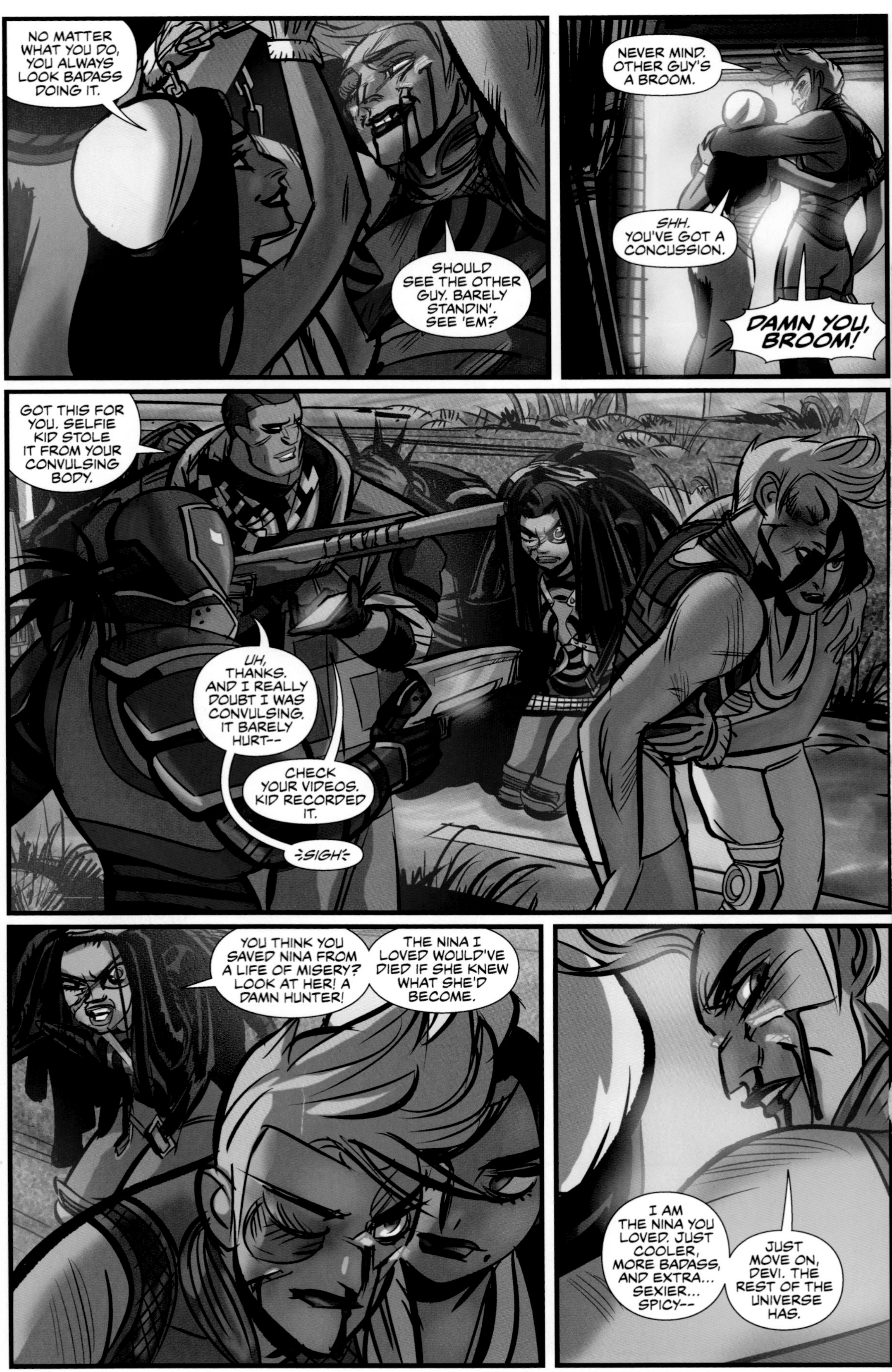
NO MATTER WHAT YOU DO, YOU ALWAYS LOOK BADASS DOING IT.
SHOULD SEE THE OTHER GUY. BARELY STANDIN'. SEE 'EM?
NEVER MIND. OTHER GUY'S A BROOM.
SHH. YOU'VE GOT A CONCUSSION.
DAMN YOU, BROOM!
GOT THIS FOR YOU. SELFIE KID STOLE IT FROM YOUR CONVULSING BODY.
UH, THANKS. AND I REALLY DOUBT I WAS CONVULSING. IT BARELY HURT--
CHECK YOUR VIDEOS. KID RECORDED IT.
SIGH
YOU THINK YOU SAVED NINA FROM A LIFE OF MISERY? LOOK AT HER! A DAMN HUNTER!
THE NINA I LOVED WOULD'VE DIED IF SHE KNEW WHAT SHE'D BECOME.
I AM THE NINA YOU LOVED. JUST COOLER, MORE BADASS, AND EXTRA... SEXIER... SPICY--
JUST MOVE ON, DEVI. THE REST OF THE UNIVERSE HAS.

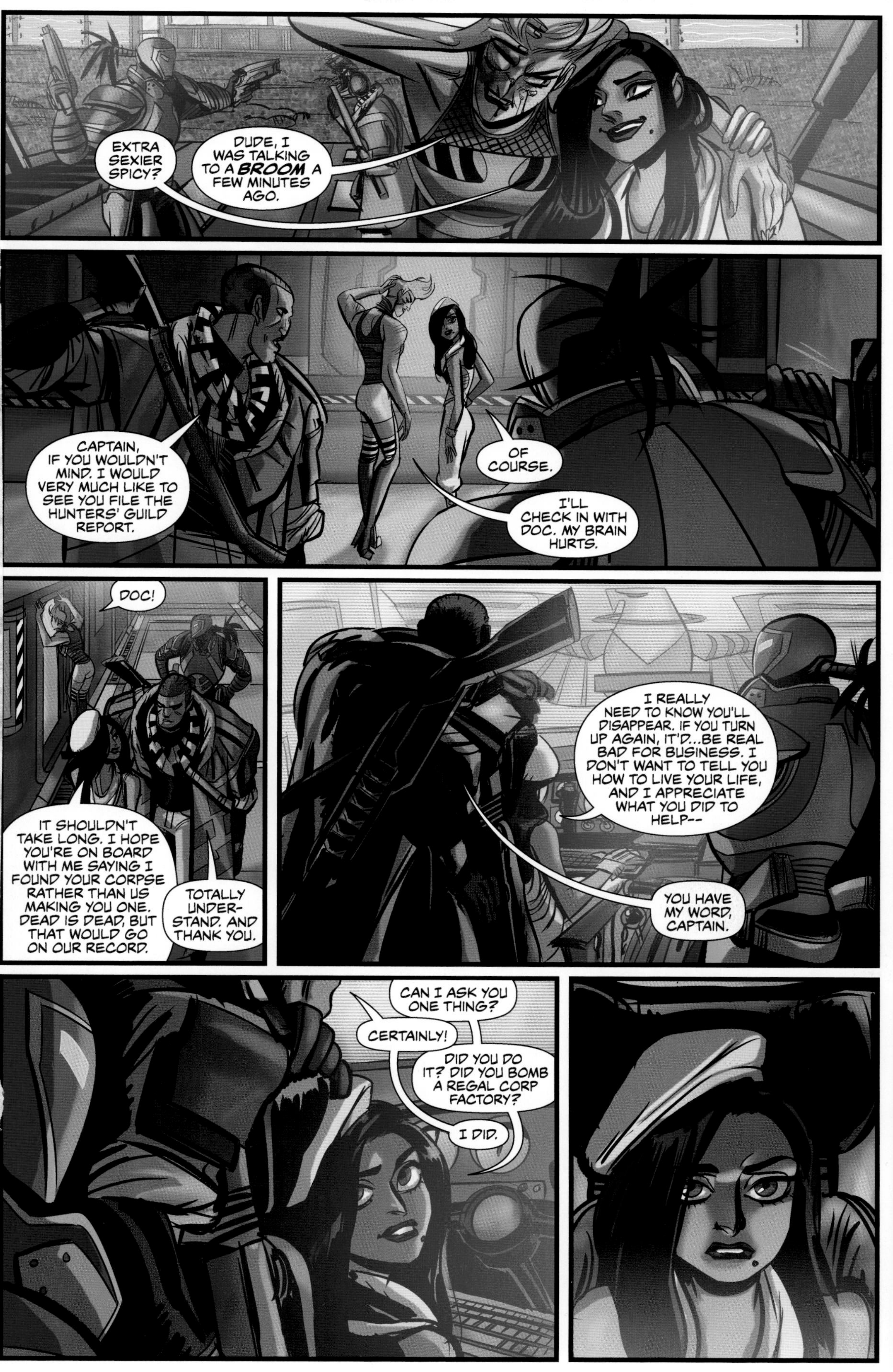
EXTRA SEXIER SPICY?
DUDE, I WAS TALKING TO A **BROOM** A FEW MINUTES AGO.
CAPTAIN, IF YOU WOULDN'T MIND, I WOULD VERY MUCH LIKE TO SEE YOU FILE THE HUNTERS' GUILD REPORT.
OF COURSE.
I'LL CHECK IN WITH DOC. MY BRAIN HURTS.
DOC!
IT SHOULDN'T TAKE LONG. I HOPE YOU'RE ON BOARD WITH ME SAYING I FOUND YOUR CORPSE RATHER THAN US MAKING YOU ONE. DEAD IS DEAD, BUT THAT WOULD GO ON OUR RECORD.
TOTALLY UNDER-STAND. AND THANK YOU.
I REALLY NEED TO KNOW YOU'LL DISAPPEAR. IF YOU TURN UP AGAIN, IT'D...BE REAL BAD FOR BUSINESS. I DON'T WANT TO TELL YOU HOW TO LIVE YOUR LIFE, AND I APPRECIATE WHAT YOU DID TO HELP--
YOU HAVE MY WORD, CAPTAIN.
CAN I ASK YOU ONE THING?
CERTAINLY!
DID YOU DO IT? DID YOU BOMB A REGAL CORP FACTORY?
I DID.

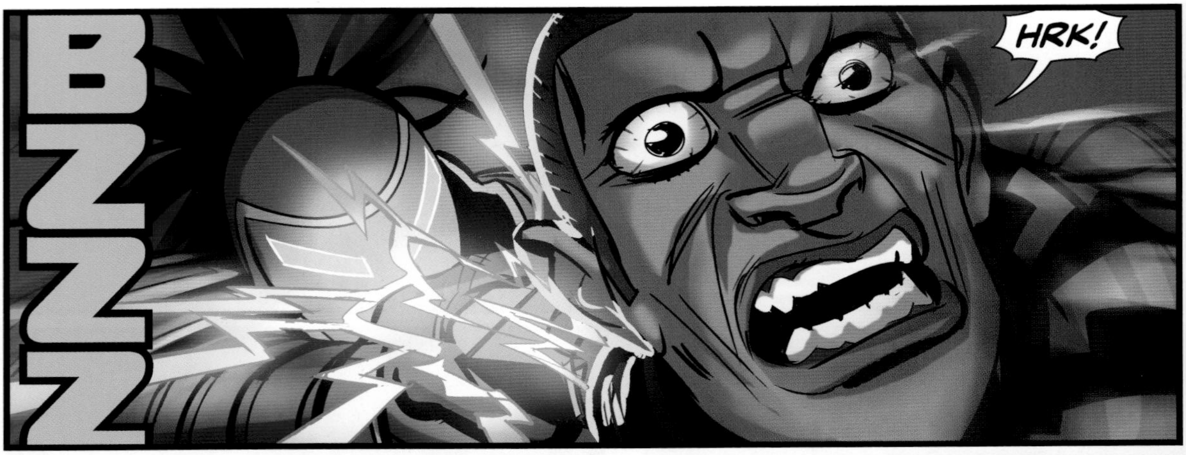
BZZZ
HRK!

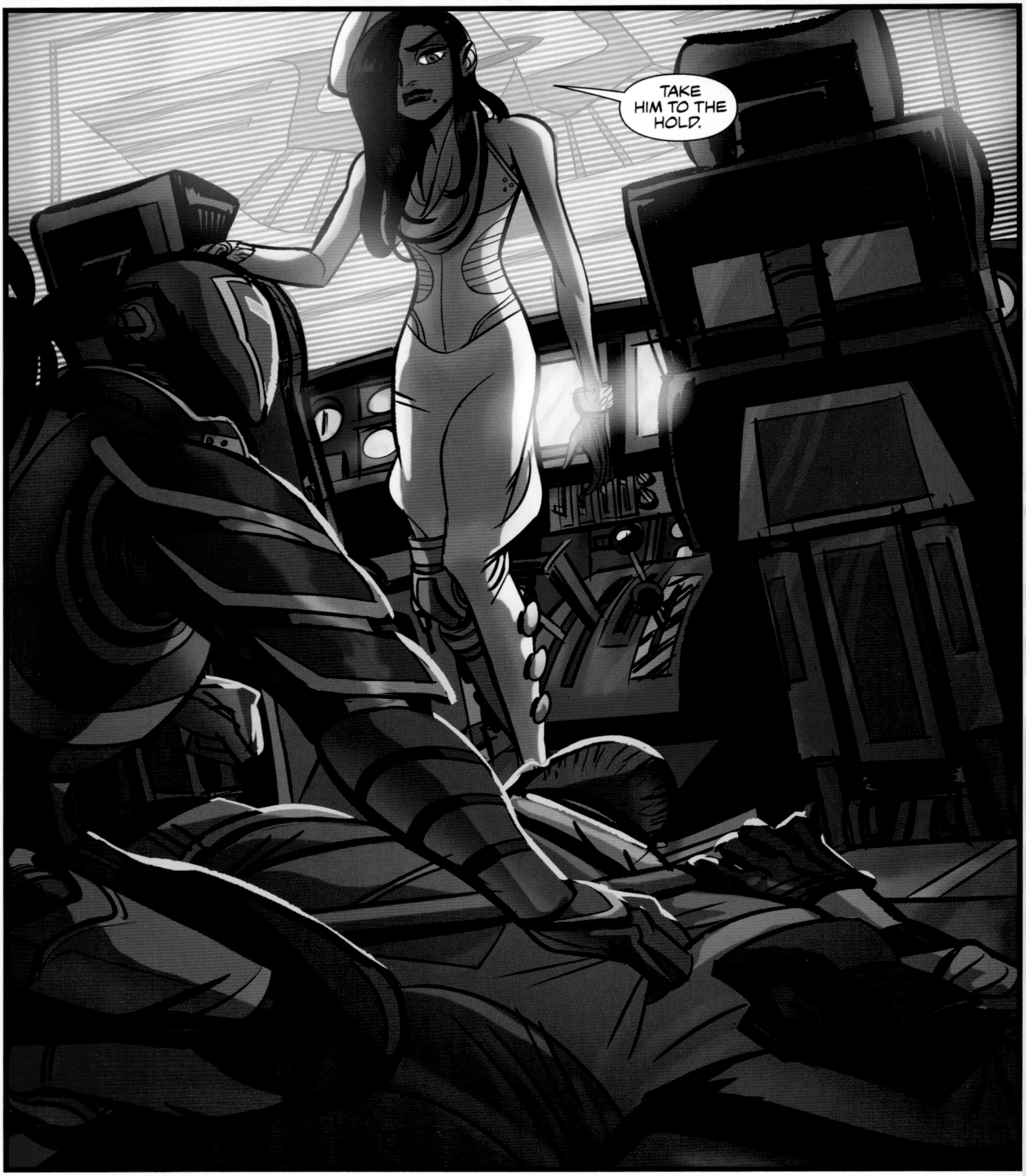
TAKE HIM TO THE HOLD.

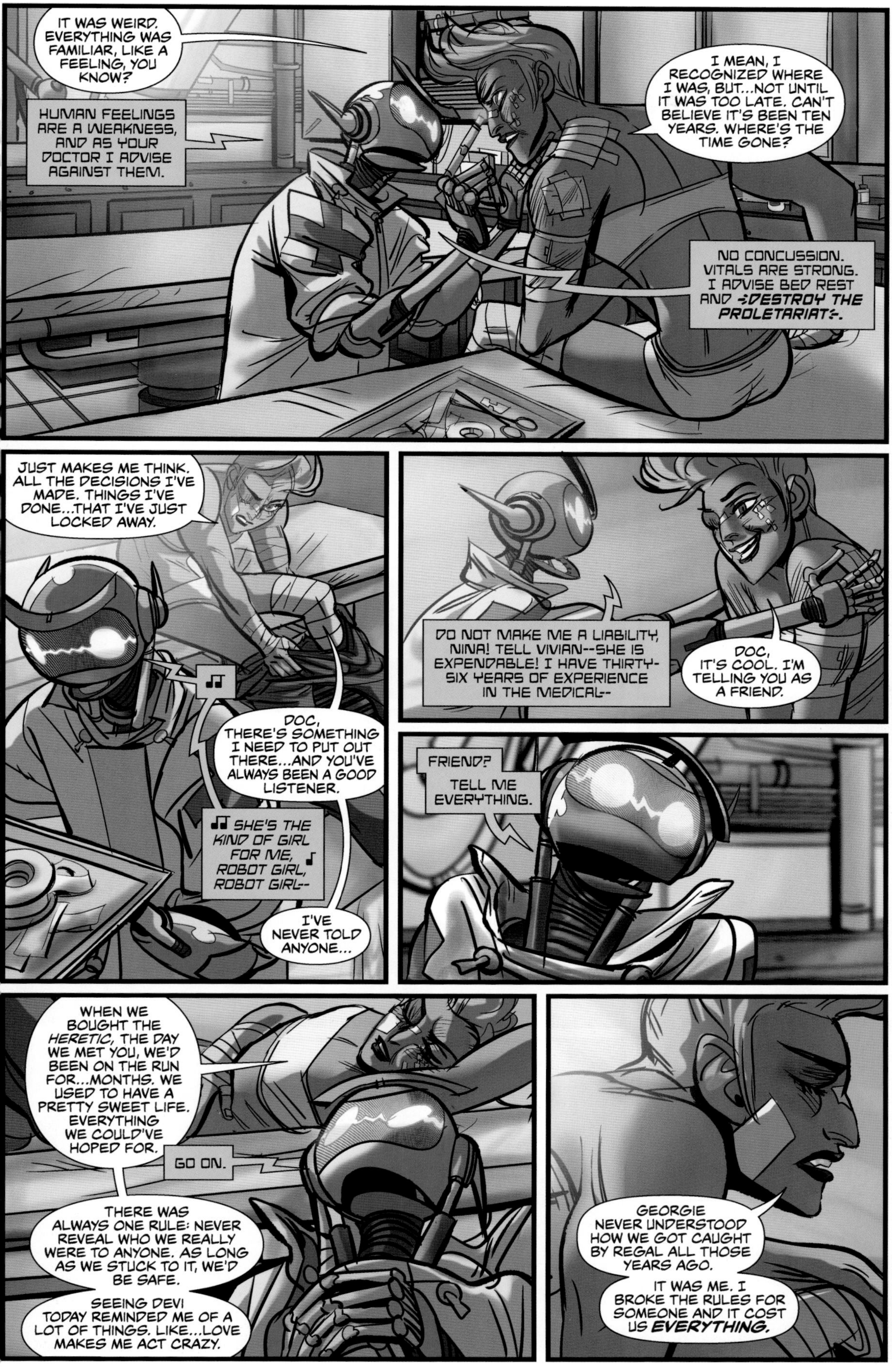

IT WAS WEIRD. EVERYTHING WAS FAMILIAR, LIKE A FEELING, YOU KNOW?
HUMAN FEELINGS ARE A WEAKNESS, AND AS YOUR DOCTOR I ADVISE AGAINST THEM.
I MEAN, I RECOGNIZED WHERE I WAS, BUT...NOT UNTIL IT WAS TOO LATE. CAN'T BELIEVE IT'S BEEN TEN YEARS. WHERE'S THE TIME GONE?
NO CONCUSSION. VITALS ARE STRONG. I ADVISE BED REST AND ÷DESTROY THE PROLETARIAT÷.
JUST MAKES ME THINK. ALL THE DECISIONS I'VE MADE. THINGS I'VE DONE...THAT I'VE JUST LOCKED AWAY.
♫
DOC, THERE'S SOMETHING I NEED TO PUT OUT THERE...AND YOU'VE ALWAYS BEEN A GOOD LISTENER.
♫ SHE'S THE KIND OF GIRL FOR ME, ROBOT GIRL, ROBOT GIRL--
I'VE NEVER TOLD ANYONE...
DO NOT MAKE ME A LIABILITY, NINA! TELL VIVIAN--SHE IS EXPENDABLE! I HAVE THIRTY-SIX YEARS OF EXPERIENCE IN THE MEDICAL--
DOC, IT'S COOL. I'M TELLING YOU AS A FRIEND.
FRIEND? TELL ME EVERYTHING.
WHEN WE BOUGHT THE HERETIC, THE DAY WE MET YOU, WE'D BEEN ON THE RUN FOR...MONTHS. WE USED TO HAVE A PRETTY SWEET LIFE. EVERYTHING WE COULD'VE HOPED FOR.
GO ON.
THERE WAS ALWAYS ONE RULE: NEVER REVEAL WHO WE REALLY WERE TO ANYONE. AS LONG AS WE STUCK TO IT, WE'D BE SAFE.
SEEING DEVI TODAY REMINDED ME OF A LOT OF THINGS. LIKE...LOVE MAKES ME ACT CRAZY.
GEORGIE NEVER UNDERSTOOD HOW WE GOT CAUGHT BY REGAL ALL THOSE YEARS AGO.
IT WAS ME. I BROKE THE RULES FOR SOMEONE AND IT COST US EVERYTHING.

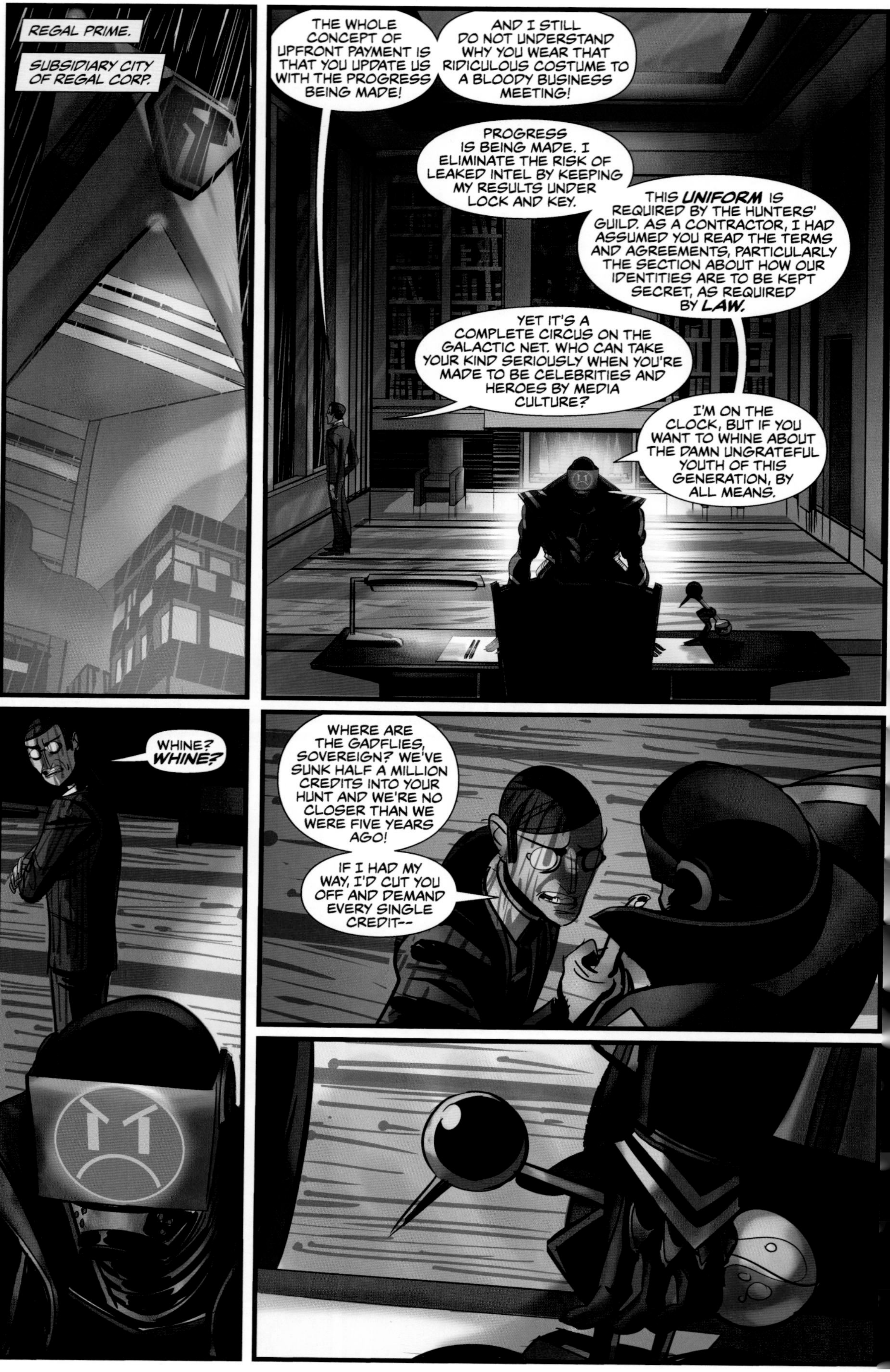
REGAL PRIME.
SUBSIDIARY CITY OF REGAL CORP.
THE WHOLE CONCEPT OF UPFRONT PAYMENT IS THAT YOU UPDATE US WITH THE PROGRESS BEING MADE!
AND I STILL DO NOT UNDERSTAND WHY YOU WEAR THAT RIDICULOUS COSTUME TO A BLOODY BUSINESS MEETING!
PROGRESS IS BEING MADE. I ELIMINATE THE RISK OF LEAKED INTEL BY KEEPING MY RESULTS UNDER LOCK AND KEY.
THIS UNIFORM IS REQUIRED BY THE HUNTERS' GUILD. AS A CONTRACTOR, I HAD ASSUMED YOU READ THE TERMS AND AGREEMENTS, PARTICULARLY THE SECTION ABOUT HOW OUR IDENTITIES ARE TO BE KEPT SECRET, AS REQUIRED BY LAW.
YET IT'S A COMPLETE CIRCUS ON THE GALACTIC NET. WHO CAN TAKE YOUR KIND SERIOUSLY WHEN YOU'RE MADE TO BE CELEBRITIES AND HEROES BY MEDIA CULTURE?
I'M ON THE CLOCK, BUT IF YOU WANT TO WHINE ABOUT THE DAMN UNGRATEFUL YOUTH OF THIS GENERATION, BY ALL MEANS.
WHINE? WHINE?
WHERE ARE THE GADFLIES, SOVEREIGN? WE'VE SUNK HALF A MILLION CREDITS INTO YOUR HUNT AND WE'RE NO CLOSER THAN WE WERE FIVE YEARS AGO!
IF I HAD MY WAY, I'D CUT YOU OFF AND DEMAND EVERY SINGLE CREDIT--

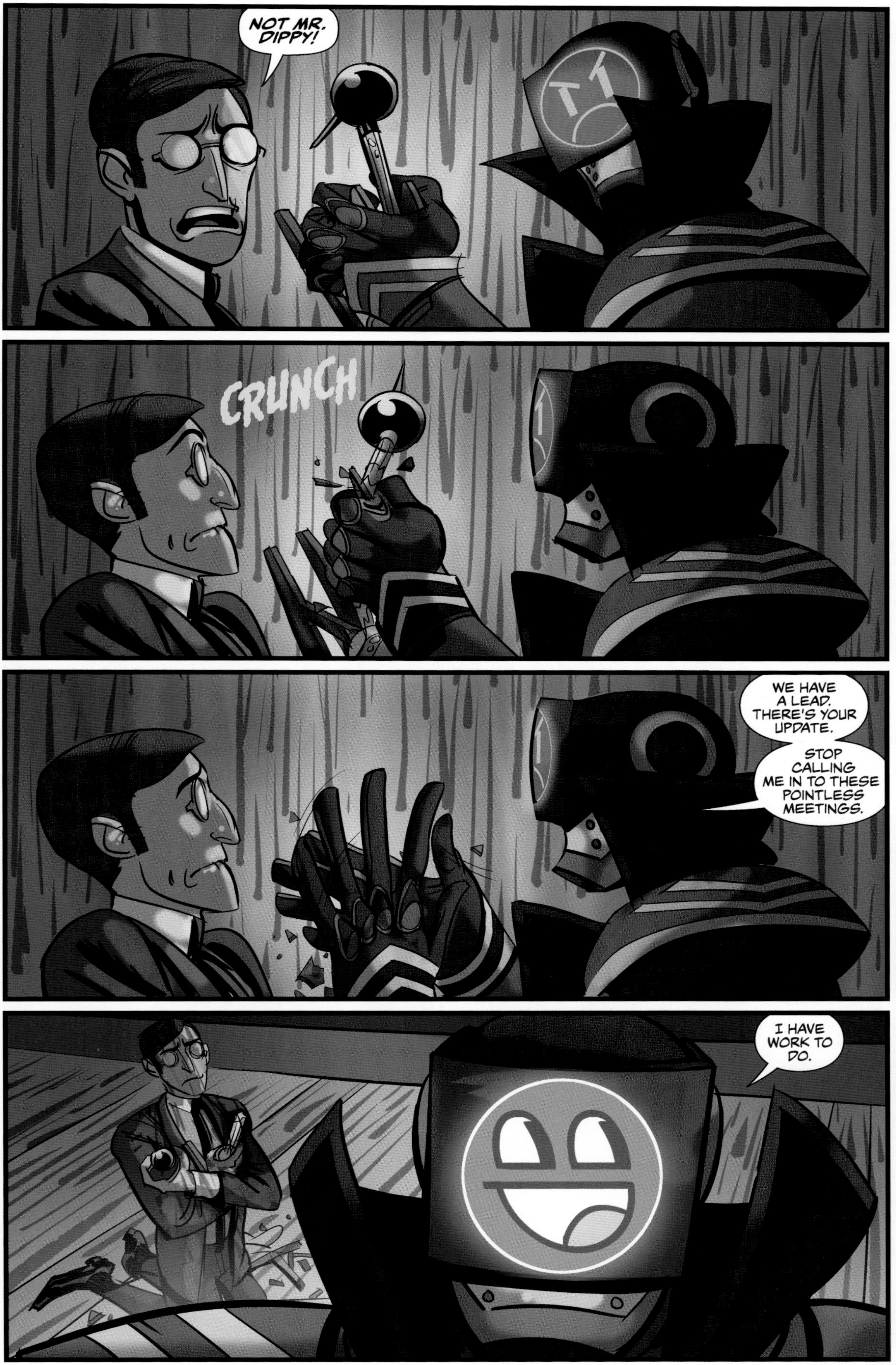
NOT MR. DIPPY!
CRUNCH
WE HAVE A LEAD. THERE'S YOUR UPDATE.
STOP CALLING ME IN TO THESE POINTLESS MEETINGS.
I HAVE WORK TO DO.

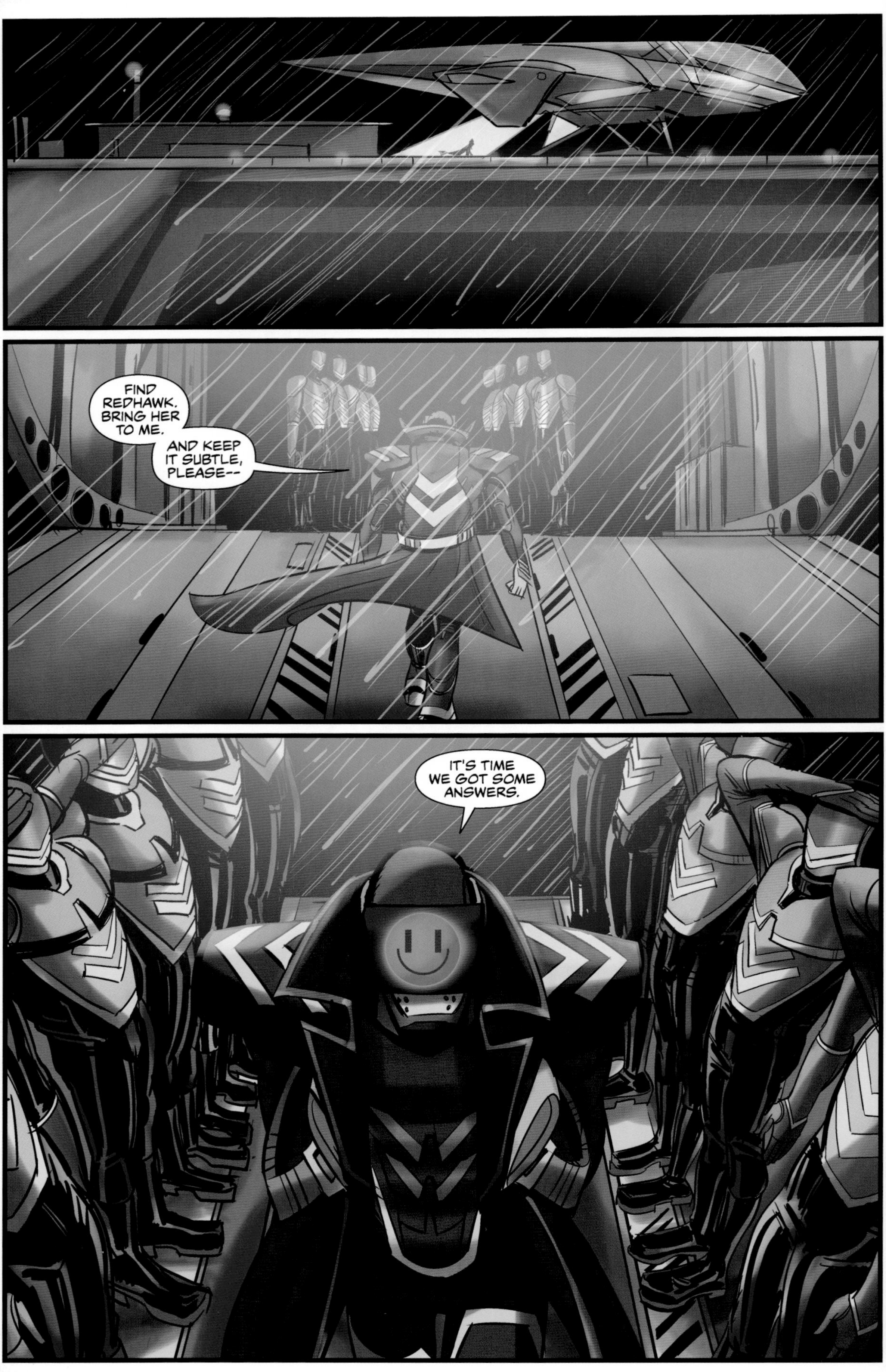
FIND REDHAWK. BRING HER TO ME.
AND KEEP IT SUBTLE, PLEASE--
IT'S TIME WE GOT SOME ANSWERS.

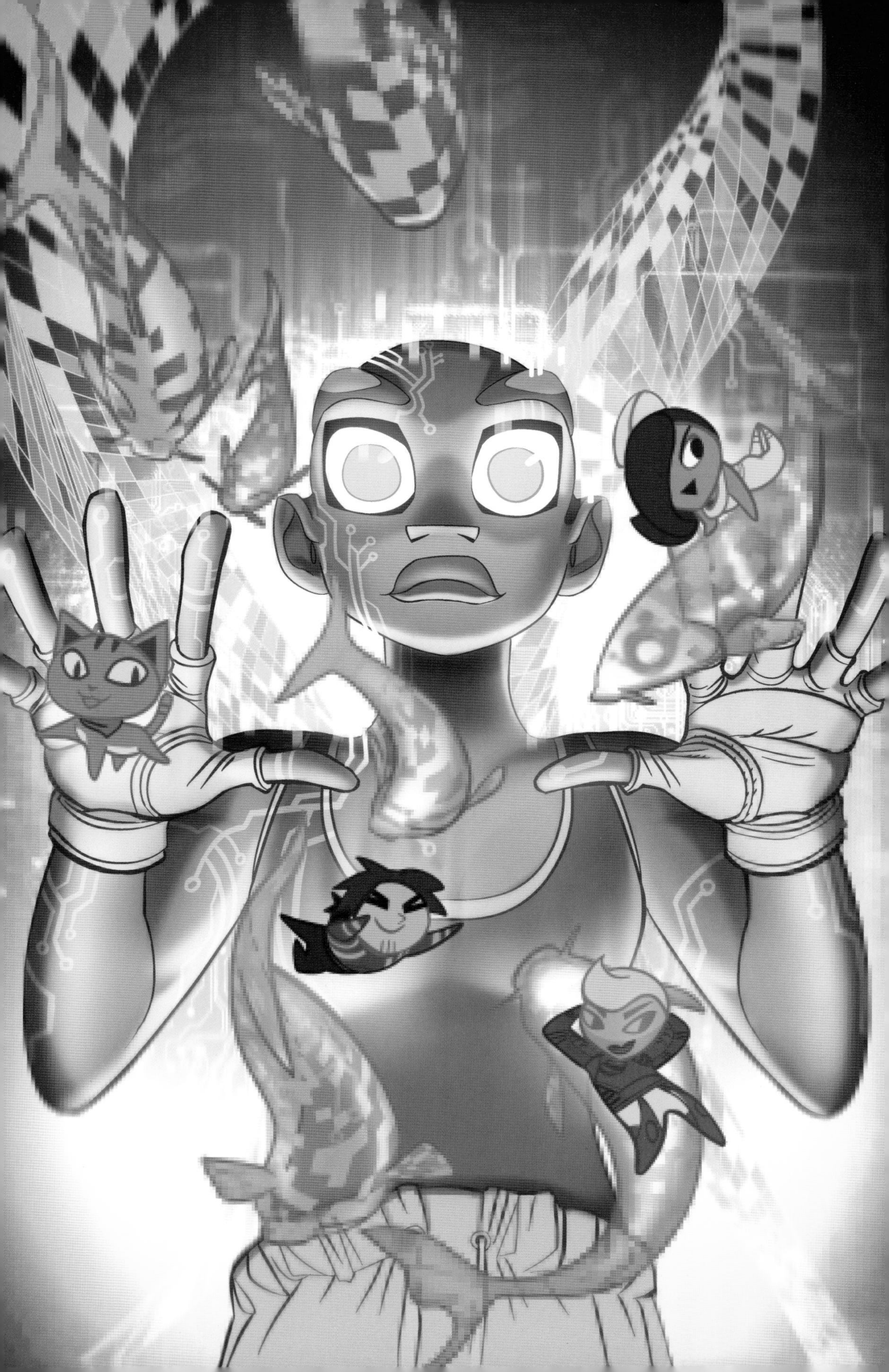

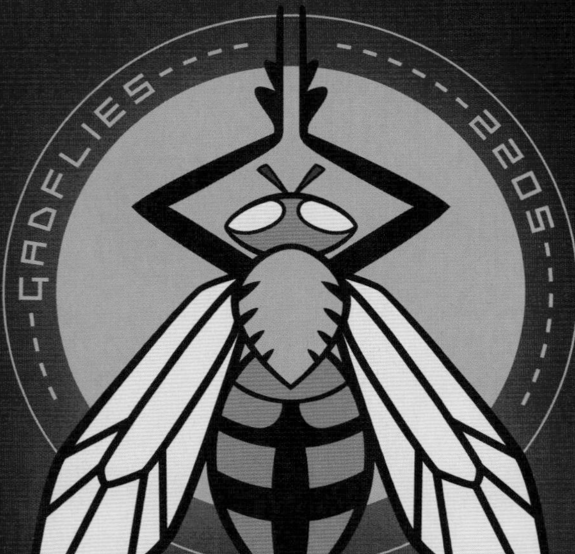
GADFLIES
2205

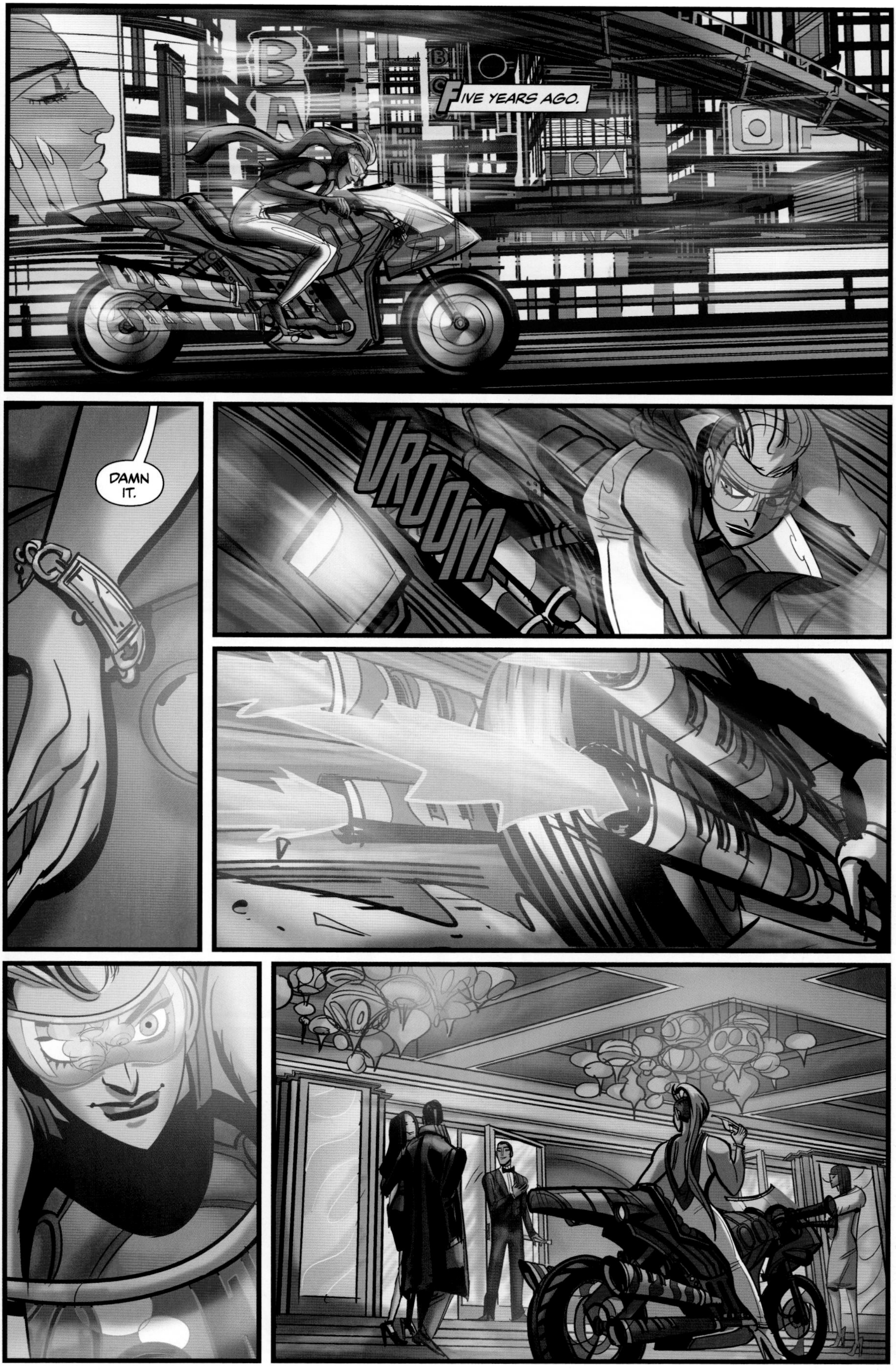
FIVE YEARS AGO.
DAMN IT.
VROOM

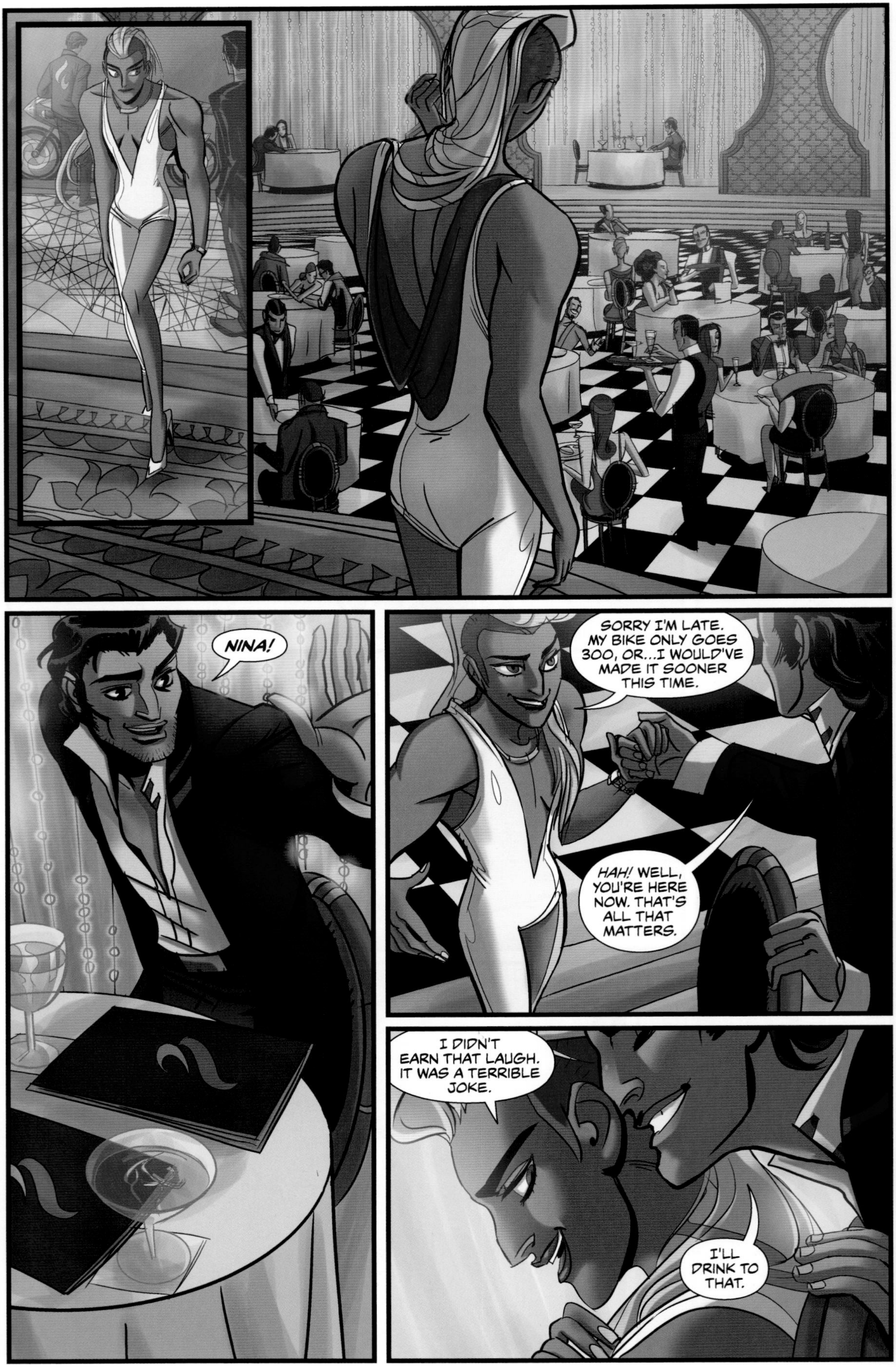
NINA!
SORRY I'M LATE. MY BIKE ONLY GOES 300, OR...I WOULD'VE MADE IT SOONER THIS TIME.
HAH! WELL, YOU'RE HERE NOW. THAT'S ALL THAT MATTERS.
I DIDN'T EARN THAT LAUGH. IT WAS A TERRIBLE JOKE.
I'LL DRINK TO THAT.

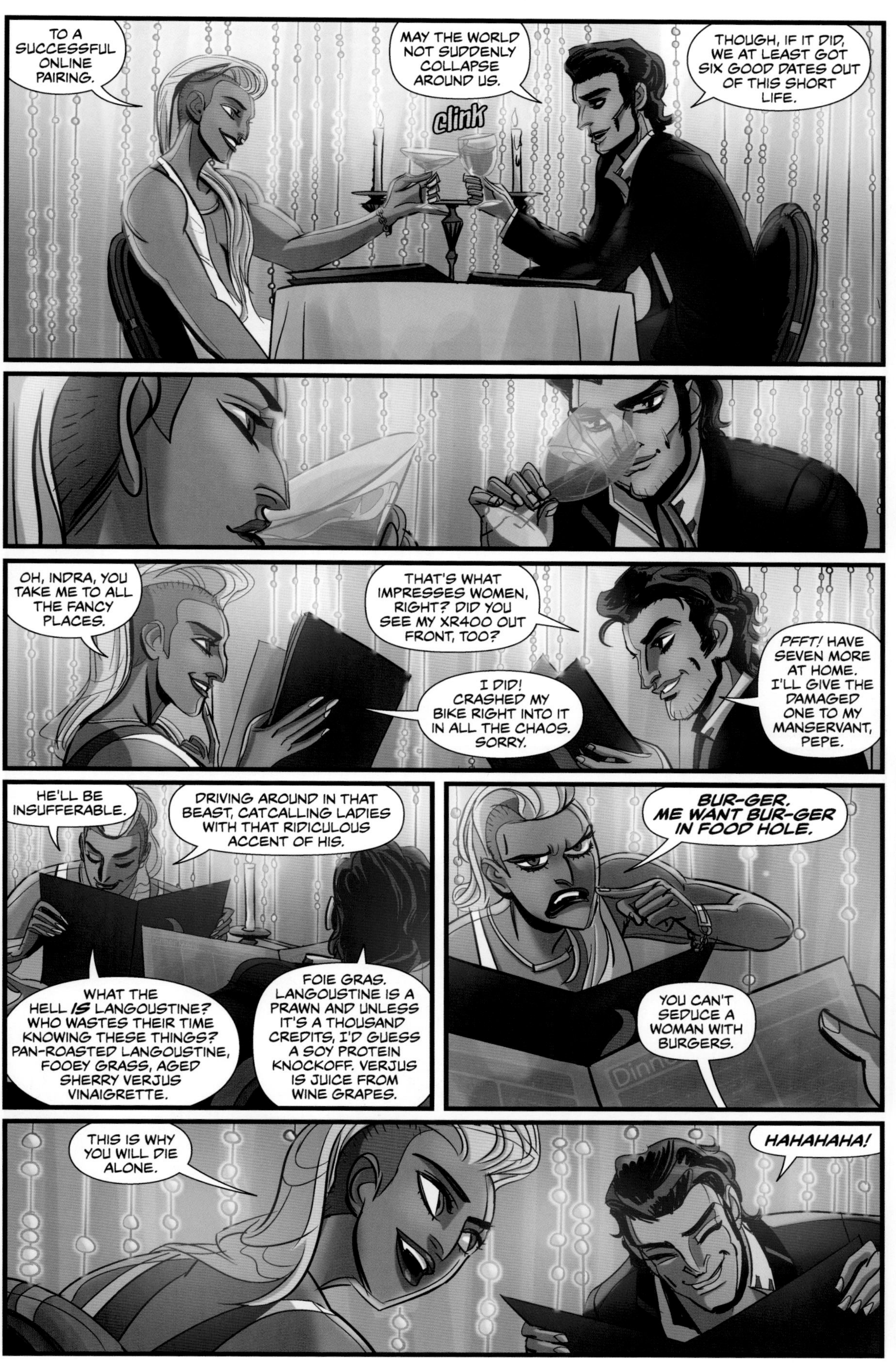
TO A SUCCESSFUL ONLINE PAIRING.
MAY THE WORLD NOT SUDDENLY COLLAPSE AROUND US.
THOUGH, IF IT DID, WE AT LEAST GOT SIX GOOD DATES OUT OF THIS SHORT LIFE.
clink
OH, INDRA, YOU TAKE ME TO ALL THE FANCY PLACES.
THAT'S WHAT IMPRESSES WOMEN, RIGHT? DID YOU SEE MY XR400 OUT FRONT, TOO?
I DID! CRASHED MY BIKE RIGHT INTO IT IN ALL THE CHAOS. SORRY.
PFFT! HAVE SEVEN MORE AT HOME. I'LL GIVE THE DAMAGED ONE TO MY MANSERVANT, PEPE.
HE'LL BE INSUFFERABLE.
DRIVING AROUND IN THAT BEAST, CATCALLING LADIES WITH THAT RIDICULOUS ACCENT OF HIS.
WHAT THE HELL *IS* LANGOUSTINE? WHO WASTES THEIR TIME KNOWING THESE THINGS? PAN-ROASTED LANGOUSTINE, FOOEY GRASS, AGED SHERRY VERJUS VINAIGRETTE.
FOIE GRAS. LANGOUSTINE IS A PRAWN AND UNLESS IT'S A THOUSAND CREDITS, I'D GUESS A SOY PROTEIN KNOCKOFF. VERJUS IS JUICE FROM WINE GRAPES.
BUR-GER. ME WANT BUR-GER IN FOOD HOLE.
YOU CAN'T SEDUCE A WOMAN WITH BURGERS.
THIS IS WHY YOU WILL DIE ALONE.
HAHAHAHA!

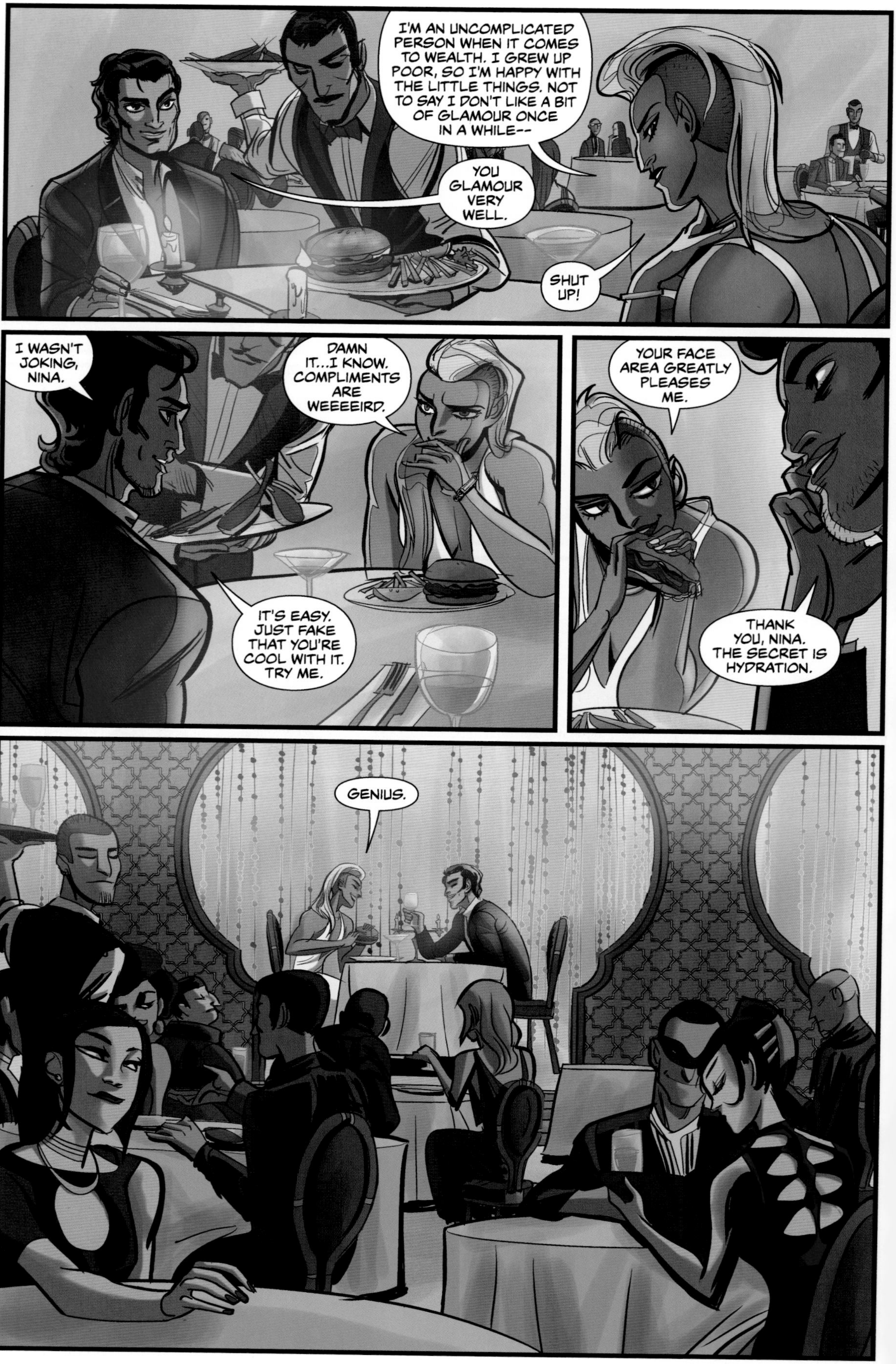
I'M AN UNCOMPLICATED PERSON WHEN IT COMES TO WEALTH. I GREW UP POOR, SO I'M HAPPY WITH THE LITTLE THINGS. NOT TO SAY I DON'T LIKE A BIT OF GLAMOUR ONCE IN A WHILE--
YOU GLAMOUR VERY WELL.
SHUT UP!
I WASN'T JOKING, NINA.
DAMN IT...I KNOW. COMPLIMENTS ARE WEEEEIRD.
IT'S EASY. JUST FAKE THAT YOU'RE COOL WITH IT. TRY ME.
YOUR FACE AREA GREATLY PLEASES ME.
THANK YOU, NINA. THE SECRET IS HYDRATION.
GENIUS.

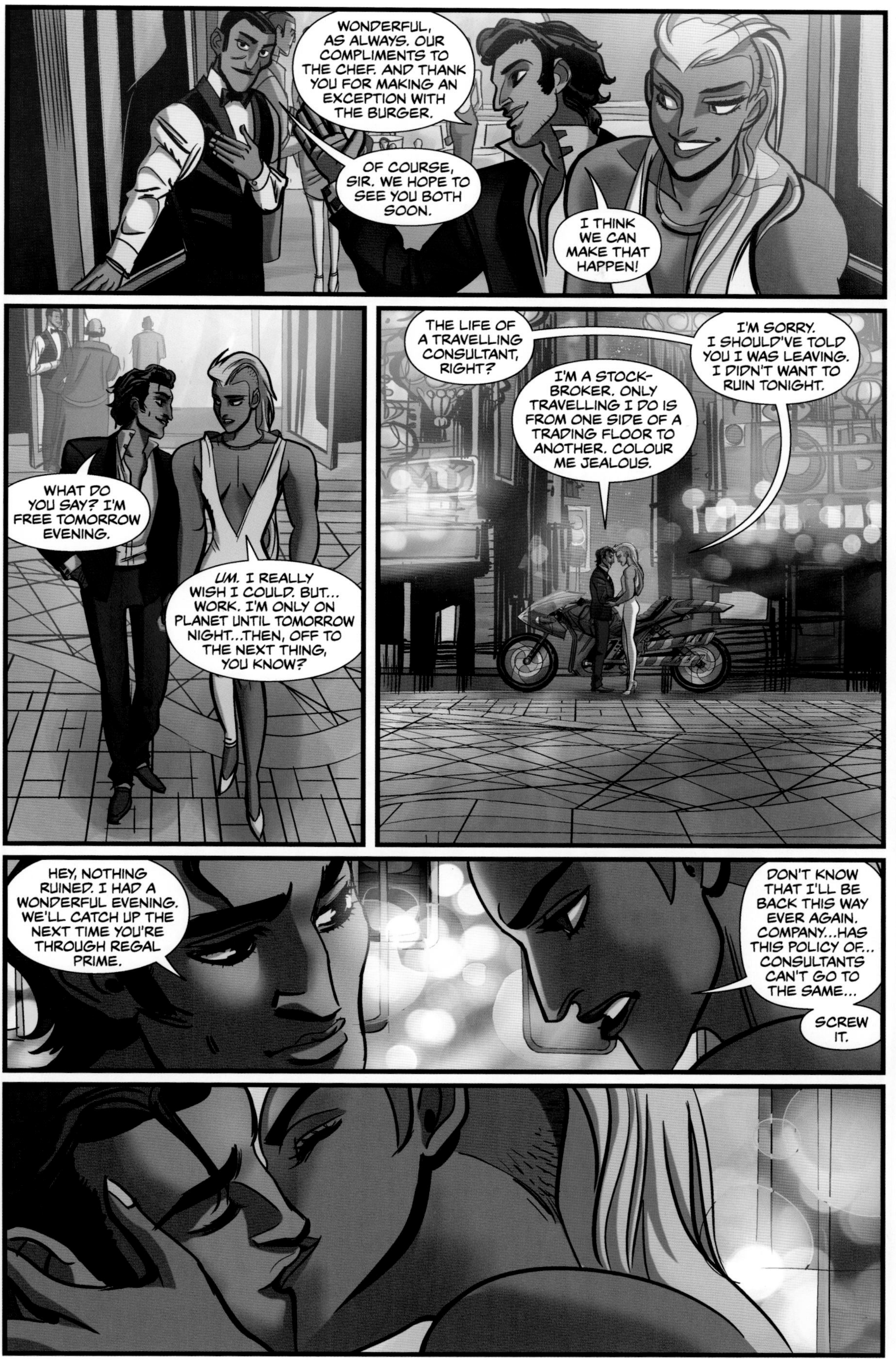
WONDERFUL, AS ALWAYS. OUR COMPLIMENTS TO THE CHEF. AND THANK YOU FOR MAKING AN EXCEPTION WITH THE BURGER.
OF COURSE, SIR. WE HOPE TO SEE YOU BOTH SOON.
I THINK WE CAN MAKE THAT HAPPEN!
WHAT DO YOU SAY? I'M FREE TOMORROW EVENING.
UM. I REALLY WISH I COULD. BUT... WORK. I'M ONLY ON PLANET UNTIL TOMORROW NIGHT...THEN, OFF TO THE NEXT THING, YOU KNOW?
THE LIFE OF A TRAVELLING CONSULTANT, RIGHT?
I'M A STOCK-BROKER. ONLY TRAVELLING I DO IS FROM ONE SIDE OF A TRADING FLOOR TO ANOTHER. COLOUR ME JEALOUS.
I'M SORRY. I SHOULD'VE TOLD YOU I WAS LEAVING. I DIDN'T WANT TO RUIN TONIGHT.
HEY, NOTHING RUINED. I HAD A WONDERFUL EVENING. WE'LL CATCH UP THE NEXT TIME YOU'RE THROUGH REGAL PRIME.
DON'T KNOW THAT I'LL BE BACK THIS WAY EVER AGAIN. COMPANY...HAS THIS POLICY OF... CONSULTANTS CAN'T GO TO THE SAME...
SCREW IT.

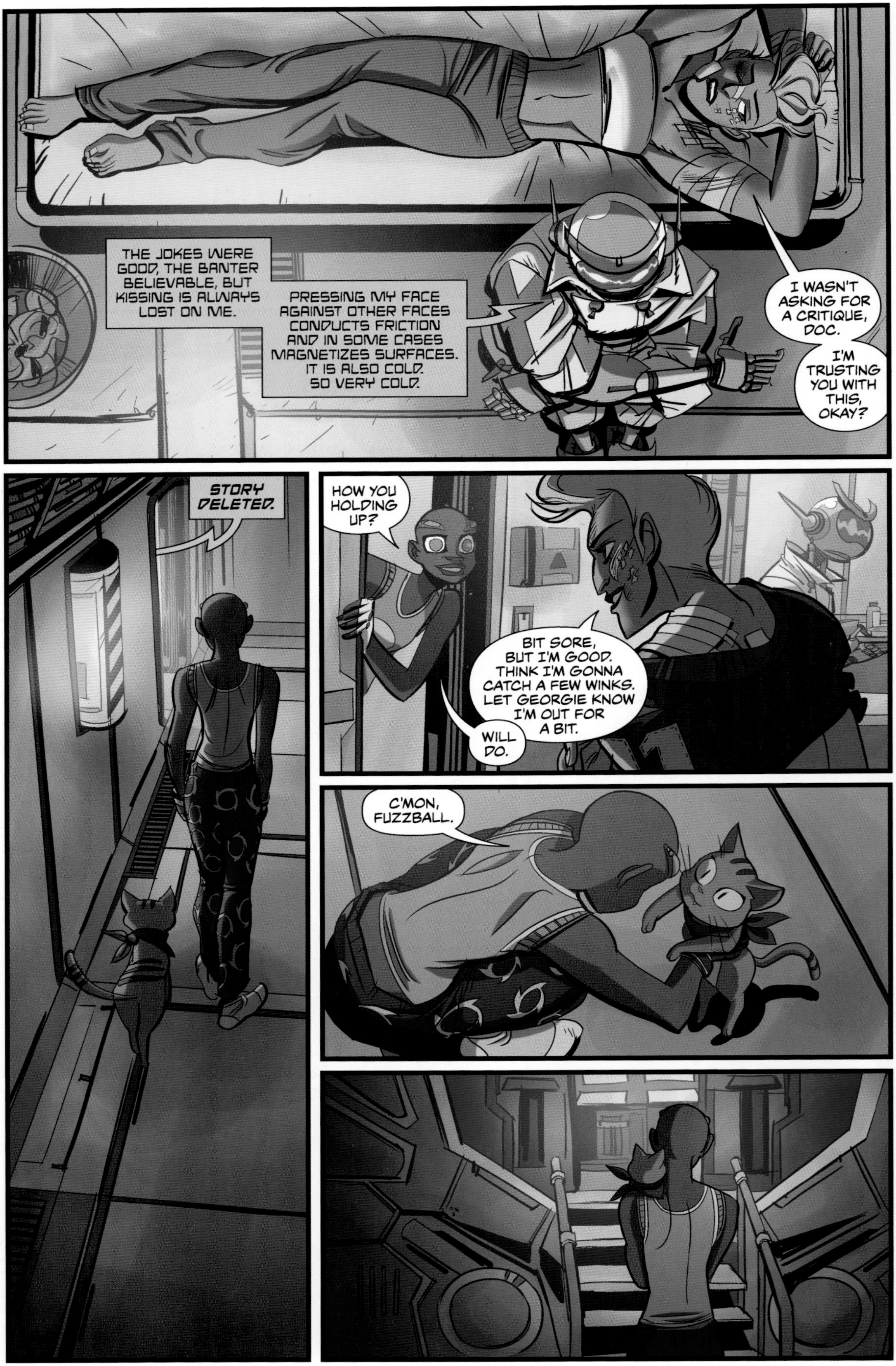
THE JOKES WERE GOOD, THE BANTER BELIEVABLE, BUT KISSING IS ALWAYS LOST ON ME.
PRESSING MY FACE AGAINST OTHER FACES CONDUCTS FRICTION AND IN SOME CASES MAGNETIZES SURFACES. IT IS ALSO COLD. SO VERY COLD.
I WASN'T ASKING FOR A CRITIQUE, DOC.
I'M TRUSTING YOU WITH THIS, OKAY?
STORY DELETED.
HOW YOU HOLDING UP?
BIT SORE, BUT I'M GOOD. THINK I'M GONNA CATCH A FEW WINKS. LET GEORGIE KNOW I'M OUT FOR A BIT.
WILL DO.
C'MON, FUZZBALL.

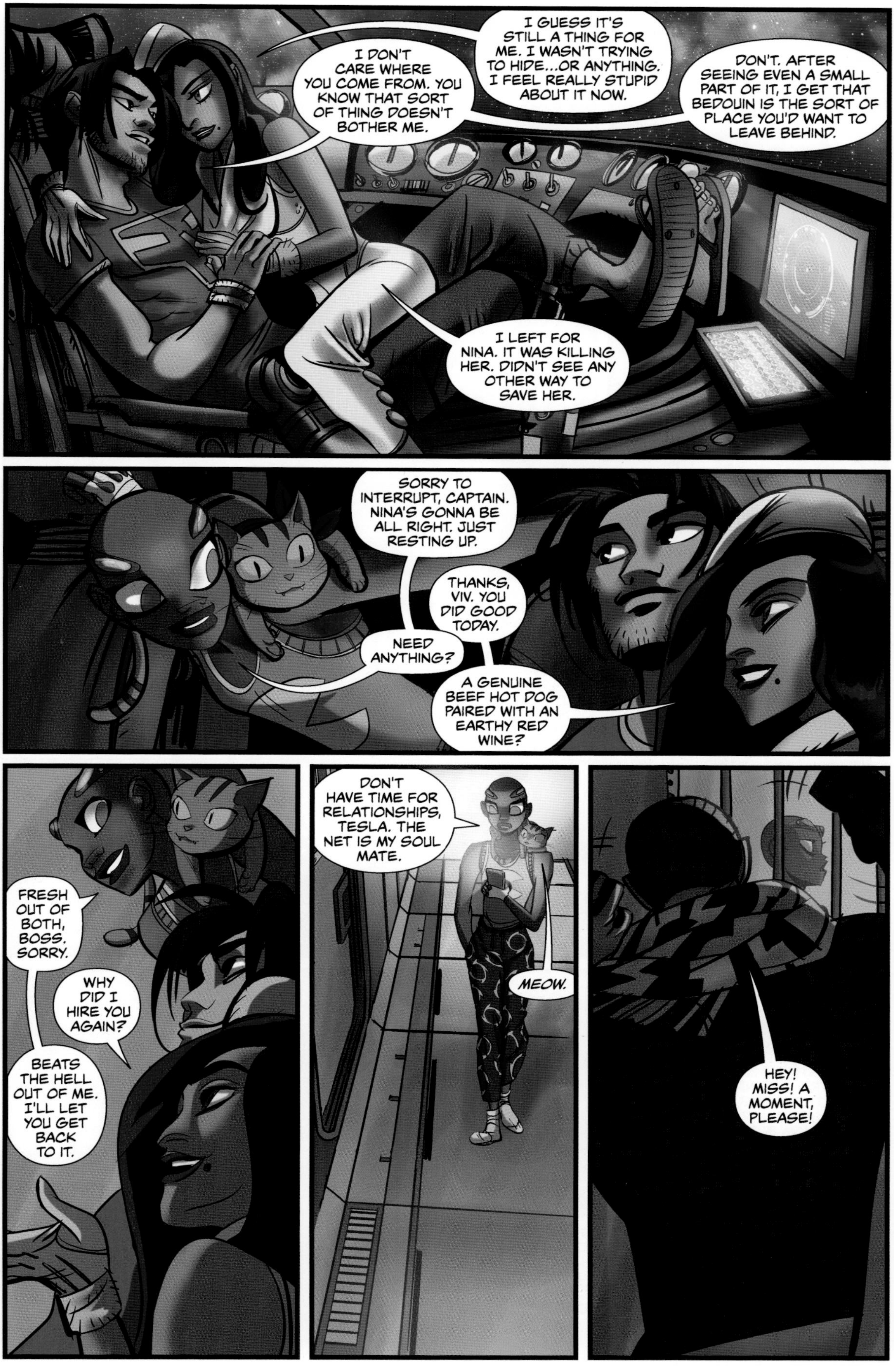
I DON'T CARE WHERE YOU COME FROM. YOU KNOW THAT SORT OF THING DOESN'T BOTHER ME.
I GUESS IT'S STILL A THING FOR ME. I WASN'T TRYING TO HIDE...OR ANYTHING. I FEEL REALLY STUPID ABOUT IT NOW.
DON'T. AFTER SEEING EVEN A SMALL PART OF IT, I GET THAT BEDOUIN IS THE SORT OF PLACE YOU'D WANT TO LEAVE BEHIND.
I LEFT FOR NINA. IT WAS KILLING HER. DIDN'T SEE ANY OTHER WAY TO SAVE HER.
SORRY TO INTERRUPT, CAPTAIN. NINA'S GONNA BE ALL RIGHT. JUST RESTING UP.
THANKS, VIV. YOU DID GOOD TODAY.
NEED ANYTHING?
A GENUINE BEEF HOT DOG PAIRED WITH AN EARTHY RED WINE?
FRESH OUT OF BOTH, BOSS. SORRY.
WHY DID I HIRE YOU AGAIN?
BEATS THE HELL OUT OF ME. I'LL LET YOU GET BACK TO IT.
DON'T HAVE TIME FOR RELATIONSHIPS, TESLA. THE NET IS MY SOUL MATE.
MEOW.
HEY! MISS! A MOMENT, PLEASE!

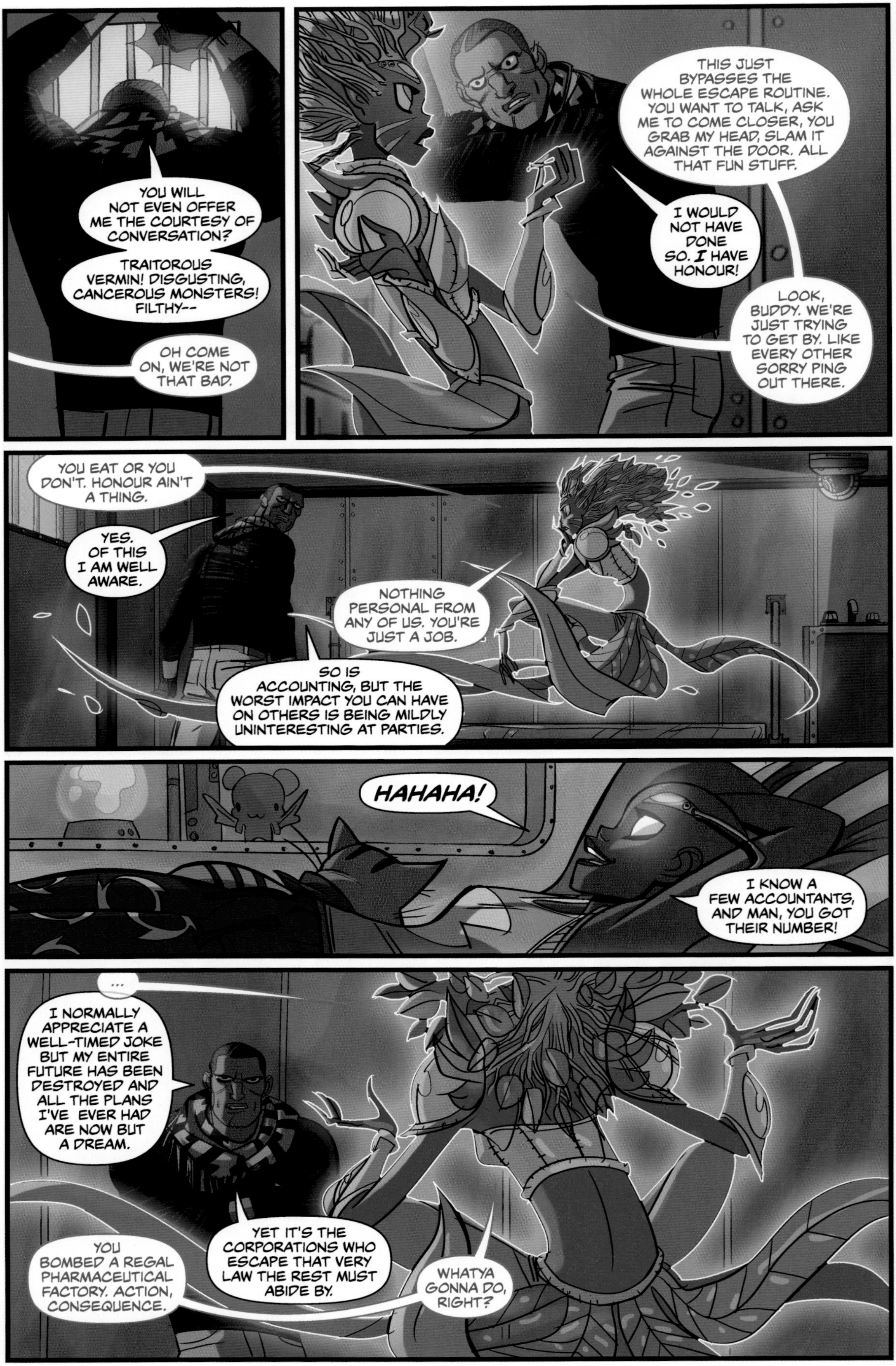
YOU WILL NOT EVEN OFFER ME THE COURTESY OF CONVERSATION?
TRAITOROUS VERMIN! DISGUSTING, CANCEROUS MONSTERS! FILTHY--
OH COME ON, WE'RE NOT THAT BAD.
THIS JUST BYPASSES THE WHOLE ESCAPE ROUTINE. YOU WANT TO TALK, ASK ME TO COME CLOSER, YOU GRAB MY HEAD, SLAM IT AGAINST THE DOOR. ALL THAT FUN STUFF.
I WOULD NOT HAVE DONE SO. I HAVE HONOUR!
LOOK, BUDDY. WE'RE JUST TRYING TO GET BY. LIKE EVERY OTHER SORRY PING OUT THERE.
YOU EAT OR YOU DON'T. HONOUR AIN'T A THING.
YES. OF THIS I AM WELL AWARE.
NOTHING PERSONAL FROM ANY OF US. YOU'RE JUST A JOB.
SO IS ACCOUNTING, BUT THE WORST IMPACT YOU CAN HAVE ON OTHERS IS BEING MILDLY UNINTERESTING AT PARTIES.
HAHAHA!
I KNOW A FEW ACCOUNTANTS, AND MAN, YOU GOT THEIR NUMBER!
...
I NORMALLY APPRECIATE A WELL-TIMED JOKE BUT MY ENTIRE FUTURE HAS BEEN DESTROYED AND ALL THE PLANS I'VE EVER HAD ARE NOW BUT A DREAM.
YOU BOMBED A REGAL PHARMACEUTICAL FACTORY. ACTION, CONSEQUENCE.
YET IT'S THE CORPORATIONS WHO ESCAPE THAT VERY LAW THE REST MUST ABIDE BY.
WHATYA GONNA DO, RIGHT?

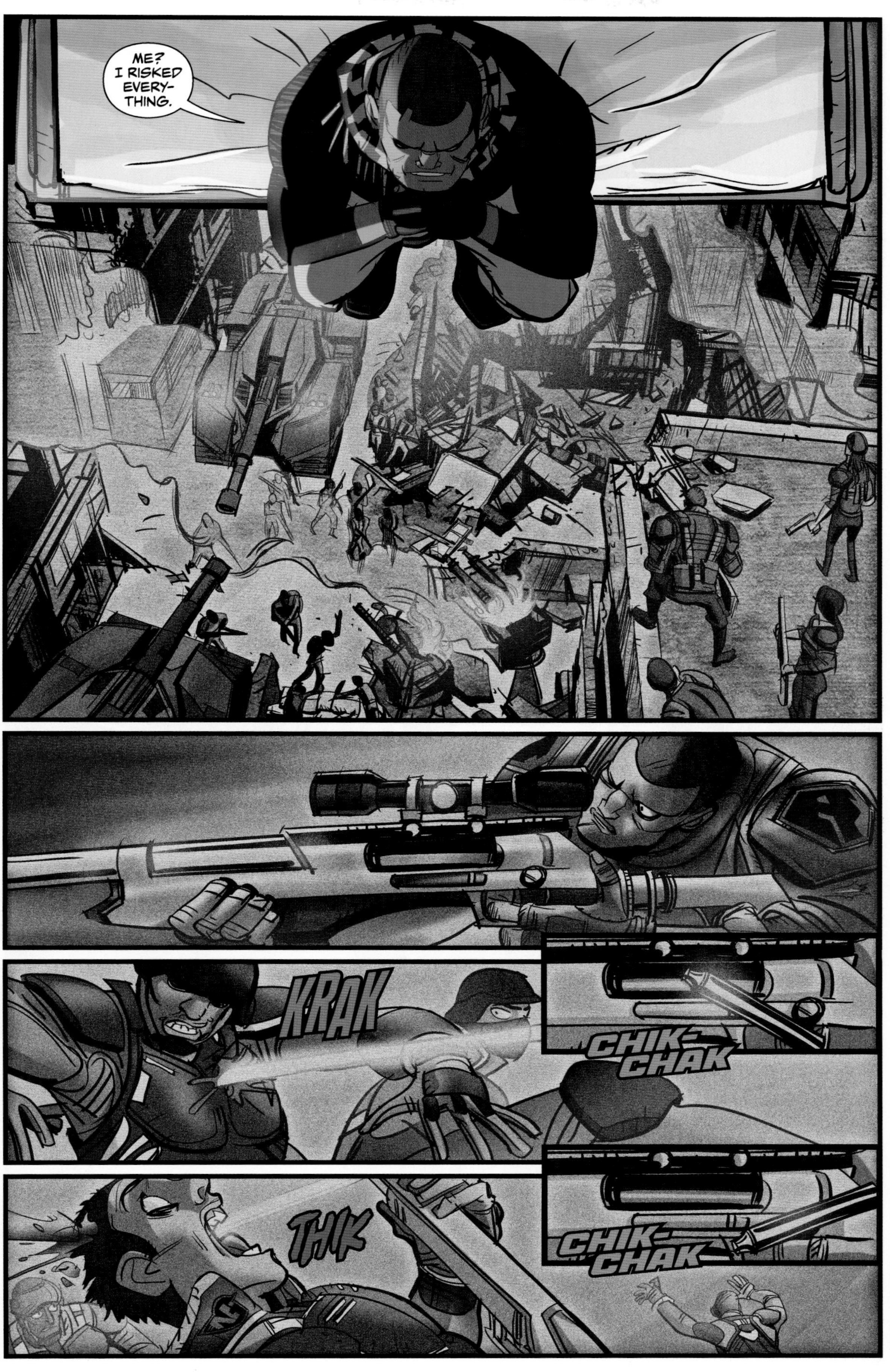
ME? I RISKED EVERYTHING.
KRAK
CHIK-CHAK
THIK
CHIK-CHAK

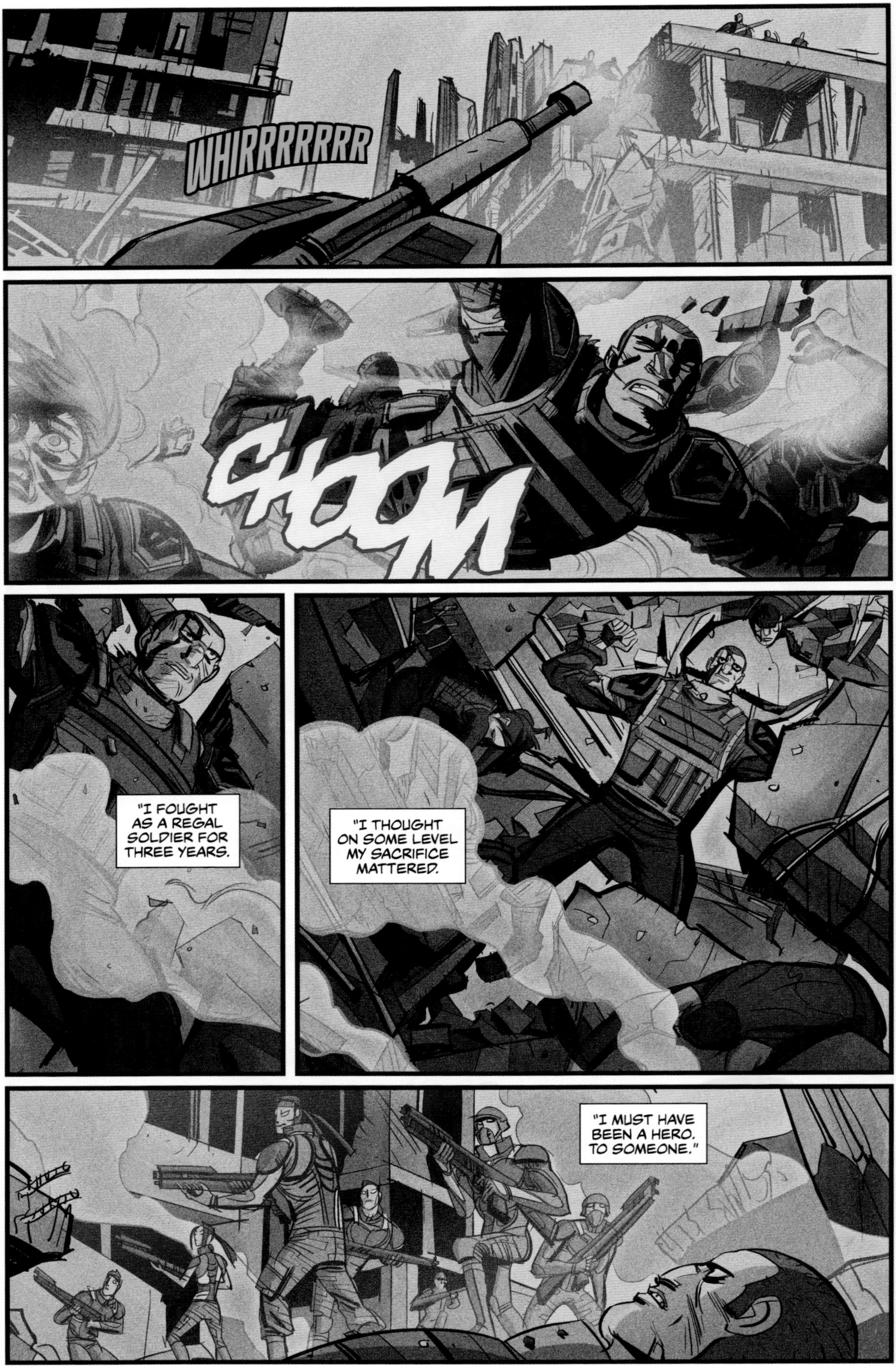
WHIRRRRRRR
CHOOM
"I FOUGHT AS A REGAL SOLDIER FOR THREE YEARS.
"I THOUGHT ON SOME LEVEL MY SACRIFICE MATTERED.
"I MUST HAVE BEEN A HERO. TO SOMEONE."

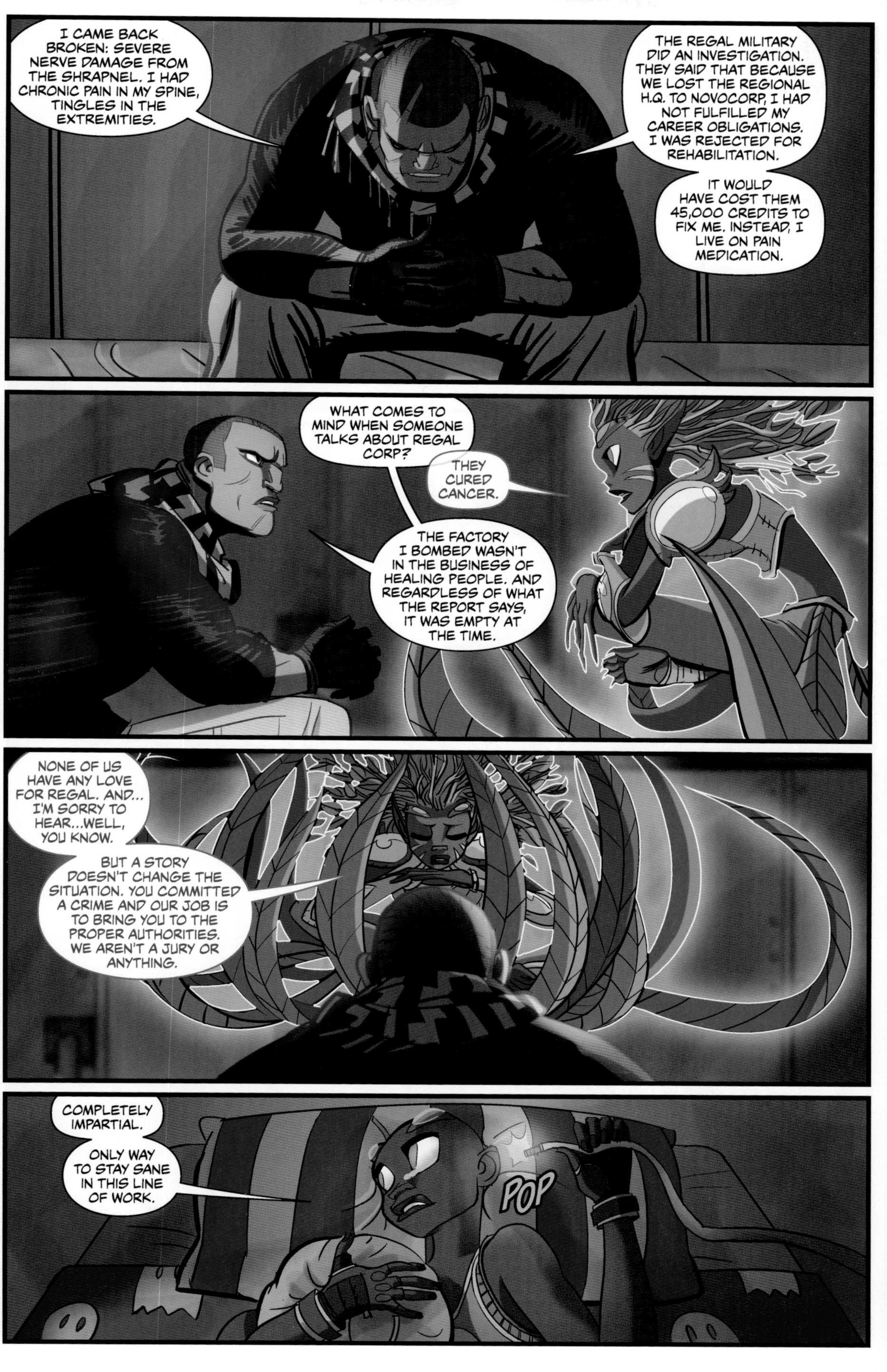
I CAME BACK BROKEN: SEVERE NERVE DAMAGE FROM THE SHRAPNEL. I HAD CHRONIC PAIN IN MY SPINE, TINGLES IN THE EXTREMITIES.
THE REGAL MILITARY DID AN INVESTIGATION. THEY SAID THAT BECAUSE WE LOST THE REGIONAL H.Q. TO NOVOCORP, I HAD NOT FULFILLED MY CAREER OBLIGATIONS. I WAS REJECTED FOR REHABILITATION.
IT WOULD HAVE COST THEM 45,000 CREDITS TO FIX ME. INSTEAD, I LIVE ON PAIN MEDICATION.
WHAT COMES TO MIND WHEN SOMEONE TALKS ABOUT REGAL CORP?
THEY CURED CANCER.
THE FACTORY I BOMBED WASN'T IN THE BUSINESS OF HEALING PEOPLE. AND REGARDLESS OF WHAT THE REPORT SAYS, IT WAS EMPTY AT THE TIME.
NONE OF US HAVE ANY LOVE FOR REGAL. AND... I'M SORRY TO HEAR...WELL, YOU KNOW.
BUT A STORY DOESN'T CHANGE THE SITUATION. YOU COMMITTED A CRIME AND OUR JOB IS TO BRING YOU TO THE PROPER AUTHORITIES. WE AREN'T A JURY OR ANYTHING.
COMPLETELY IMPARTIAL.
ONLY WAY TO STAY SANE IN THIS LINE OF WORK.
POP

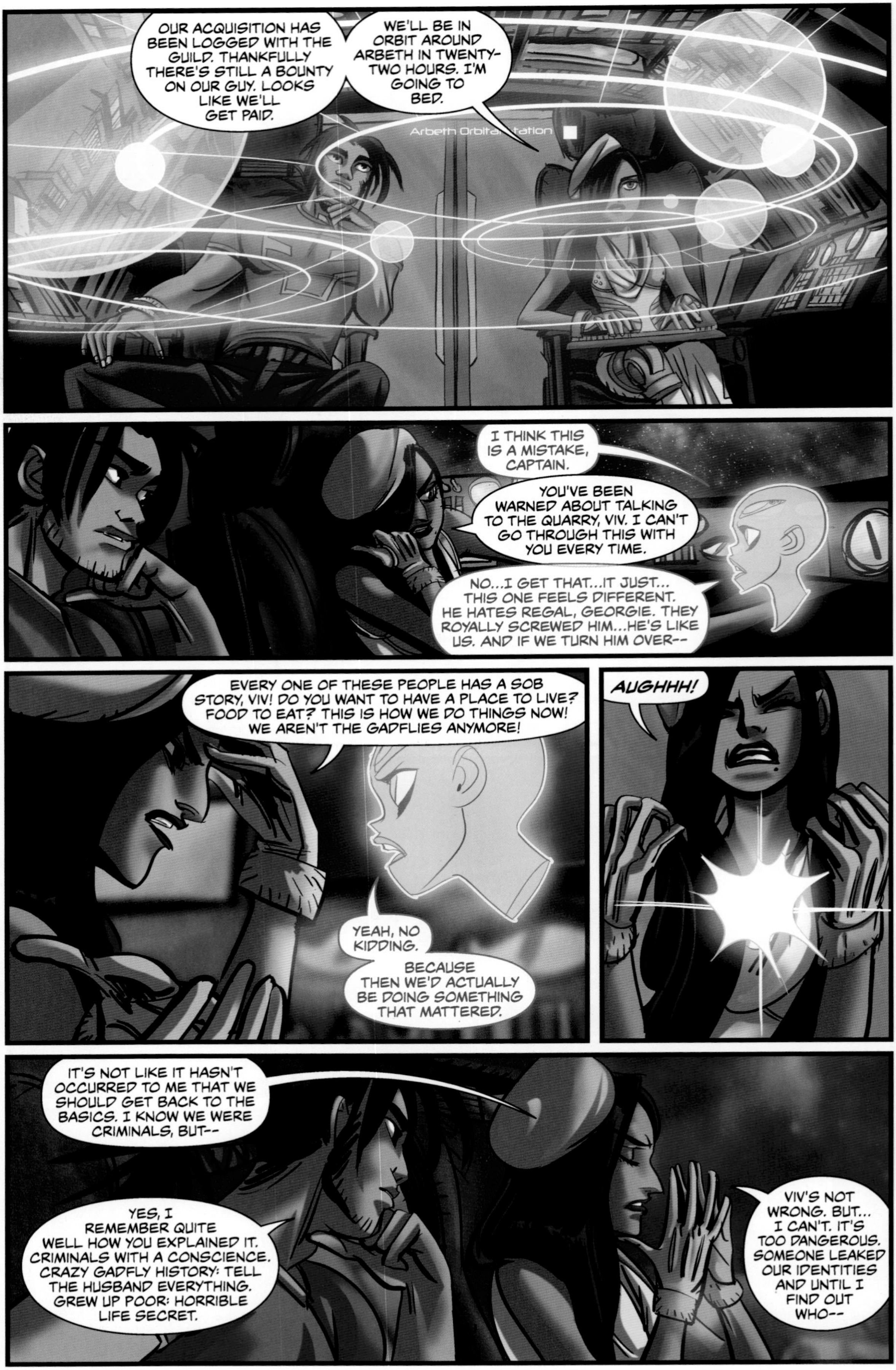
OUR ACQUISITION HAS BEEN LOGGED WITH THE GUILD. THANKFULLY THERE'S STILL A BOUNTY ON OUR GUY. LOOKS LIKE WE'LL GET PAID.
WE'LL BE IN ORBIT AROUND ARBETH IN TWENTY-TWO HOURS. I'M GOING TO BED.
I THINK THIS IS A MISTAKE, CAPTAIN.
YOU'VE BEEN WARNED ABOUT TALKING TO THE QUARRY, VIV. I CAN'T GO THROUGH THIS WITH YOU EVERY TIME.
NO...I GET THAT...IT JUST... THIS ONE FEELS DIFFERENT. HE HATES REGAL, GEORGIE. THEY ROYALLY SCREWED HIM...HE'S LIKE US. AND IF WE TURN HIM OVER--
EVERY ONE OF THESE PEOPLE HAS A SOB STORY, VIV! DO YOU WANT TO HAVE A PLACE TO LIVE? FOOD TO EAT? THIS IS HOW WE DO THINGS NOW! WE AREN'T THE GADFLIES ANYMORE!
YEAH, NO KIDDING.
BECAUSE THEN WE'D ACTUALLY BE DOING SOMETHING THAT MATTERED.
AUGHHH!
IT'S NOT LIKE IT HASN'T OCCURRED TO ME THAT WE SHOULD GET BACK TO THE BASICS. I KNOW WE WERE CRIMINALS, BUT--
YES, I REMEMBER QUITE WELL HOW YOU EXPLAINED IT. CRIMINALS WITH A CONSCIENCE. CRAZY GADFLY HISTORY: TELL THE HUSBAND EVERYTHING. GREW UP POOR: HORRIBLE LIFE SECRET.
VIV'S NOT WRONG. BUT... I CAN'T. IT'S TOO DANGEROUS. SOMEONE LEAKED OUR IDENTITIES AND UNTIL I FIND OUT WHO--

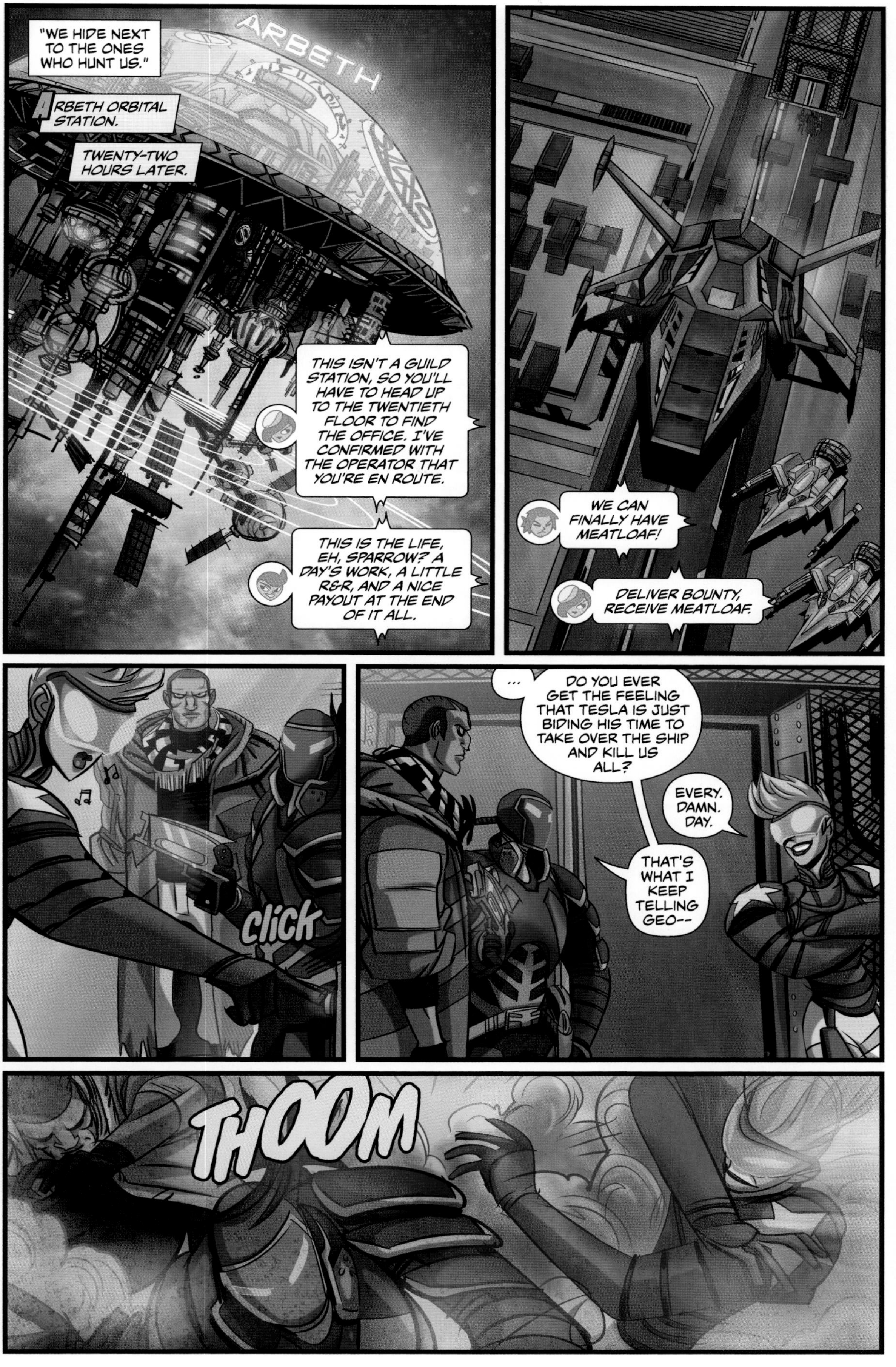

"WE HIDE NEXT TO THE ONES WHO HUNT US."
ARBETH
ARBETH ORBITAL STATION.
TWENTY-TWO HOURS LATER.
THIS ISN'T A GUILD STATION, SO YOU'LL HAVE TO HEAD UP TO THE TWENTIETH FLOOR TO FIND THE OFFICE. I'VE CONFIRMED WITH THE OPERATOR THAT YOU'RE EN ROUTE.
THIS IS THE LIFE, EH, SPARROW? A DAY'S WORK, A LITTLE R&R, AND A NICE PAYOUT AT THE END OF IT ALL.
WE CAN FINALLY HAVE MEATLOAF!
DELIVER BOUNTY, RECEIVE MEATLOAF.
CLICK
...
DO YOU EVER GET THE FEELING THAT TESLA IS JUST BIDING HIS TIME TO TAKE OVER THE SHIP AND KILL US ALL?
EVERY. DAMN. DAY.
THAT'S WHAT I KEEP TELLING GEO--
THOOM

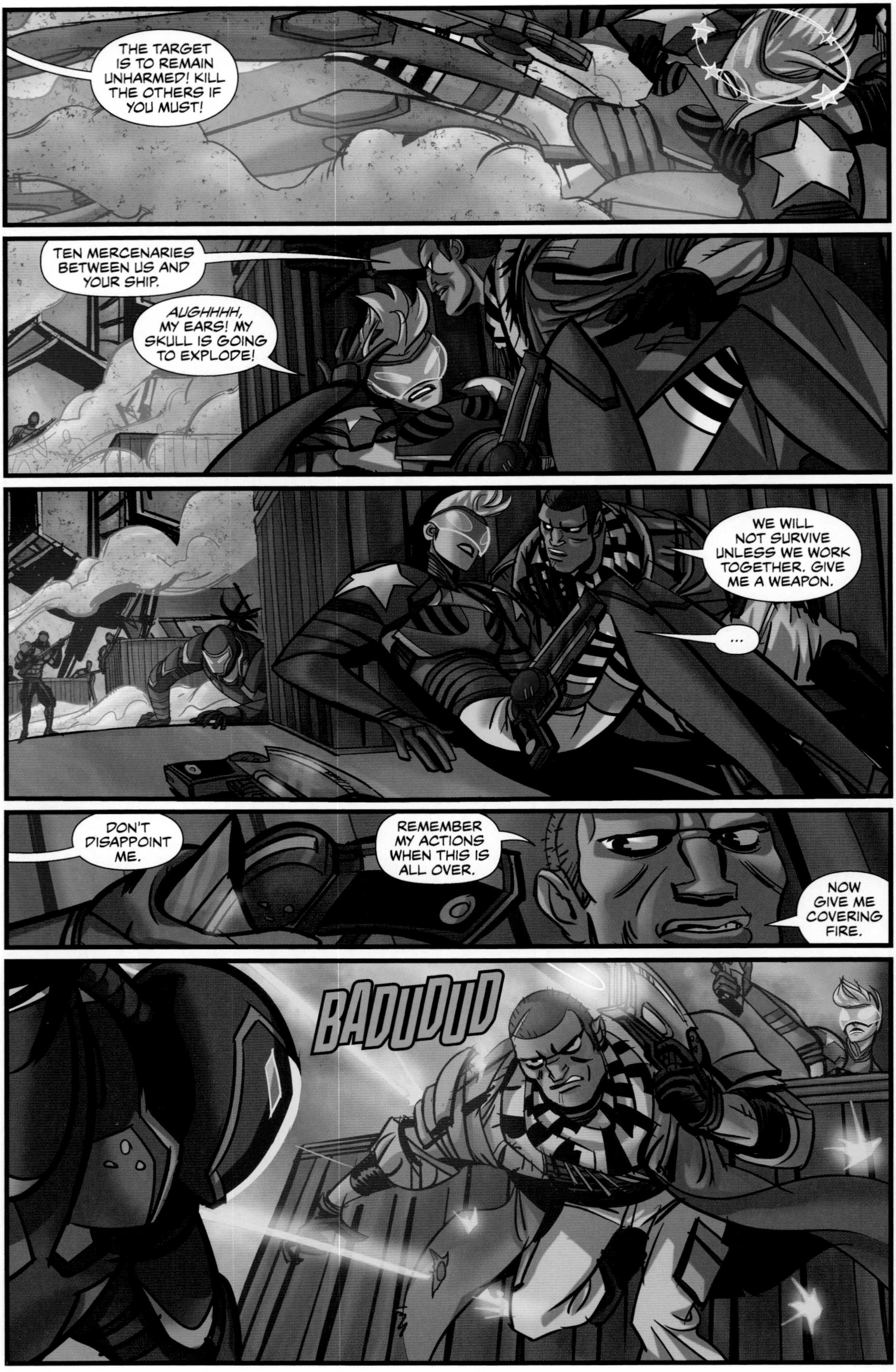
THE TARGET IS TO REMAIN UNHARMED! KILL THE OTHERS IF YOU MUST!
TEN MERCENARIES BETWEEN US AND YOUR SHIP.
AUGHHHH, MY EARS! MY SKULL IS GOING TO EXPLODE!
WE WILL NOT SURVIVE UNLESS WE WORK TOGETHER. GIVE ME A WEAPON.
...
DON'T DISAPPOINT ME.
REMEMBER MY ACTIONS WHEN THIS IS ALL OVER.
NOW GIVE ME COVERING FIRE.
BADUDUD

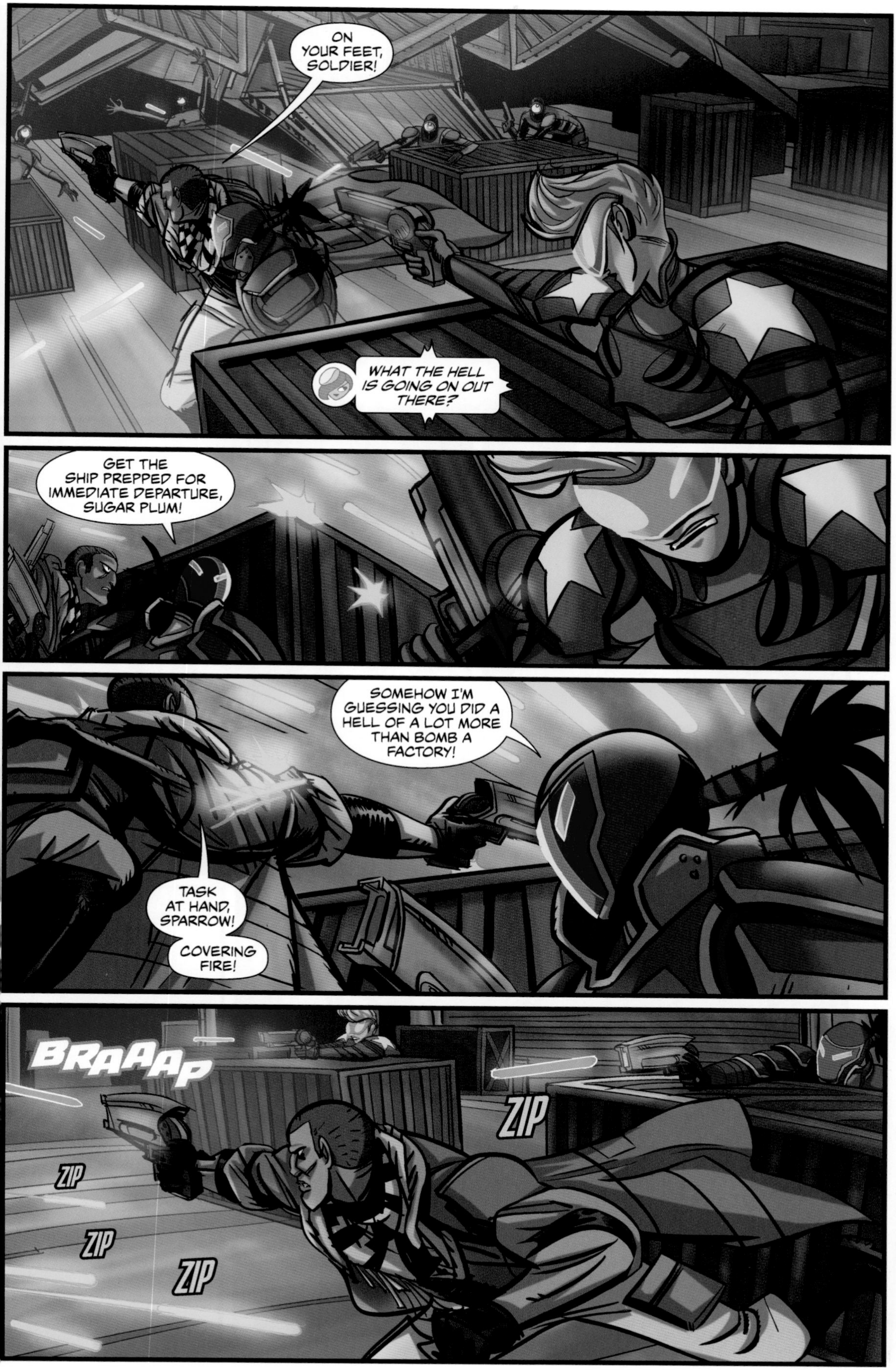
ON YOUR FEET, SOLDIER!
WHAT THE HELL IS GOING ON OUT THERE?
GET THE SHIP PREPPED FOR IMMEDIATE DEPARTURE, SUGAR PLUM!
SOMEHOW I'M GUESSING YOU DID A HELL OF A LOT MORE THAN BOMB A FACTORY!
TASK AT HAND, SPARROW!
COVERING FIRE!
BRAAAP
ZIP
ZIP
ZIP
ZIP

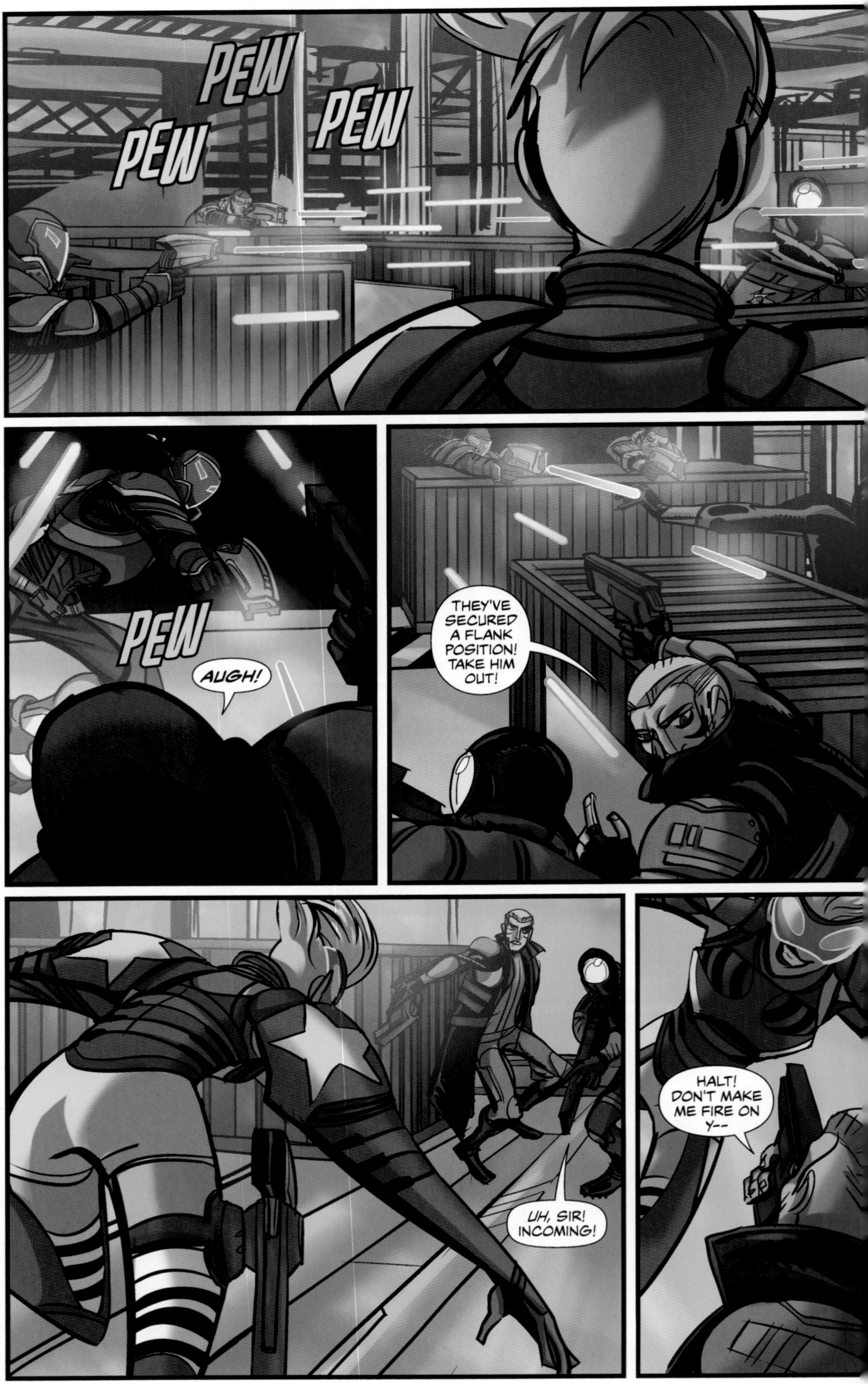
PEW
PEW
PEW
PEW
AUGH!
THEY'VE SECURED A FLANK POSITION! TAKE HIM OUT!
UH, SIR! INCOMING!
HALT! DON'T MAKE ME FIRE ON Y--

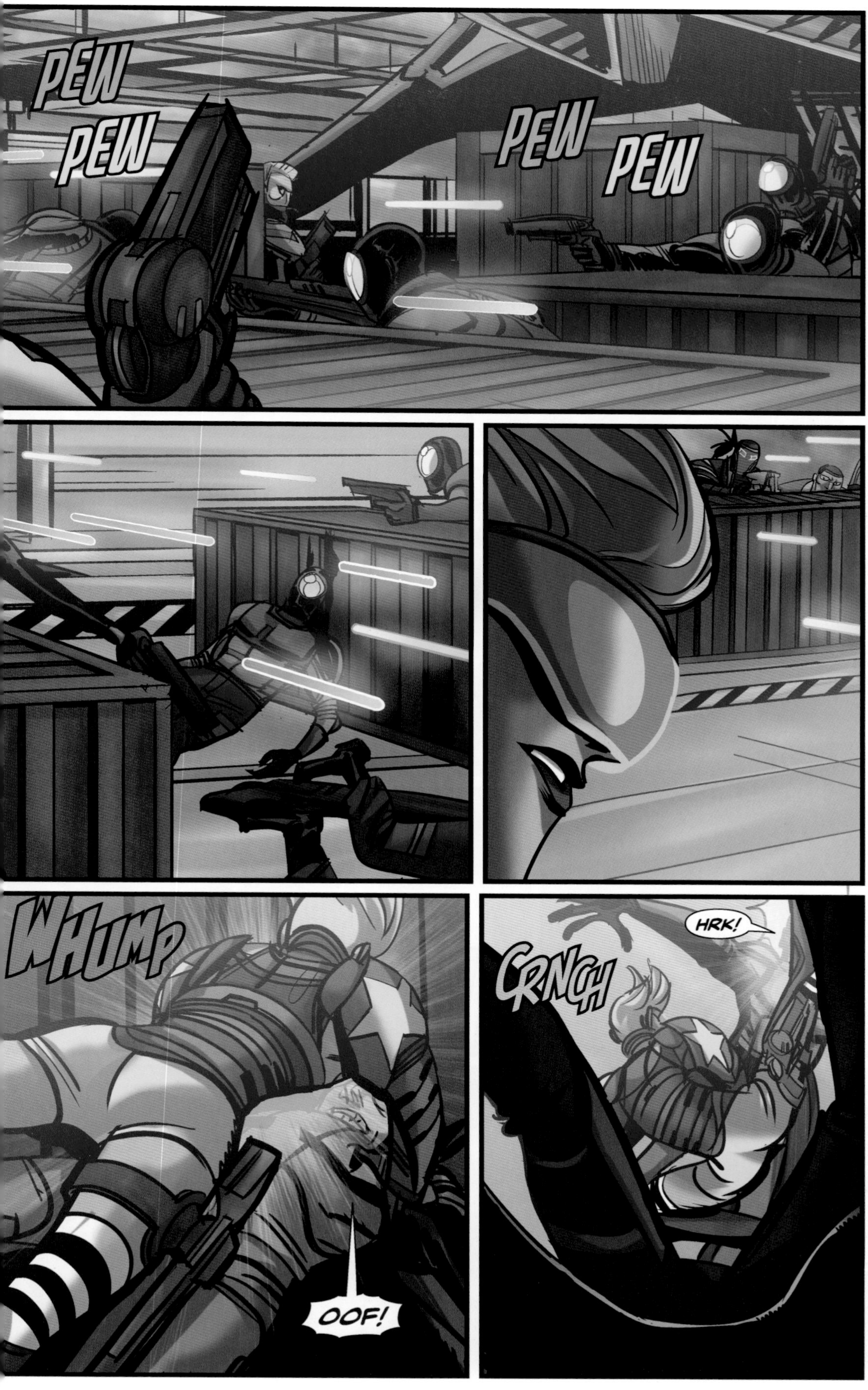
PEW
PEW
PEW
PEW
WHUMP
OOF!
HRK!
CRNCH

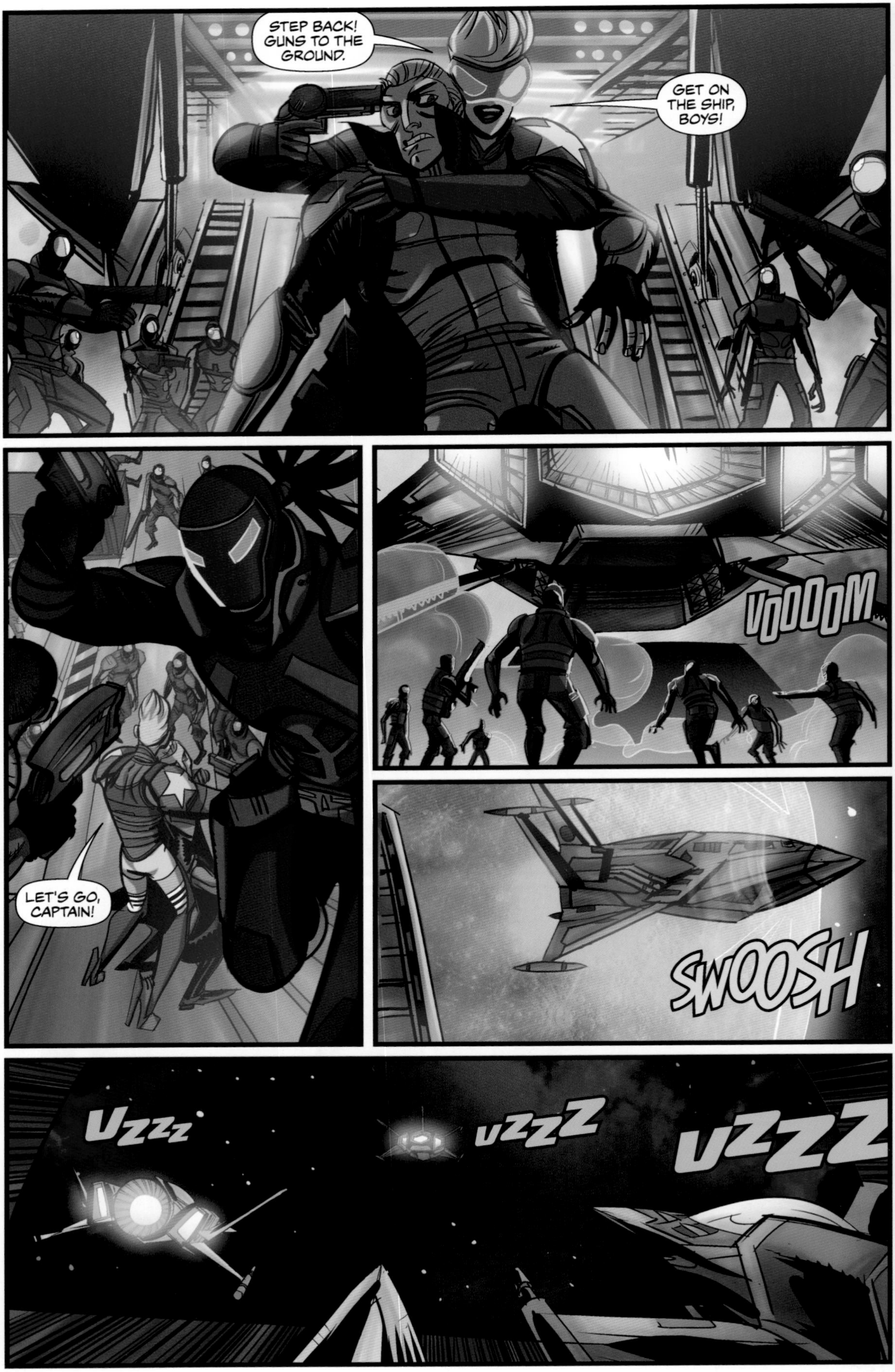
STEP BACK! GUNS TO THE GROUND.
GET ON THE SHIP, BOYS!
LET'S GO, CAPTAIN!
VOOOOM
SWOOSH
UZZZ
UZZZ
UZZZ

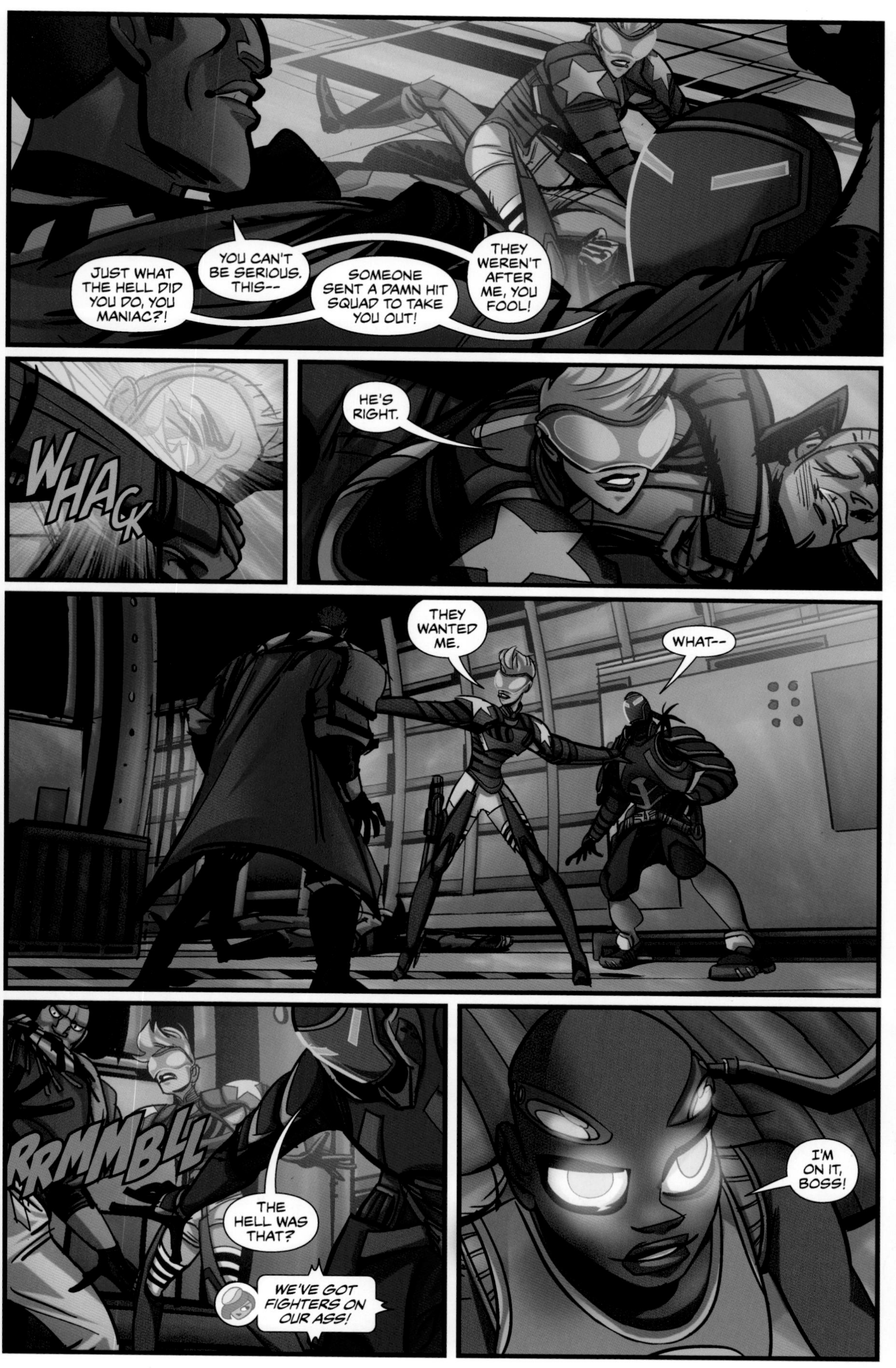
JUST WHAT THE HELL DID YOU DO, YOU MANIAC?!
YOU CAN'T BE SERIOUS. THIS--
SOMEONE SENT A DAMN HIT SQUAD TO TAKE YOU OUT!
THEY WEREN'T AFTER ME, YOU FOOL!
WHACK
HE'S RIGHT.
THEY WANTED ME.
WHAT--
RRMMBLL
THE HELL WAS THAT?
WE'VE GOT FIGHTERS ON OUR ASS!
I'M ON IT, BOSS!

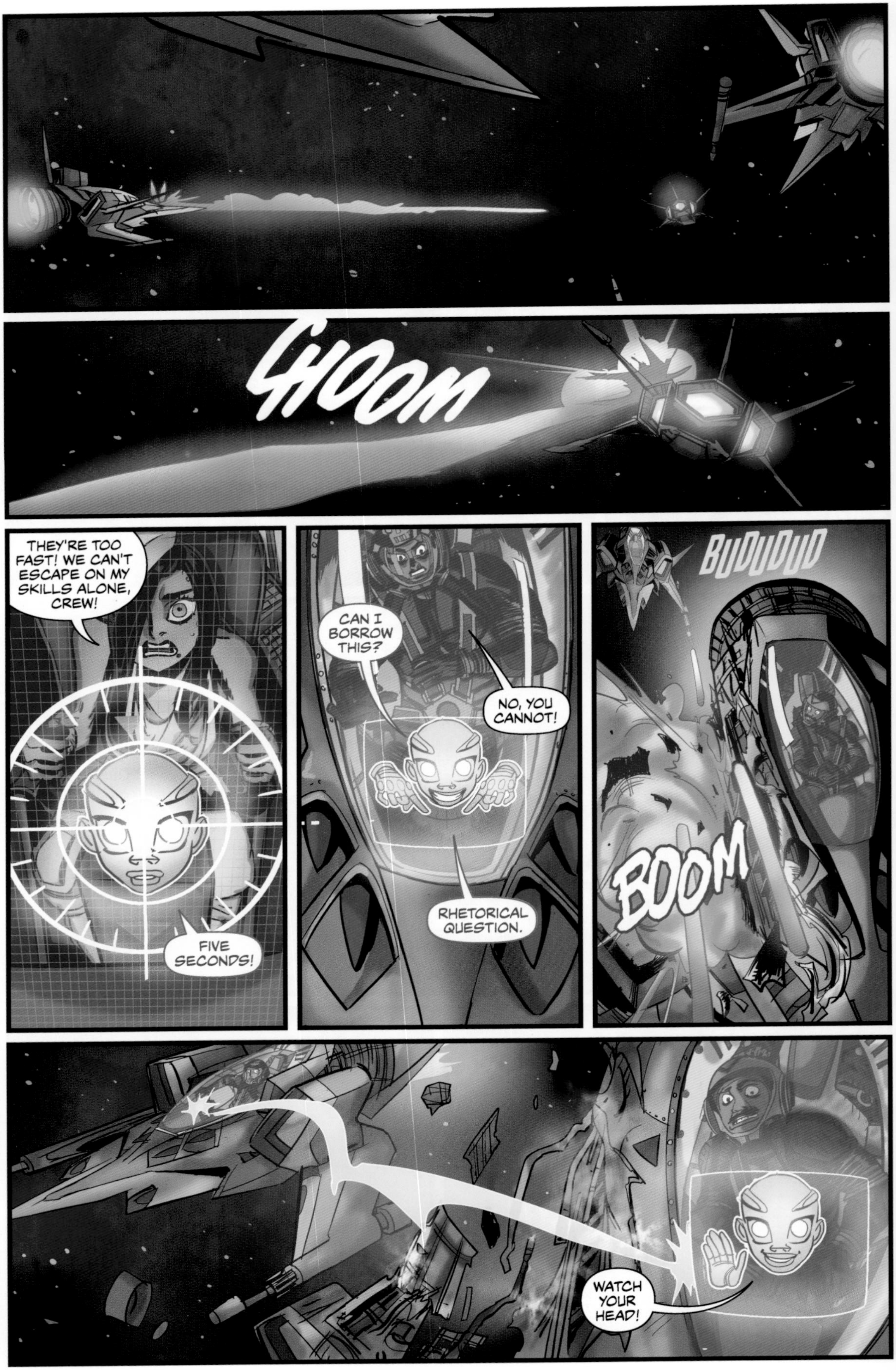
CHOOM
THEY'RE TOO FAST! WE CAN'T ESCAPE ON MY SKILLS ALONE, CREW!
FIVE SECONDS!
CAN I BORROW THIS?
NO, YOU CANNOT!
RHETORICAL QUESTION.
BUDUDUD
BOOM
WATCH YOUR HEAD!

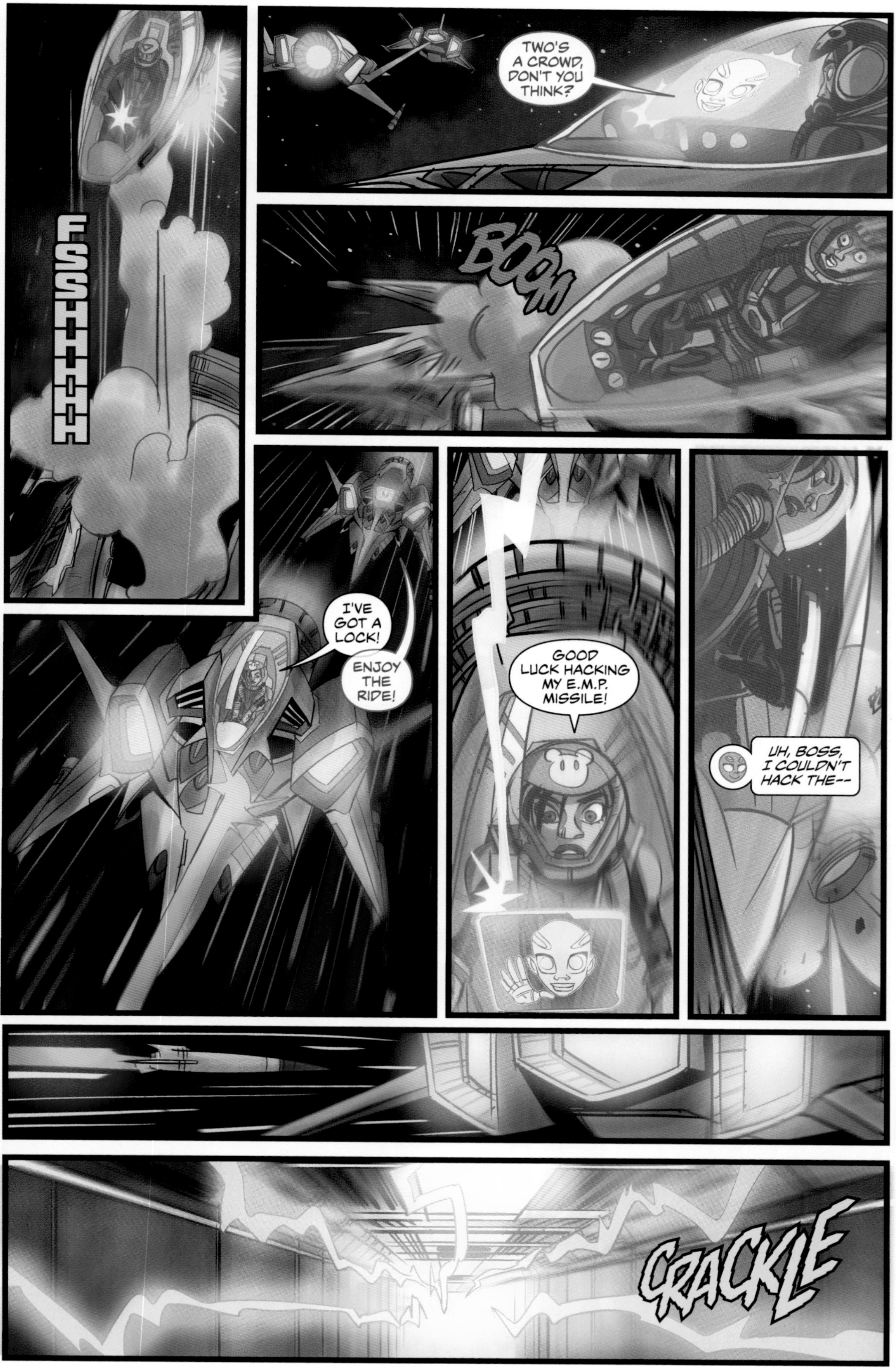
FSSHHHHH
TWO'S A CROWD, DON'T YOU THINK?
BOOM
I'VE GOT A LOCK!
ENJOY THE RIDE!
GOOD LUCK HACKING MY E.M.P. MISSILE!
UH, BOSS, I COULDN'T HACK THE--
CRACKLE

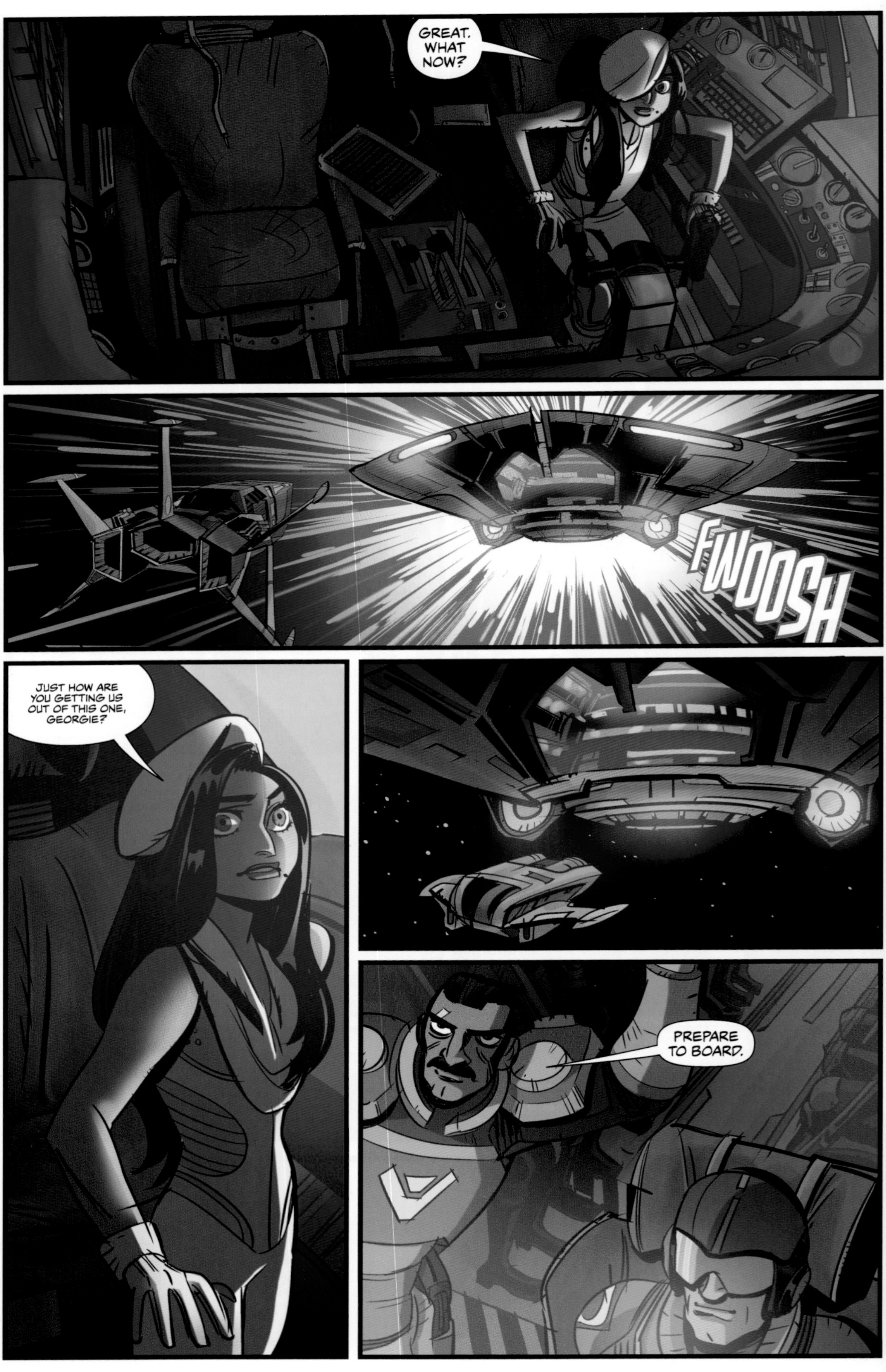
GREAT. WHAT NOW?
FWOOSH
JUST HOW ARE YOU GETTING US OUT OF THIS ONE, GEORGIE?
PREPARE TO BOARD.

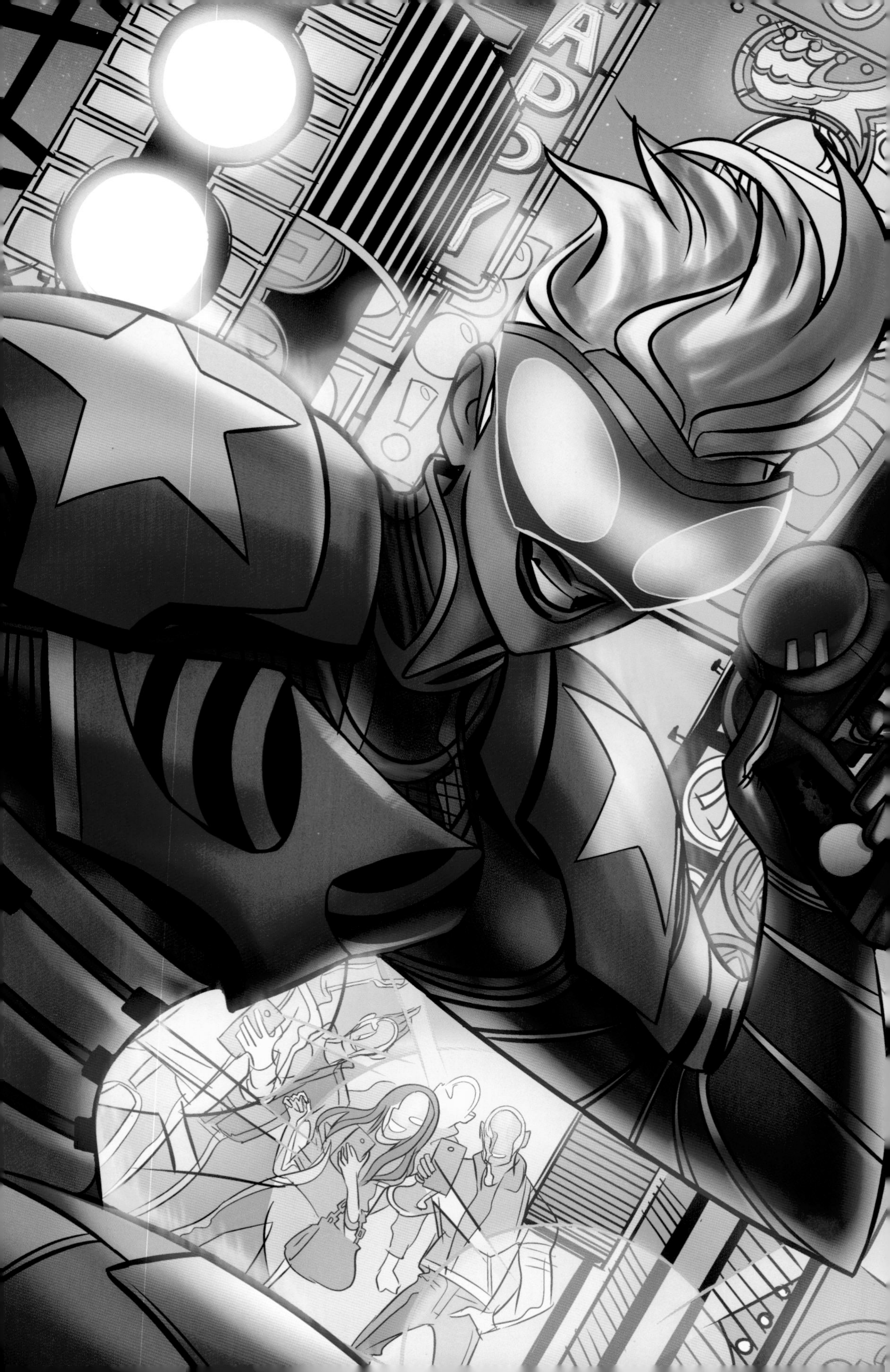

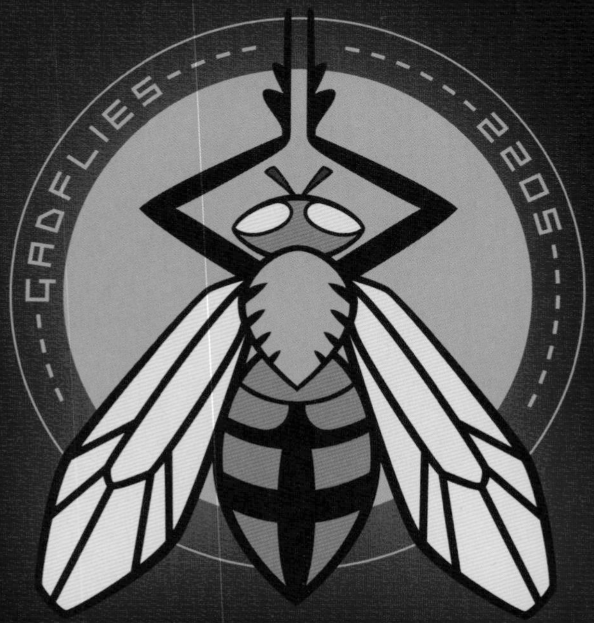
GADFLIES
2205

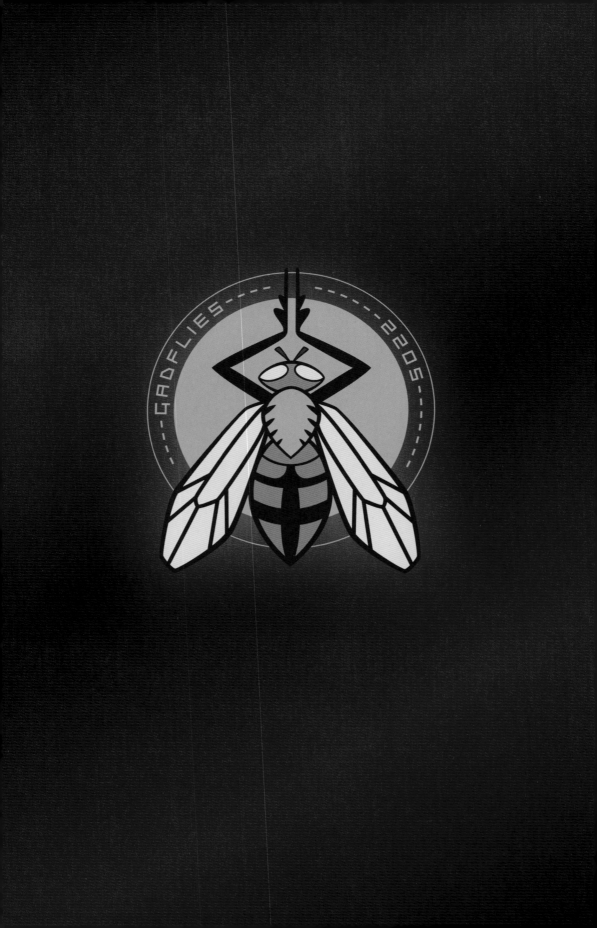

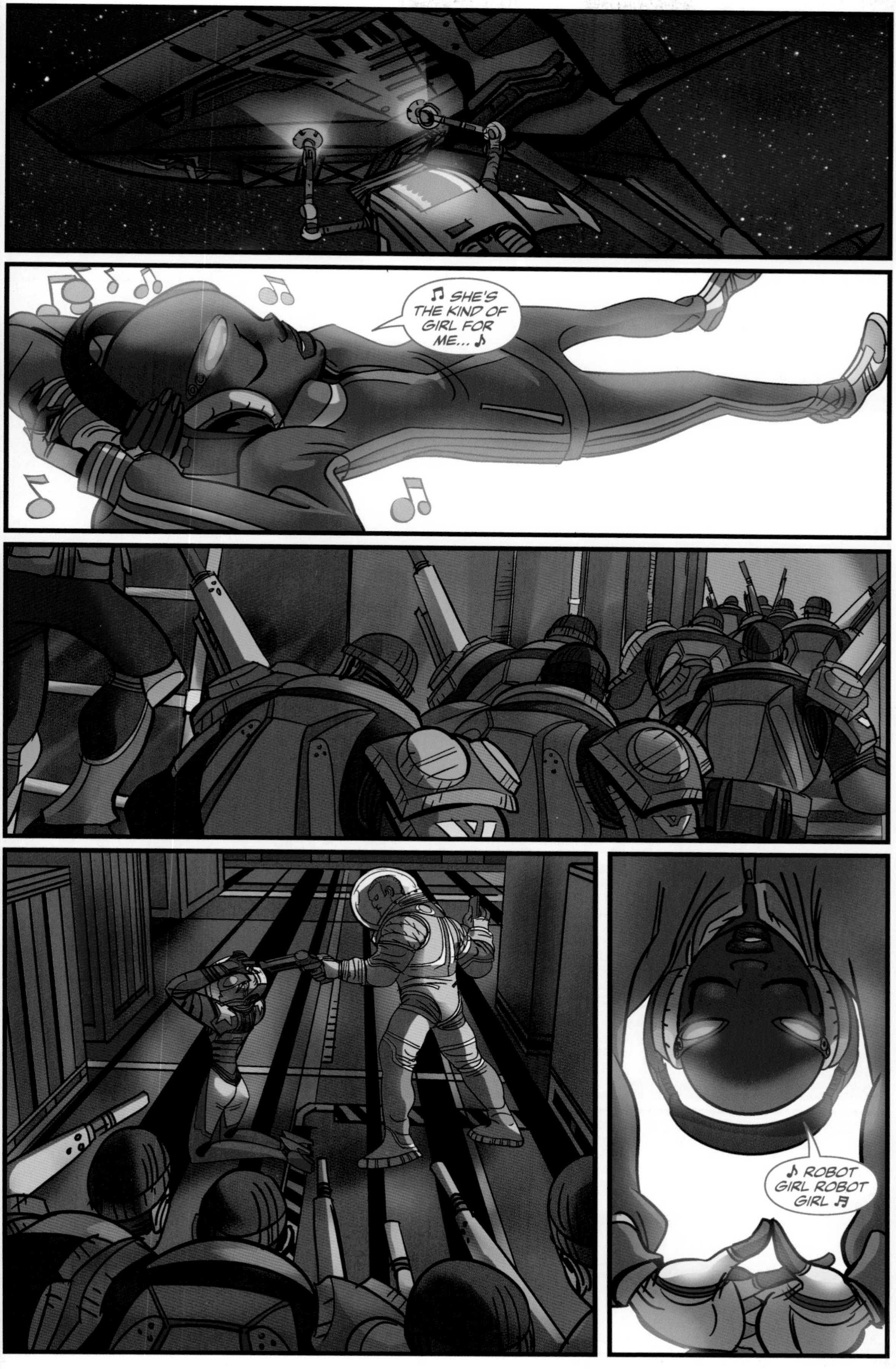
♫ SHE'S THE KIND OF GIRL FOR ME... ♪
♪ ROBOT GIRL ROBOT GIRL ♫

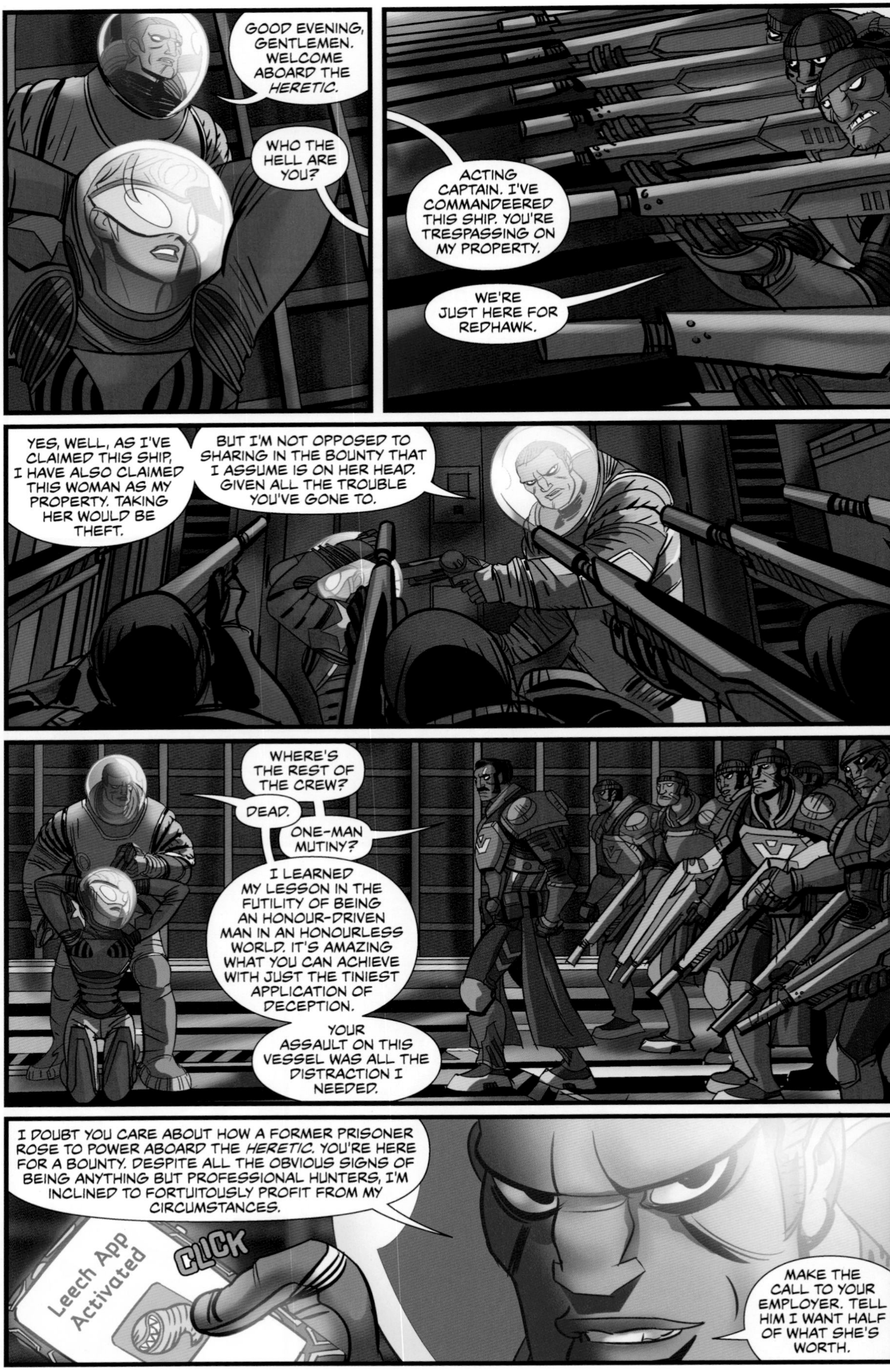
GOOD EVENING, GENTLEMEN. WELCOME ABOARD THE *HERETIC.*
WHO THE HELL ARE YOU?
ACTING CAPTAIN. I'VE COMMANDEERED THIS SHIP. YOU'RE TRESPASSING ON MY PROPERTY.
WE'RE JUST HERE FOR REDHAWK.
YES, WELL, AS I'VE CLAIMED THIS SHIP, I HAVE ALSO CLAIMED THIS WOMAN AS MY PROPERTY. TAKING HER WOULD BE THEFT.
BUT I'M NOT OPPOSED TO SHARING IN THE BOUNTY THAT I ASSUME IS ON HER HEAD. GIVEN ALL THE TROUBLE YOU'VE GONE TO.
WHERE'S THE REST OF THE CREW?
DEAD.
ONE-MAN MUTINY?
I LEARNED MY LESSON IN THE FUTILITY OF BEING AN HONOUR-DRIVEN MAN IN AN HONOURLESS WORLD. IT'S AMAZING WHAT YOU CAN ACHIEVE WITH JUST THE TINIEST APPLICATION OF DECEPTION.
YOUR ASSAULT ON THIS VESSEL WAS ALL THE DISTRACTION I NEEDED.
I DOUBT YOU CARE ABOUT HOW A FORMER PRISONER ROSE TO POWER ABOARD THE *HERETIC*. YOU'RE HERE FOR A BOUNTY. DESPITE ALL THE OBVIOUS SIGNS OF BEING ANYTHING BUT PROFESSIONAL HUNTERS, I'M INCLINED TO FORTUITOUSLY PROFIT FROM MY CIRCUMSTANCES.
Leech App Activated
CLICK
MAKE THE CALL TO YOUR EMPLOYER. TELL HIM I WANT HALF OF WHAT SHE'S WORTH.

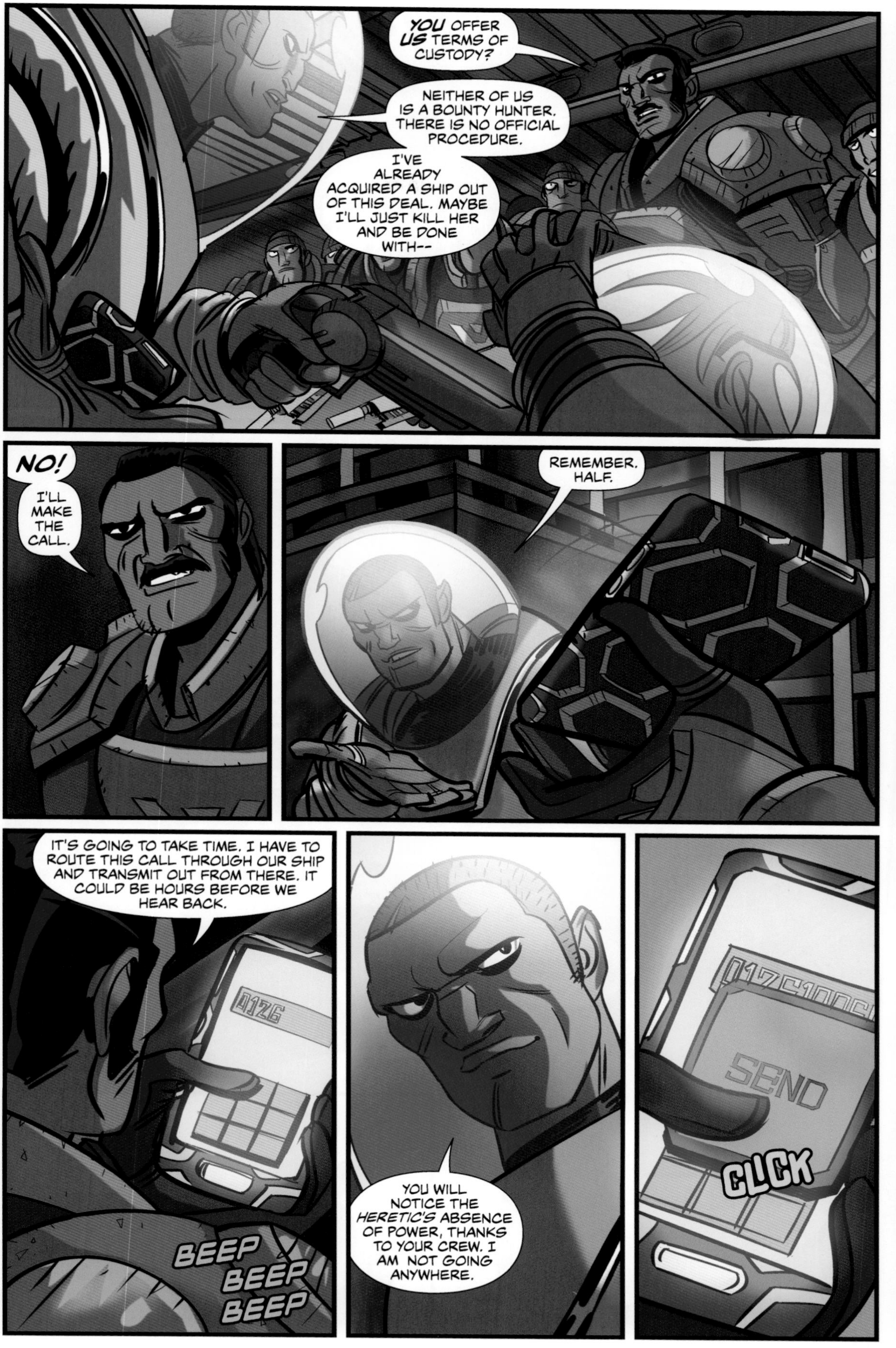

YOU OFFER US TERMS OF CUSTODY?
NEITHER OF US IS A BOUNTY HUNTER. THERE IS NO OFFICIAL PROCEDURE.
I'VE ALREADY ACQUIRED A SHIP OUT OF THIS DEAL. MAYBE I'LL JUST KILL HER AND BE DONE WITH--
NO!
I'LL MAKE THE CALL.
REMEMBER. HALF.
IT'S GOING TO TAKE TIME. I HAVE TO ROUTE THIS CALL THROUGH OUR SHIP AND TRANSMIT OUT FROM THERE. IT COULD BE HOURS BEFORE WE HEAR BACK.
0126
BEEP BEEP BEEP
YOU WILL NOTICE THE *HERETIC'S* ABSENCE OF POWER, THANKS TO YOUR CREW. I AM NOT GOING ANYWHERE.
SEND
CLICK

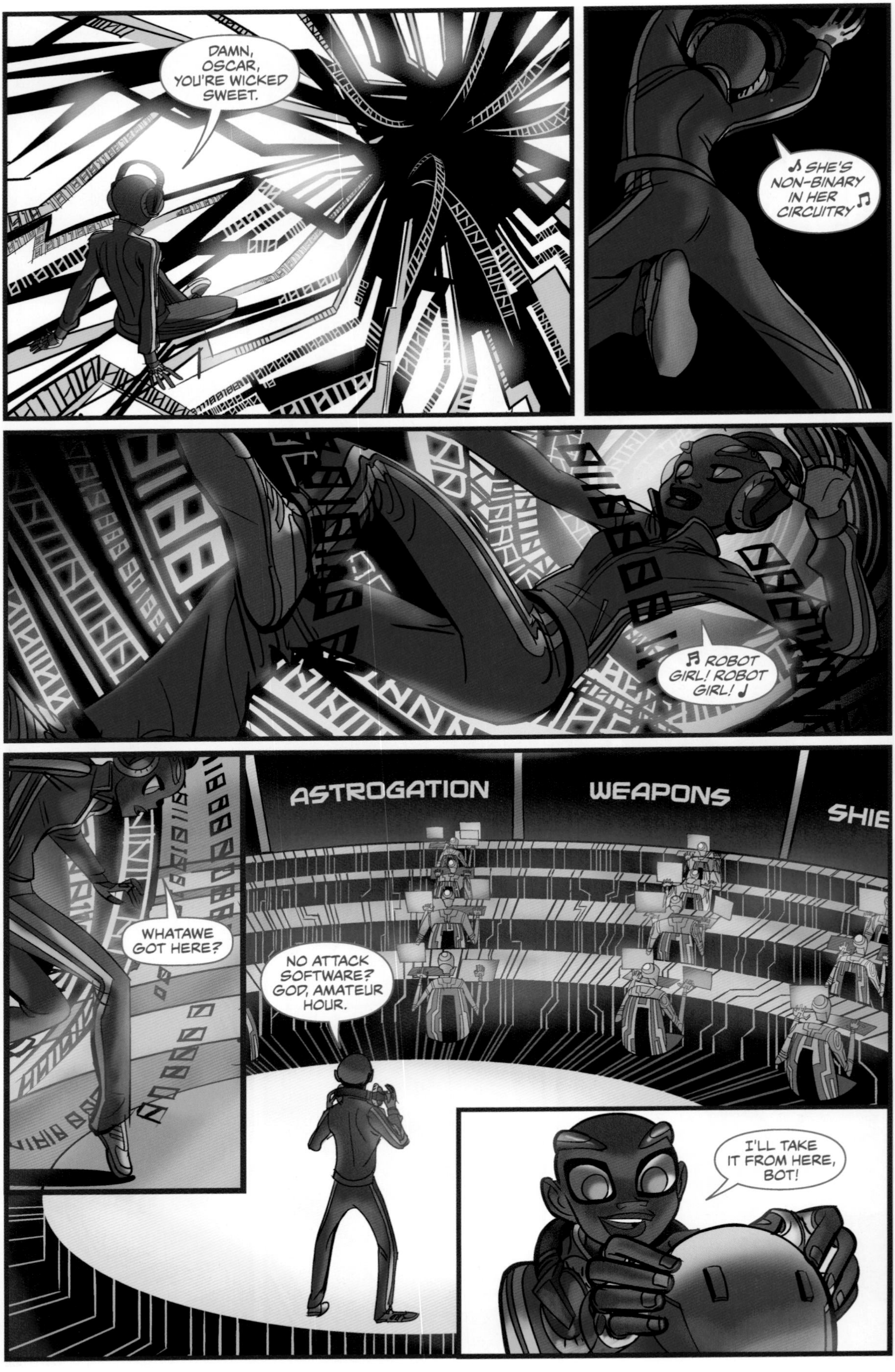
DAMN, OSCAR, YOU'RE WICKED SWEET.
♪ SHE'S NON-BINARY IN HER CIRCUITRY ♫
♬ ROBOT GIRL! ROBOT GIRL! ♩
WHATAWE GOT HERE?
ASTROGATION
WEAPONS
SHIE
NO ATTACK SOFTWARE? GOD, AMATEUR HOUR.
I'LL TAKE IT FROM HERE, BOT!

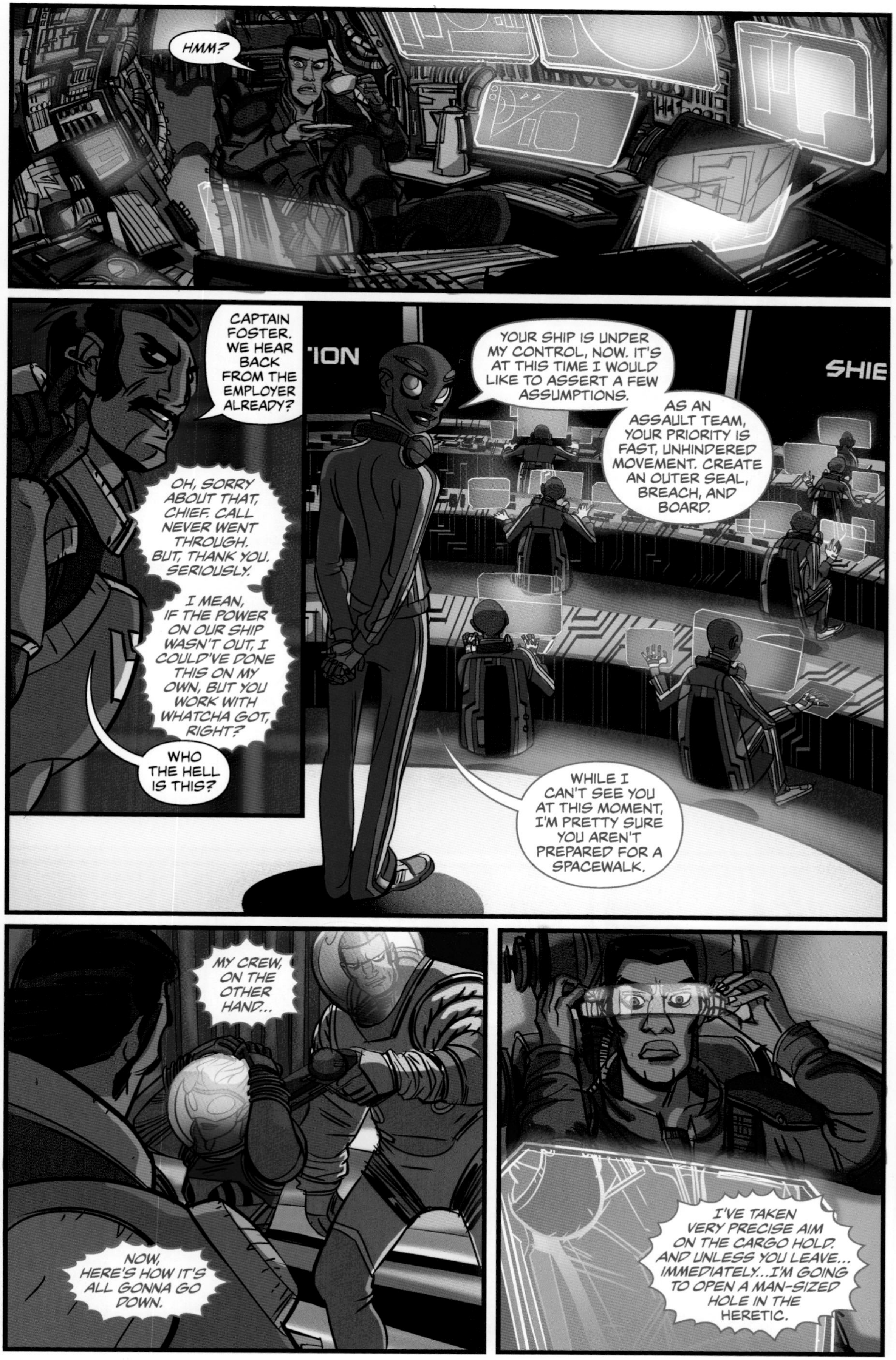
HMM?
CAPTAIN FOSTER. WE HEAR BACK FROM THE EMPLOYER ALREADY?
YOUR SHIP IS UNDER MY CONTROL, NOW. IT'S AT THIS TIME I WOULD LIKE TO ASSERT A FEW ASSUMPTIONS.
AS AN ASSAULT TEAM, YOUR PRIORITY IS FAST, UNHINDERED MOVEMENT. CREATE AN OUTER SEAL, BREACH, AND BOARD.
OH, SORRY ABOUT THAT, CHIEF. CALL NEVER WENT THROUGH. BUT, THANK YOU. SERIOUSLY.
I MEAN, IF THE POWER ON OUR SHIP WASN'T OUT, I COULD'VE DONE THIS ON MY OWN, BUT YOU WORK WITH WHATCHA GOT, RIGHT?
WHO THE HELL IS THIS?
WHILE I CAN'T SEE YOU AT THIS MOMENT, I'M PRETTY SURE YOU AREN'T PREPARED FOR A SPACEWALK.
MY CREW, ON THE OTHER HAND...
NOW, HERE'S HOW IT'S ALL GONNA GO DOWN.
I'VE TAKEN VERY PRECISE AIM ON THE CARGO HOLD. AND UNLESS YOU LEAVE... IMMEDIATELY...I'M GOING TO OPEN A MAN-SIZED HOLE IN THE HERETIC.

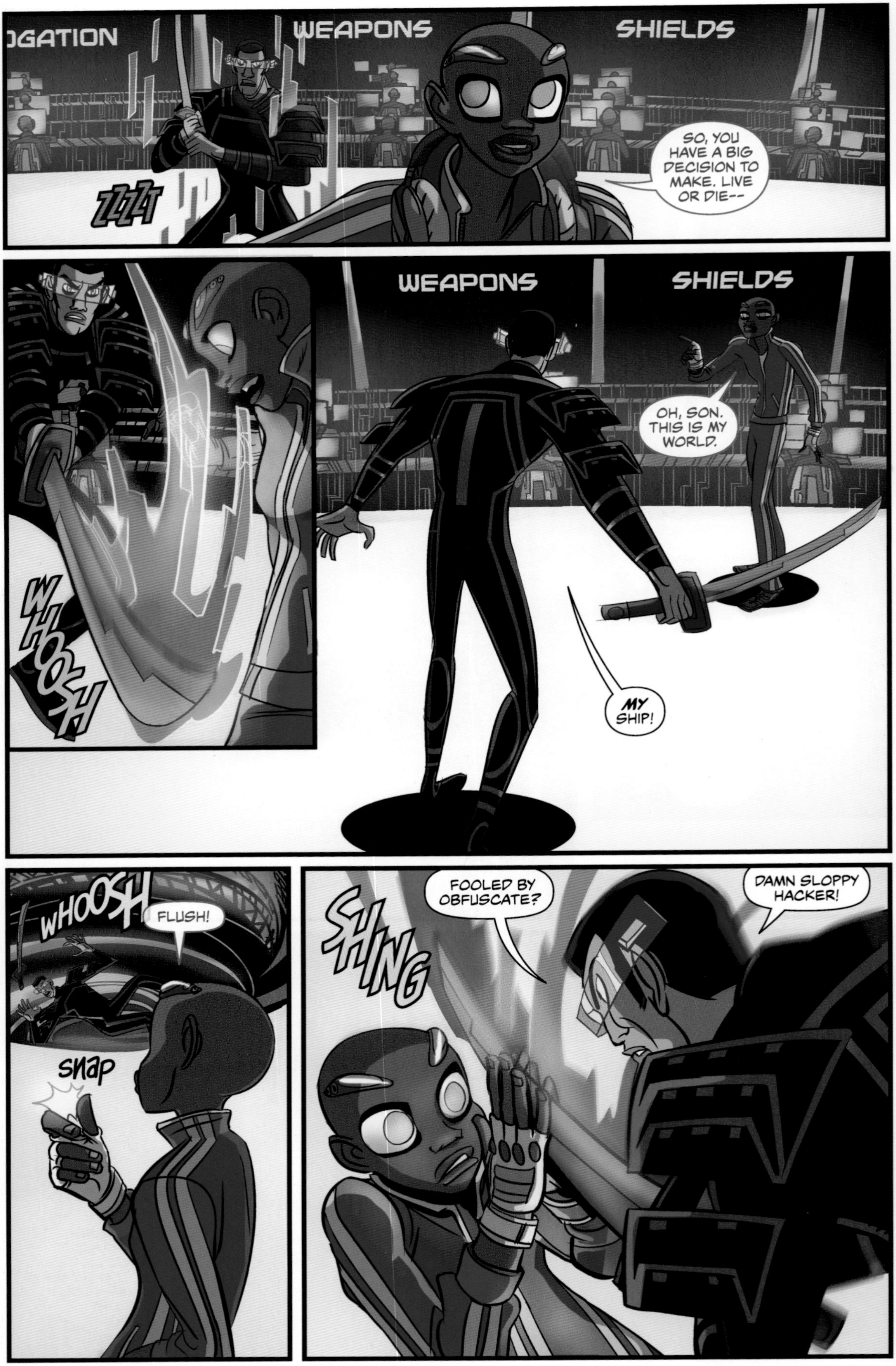
OGATION
WEAPONS
SHIELDS
SO, YOU HAVE A BIG DECISION TO MAKE. LIVE OR DIE--
ZZZZT
WHOOSH
WEAPONS
SHIELDS
OH, SON. THIS IS MY WORLD.
MY SHIP!
WHOOSH
FLUSH!
snap
SHING
FOOLED BY OBFUSCATE?
DAMN SLOPPY HACKER!

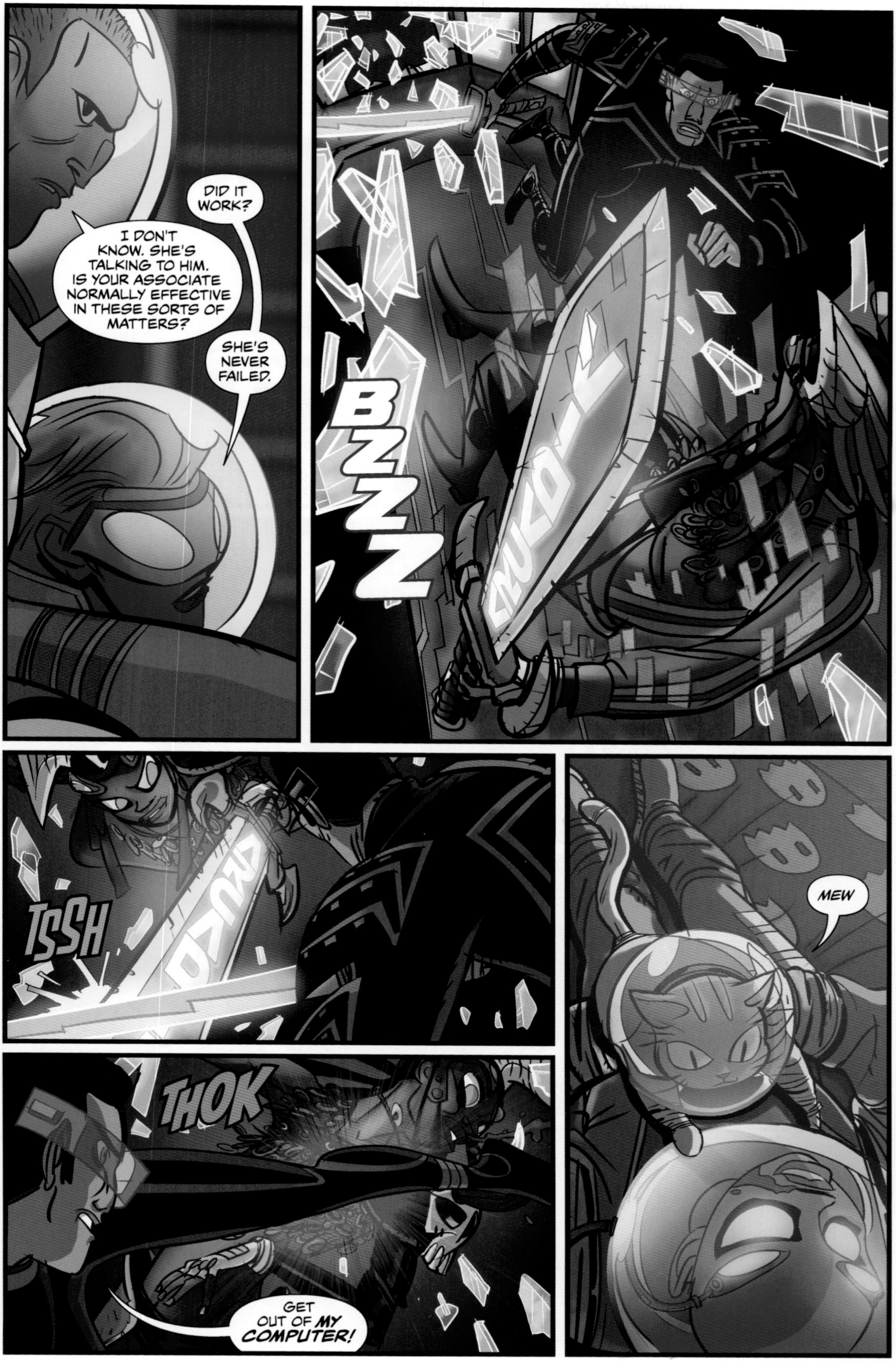
DID IT WORK?
I DON'T KNOW. SHE'S TALKING TO HIM. IS YOUR ASSOCIATE NORMALLY EFFECTIVE IN THESE SORTS OF MATTERS?
SHE'S NEVER FAILED.
BZZZ
TSSH
THOK
GET OUT OF MY COMPUTER!
MEW

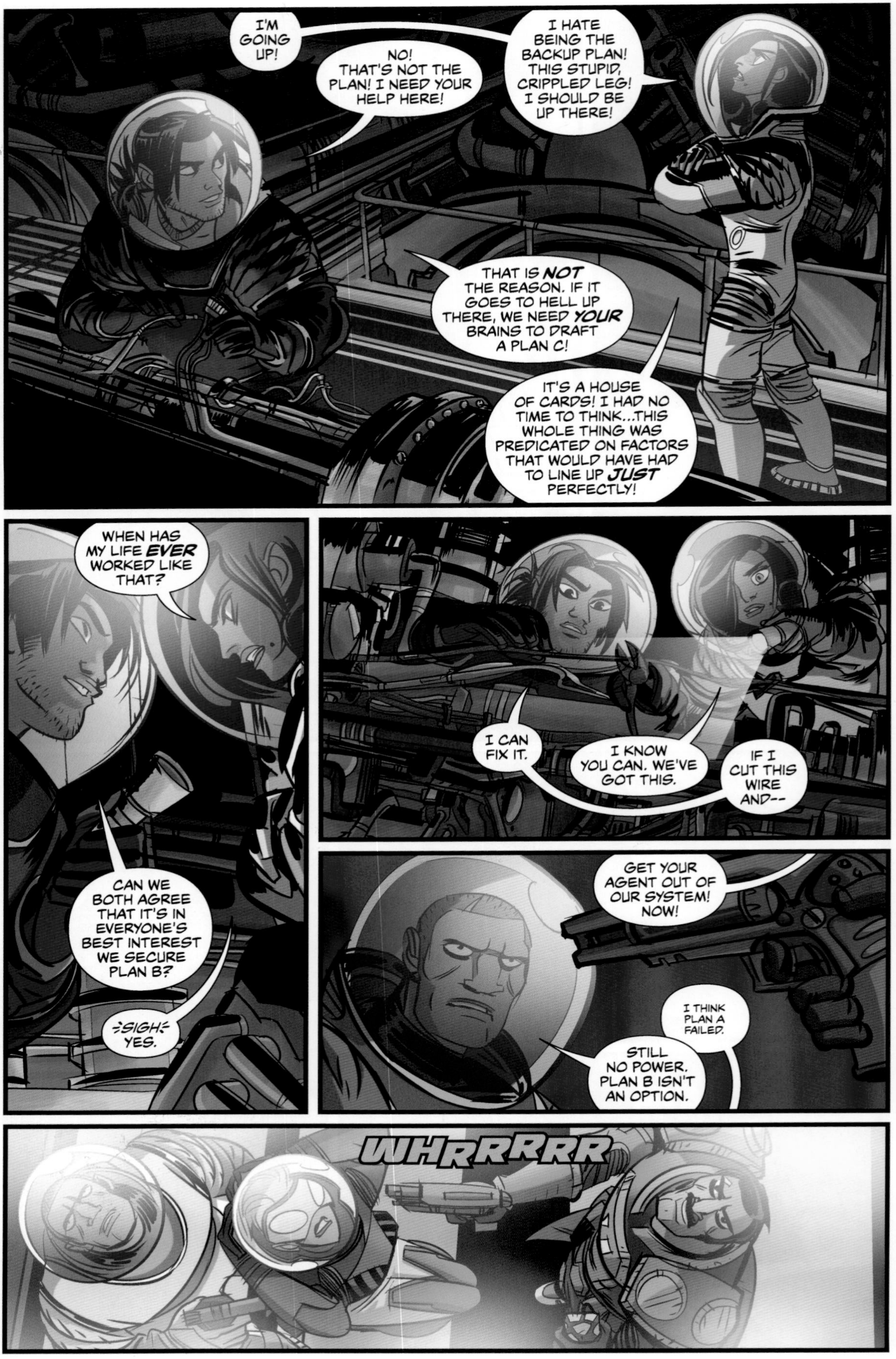
I'M GOING UP!
NO! THAT'S NOT THE PLAN! I NEED YOUR HELP HERE!
I HATE BEING THE BACKUP PLAN! THIS STUPID, CRIPPLED LEG! I SHOULD BE UP THERE!
THAT IS NOT THE REASON. IF IT GOES TO HELL UP THERE, WE NEED YOUR BRAINS TO DRAFT A PLAN C!
IT'S A HOUSE OF CARDS! I HAD NO TIME TO THINK...THIS WHOLE THING WAS PREDICATED ON FACTORS THAT WOULD HAVE HAD TO LINE UP JUST PERFECTLY!
WHEN HAS MY LIFE EVER WORKED LIKE THAT?
CAN WE BOTH AGREE THAT IT'S IN EVERYONE'S BEST INTEREST WE SECURE PLAN B?
SIGH YES.
I CAN FIX IT.
I KNOW YOU CAN. WE'VE GOT THIS.
IF I CUT THIS WIRE AND--
GET YOUR AGENT OUT OF OUR SYSTEM! NOW!
I THINK PLAN A FAILED.
STILL NO POWER. PLAN B ISN'T AN OPTION.
WHRRRRR

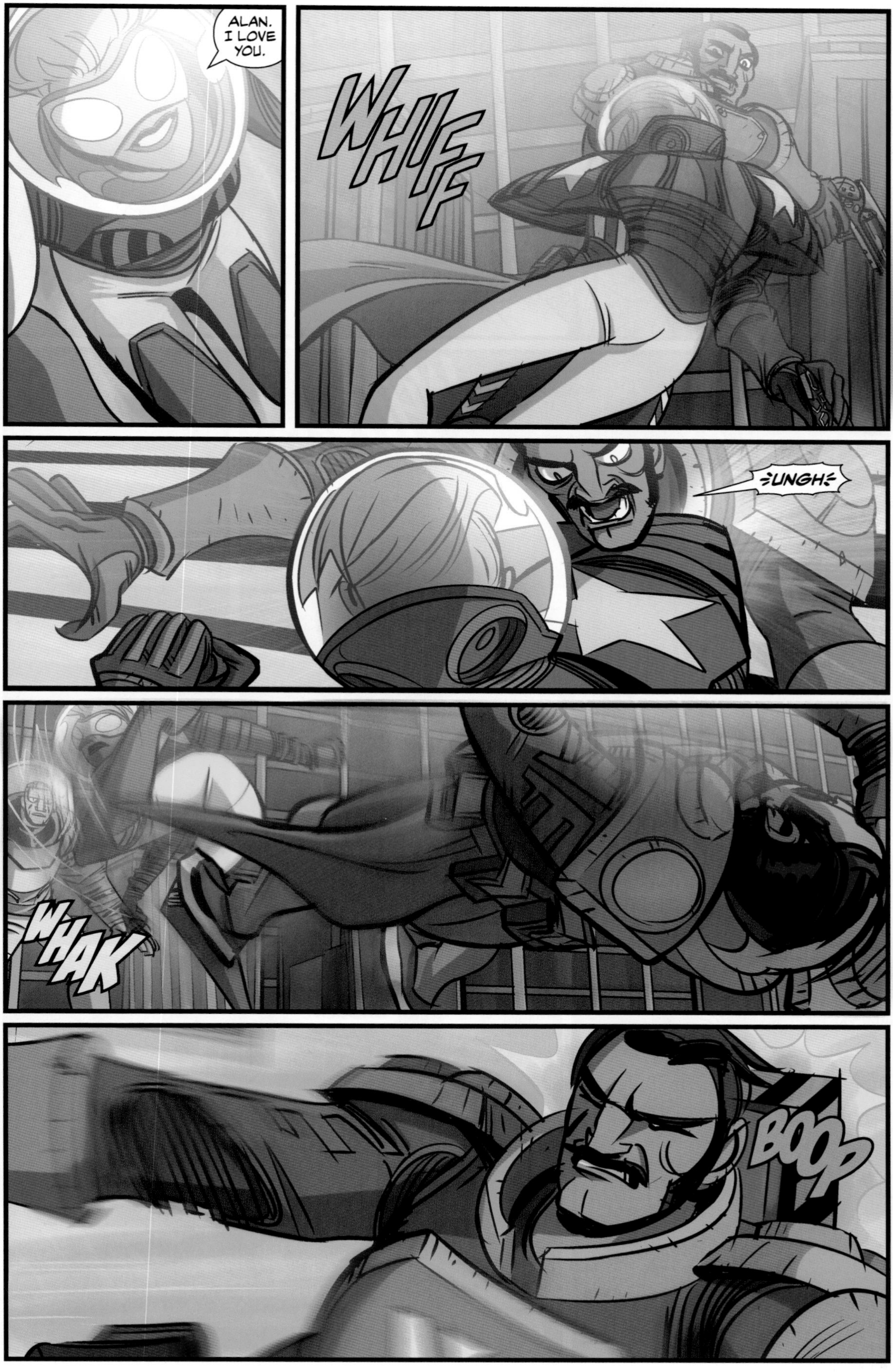
ALAN. I LOVE YOU.
WHIFF
UNGH
WHAK
BOOP

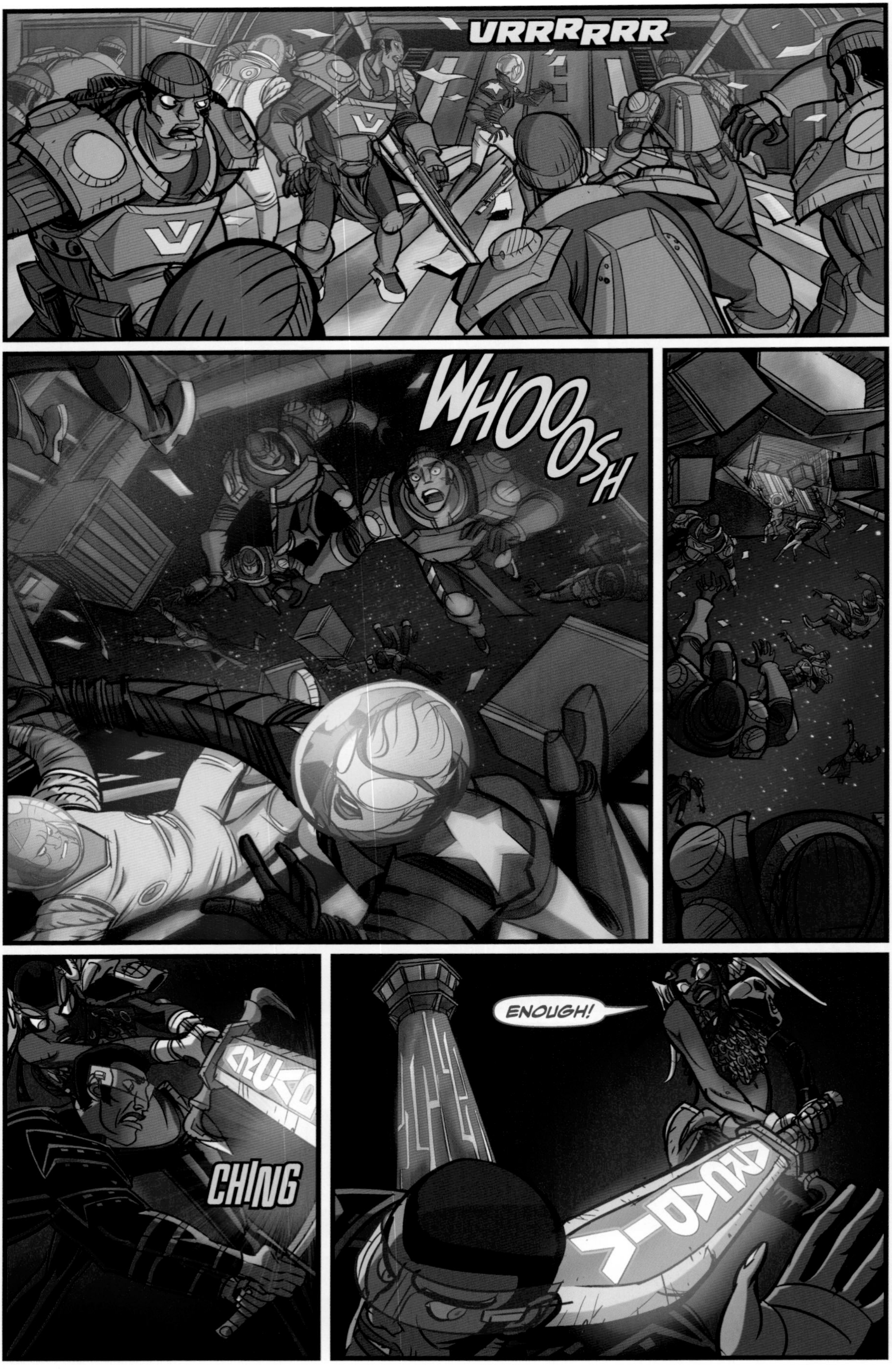

URRRRRRR
WHOOOSH
CHING
ENOUGH!

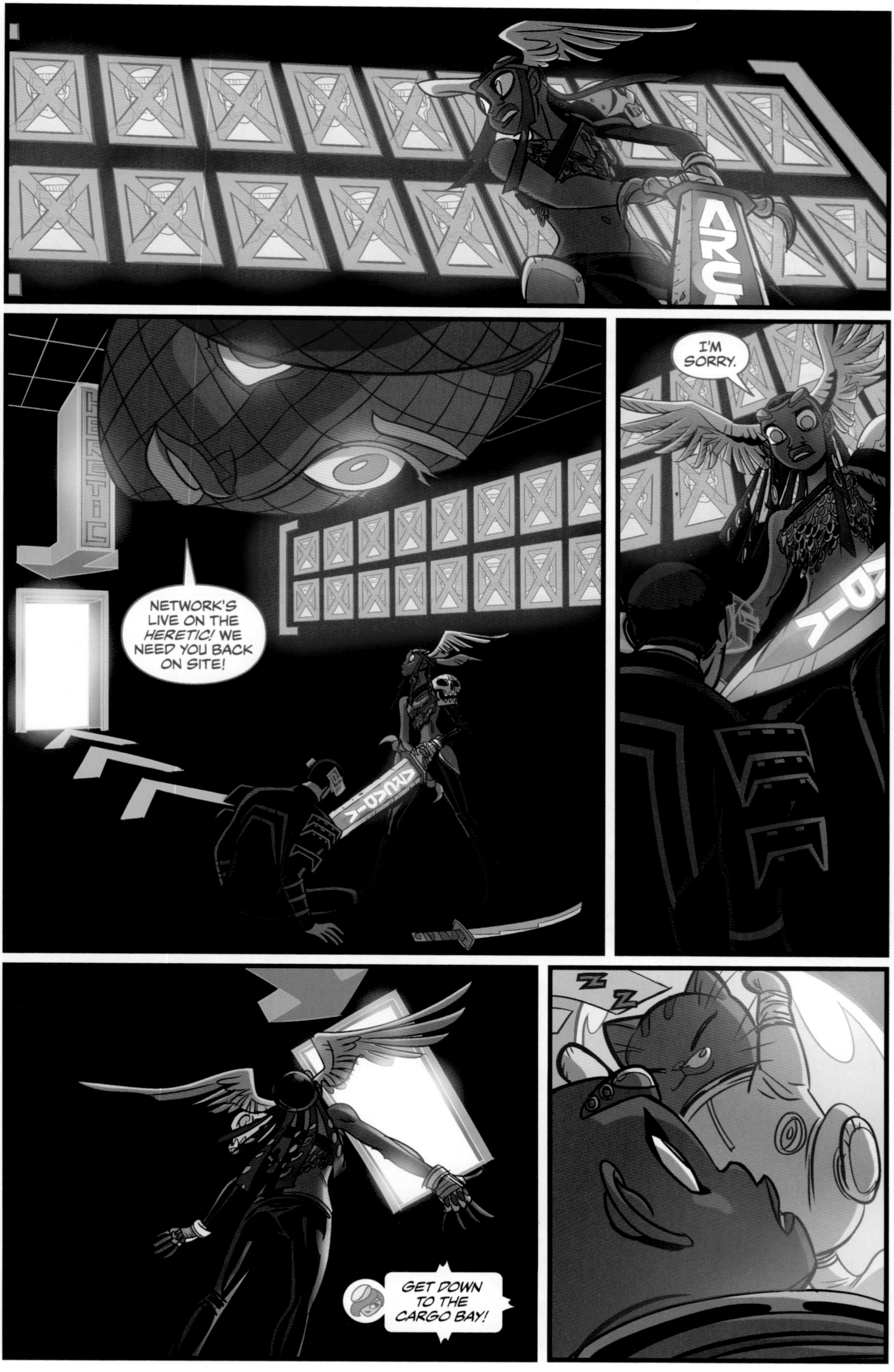
HERETIC
NETWORK'S LIVE ON THE *HERETIC!* WE NEED YOU BACK ON SITE!
I'M SORRY.
GET DOWN TO THE CARGO BAY!

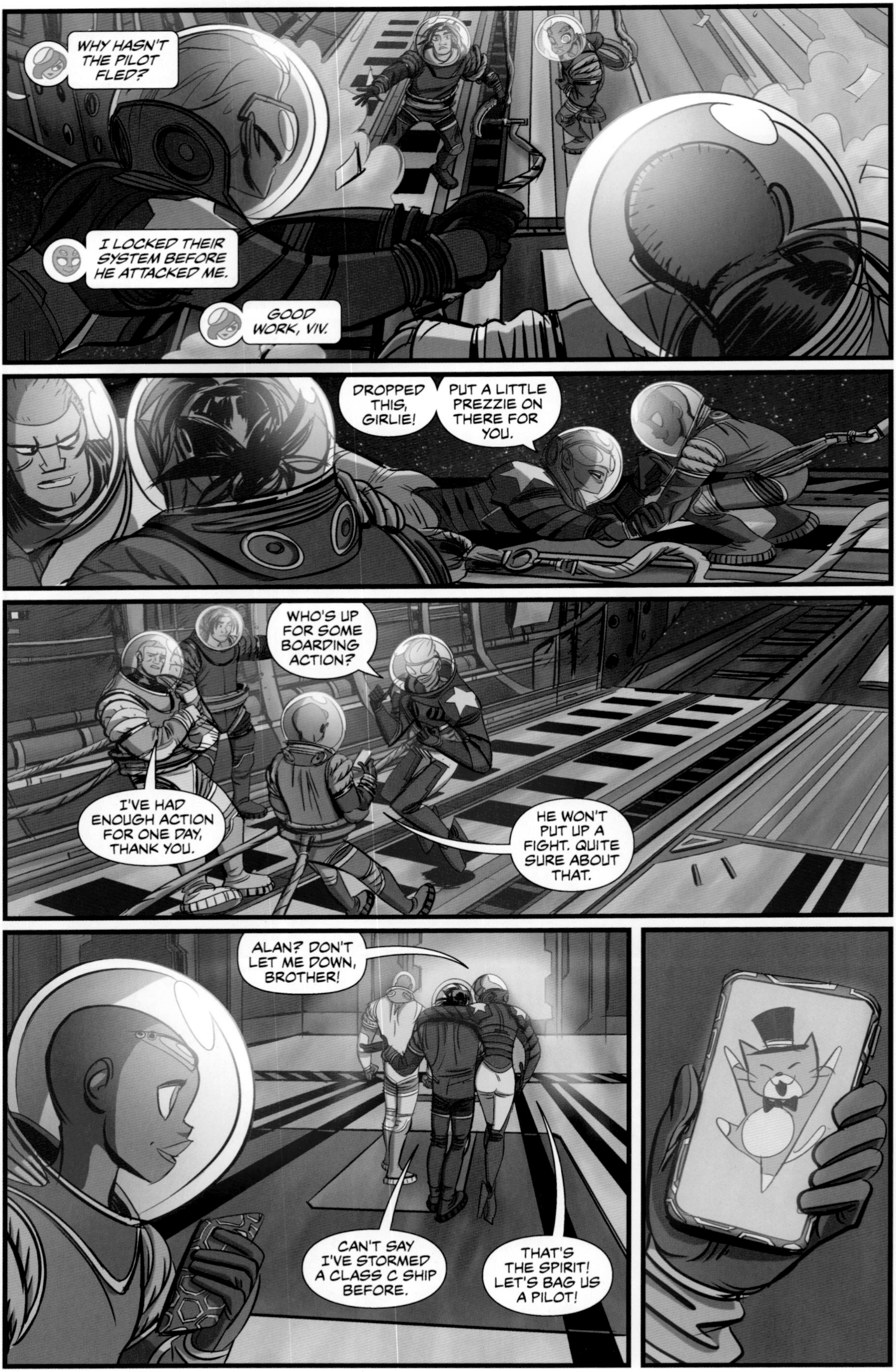
WHY HASN'T THE PILOT FLED?
I LOCKED THEIR SYSTEM BEFORE HE ATTACKED ME.
GOOD WORK, VIV.
DROPPED THIS, GIRLIE!
PUT A LITTLE PREZZIE ON THERE FOR YOU.
WHO'S UP FOR SOME BOARDING ACTION?
I'VE HAD ENOUGH ACTION FOR ONE DAY, THANK YOU.
HE WON'T PUT UP A FIGHT. QUITE SURE ABOUT THAT.
ALAN? DON'T LET ME DOWN, BROTHER!
CAN'T SAY I'VE STORMED A CLASS C SHIP BEFORE.
THAT'S THE SPIRIT! LET'S BAG US A PILOT!

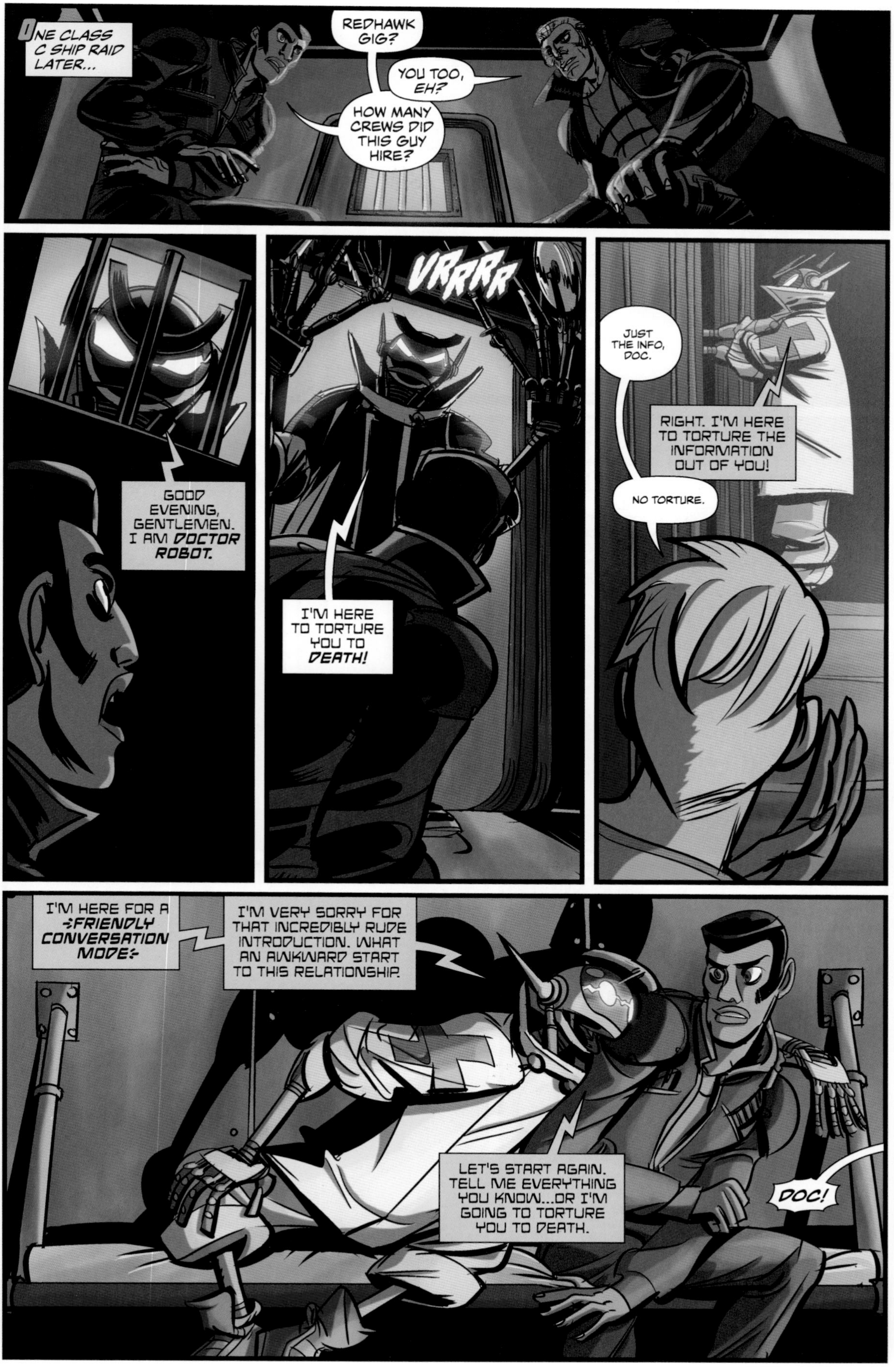
ONE CLASS C SHIP RAID LATER...
REDHAWK GIG?
YOU TOO, EH?
HOW MANY CREWS DID THIS GUY HIRE?
GOOD EVENING, GENTLEMEN. I AM DOCTOR ROBOT.
VRRRR
I'M HERE TO TORTURE YOU TO DEATH!
JUST THE INFO, DOC.
RIGHT. I'M HERE TO TORTURE THE INFORMATION OUT OF YOU!
NO TORTURE.
I'M HERE FOR A FRIENDLY CONVERSATION MODE
I'M VERY SORRY FOR THAT INCREDIBLY RUDE INTRODUCTION. WHAT AN AWKWARD START TO THIS RELATIONSHIP.
LET'S START AGAIN. TELL ME EVERYTHING YOU KNOW...OR I'M GOING TO TORTURE YOU TO DEATH.
DOC!

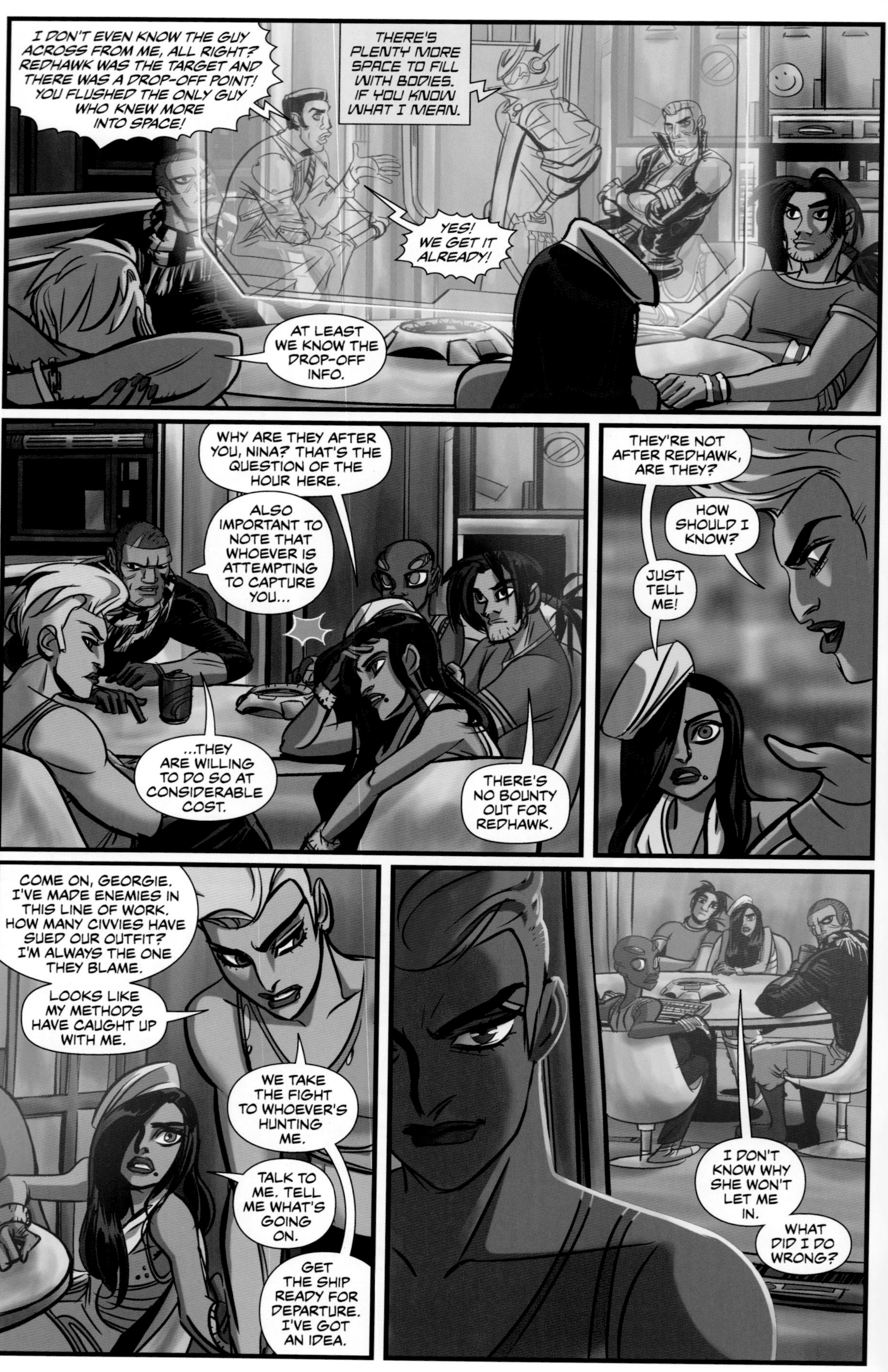
I DON'T EVEN KNOW THE GUY ACROSS FROM ME, ALL RIGHT? REDHAWK WAS THE TARGET AND THERE WAS A DROP-OFF POINT! YOU FLUSHED THE ONLY GUY WHO KNEW MORE INTO SPACE!
THERE'S PLENTY MORE SPACE TO FILL WITH BODIES. IF YOU KNOW WHAT I MEAN.
YES! WE GET IT ALREADY!
AT LEAST WE KNOW THE DROP-OFF INFO.
WHY ARE THEY AFTER YOU, NINA? THAT'S THE QUESTION OF THE HOUR HERE.
ALSO IMPORTANT TO NOTE THAT WHOEVER IS ATTEMPTING TO CAPTURE YOU...
...THEY ARE WILLING TO DO SO AT CONSIDERABLE COST.
THERE'S NO BOUNTY OUT FOR REDHAWK.
THEY'RE NOT AFTER REDHAWK, ARE THEY?
HOW SHOULD I KNOW?
JUST TELL ME!
COME ON, GEORGIE. I'VE MADE ENEMIES IN THIS LINE OF WORK. HOW MANY CIVVIES HAVE SUED OUR OUTFIT? I'M ALWAYS THE ONE THEY BLAME.
LOOKS LIKE MY METHODS HAVE CAUGHT UP WITH ME.
WE TAKE THE FIGHT TO WHOEVER'S HUNTING ME.
TALK TO ME. TELL ME WHAT'S GOING ON.
GET THE SHIP READY FOR DEPARTURE. I'VE GOT AN IDEA.
I DON'T KNOW WHY SHE WON'T LET ME IN.
WHAT DID I DO WRONG?

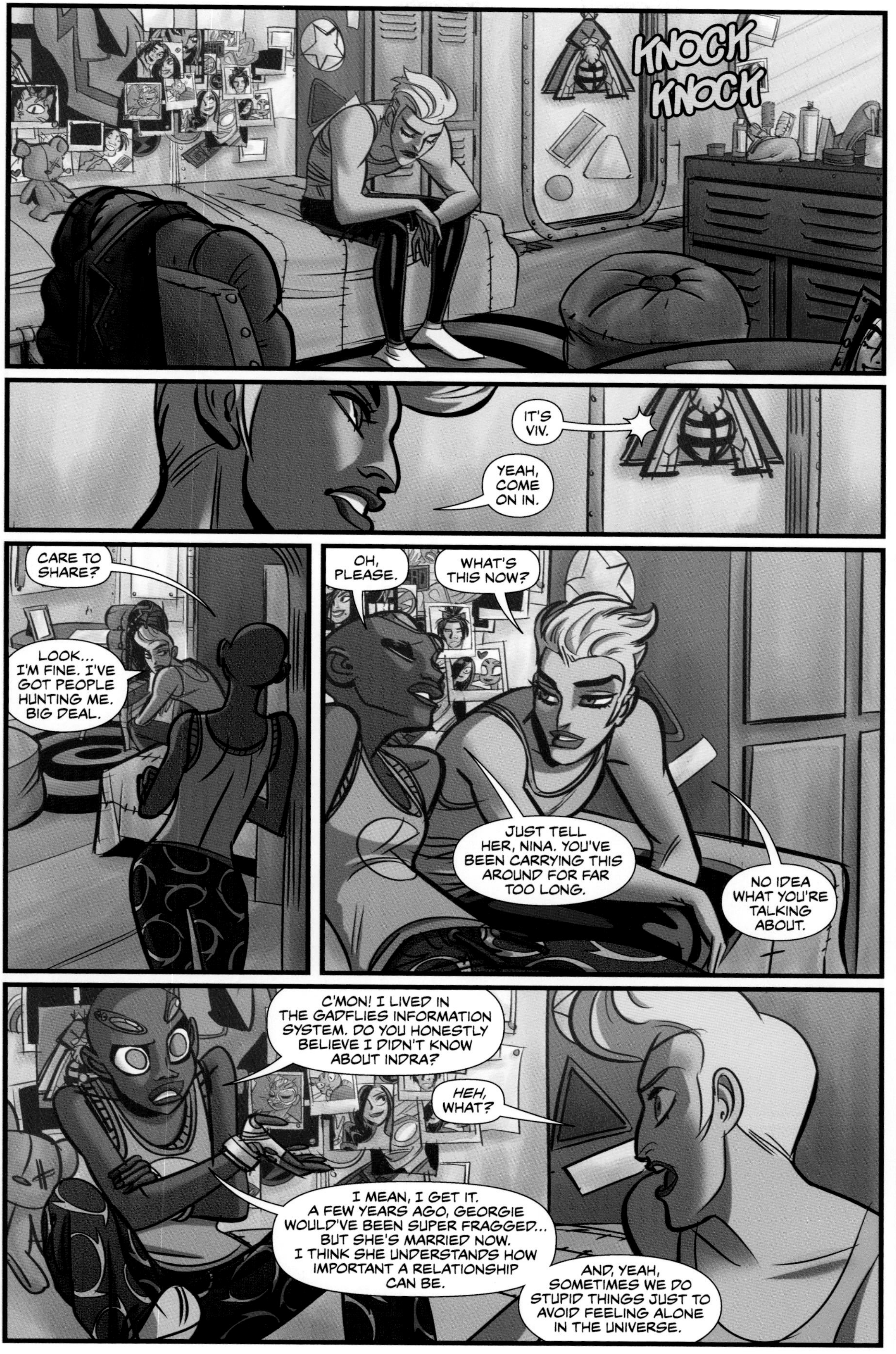
KNOCK KNOCK
IT'S VIV.
YEAH, COME ON IN.
CARE TO SHARE?
LOOK... I'M FINE. I'VE GOT PEOPLE HUNTING ME. BIG DEAL.
OH, PLEASE.
WHAT'S THIS NOW?
JUST TELL HER, NINA. YOU'VE BEEN CARRYING THIS AROUND FOR FAR TOO LONG.
NO IDEA WHAT YOU'RE TALKING ABOUT.
C'MON! I LIVED IN THE GADFLIES INFORMATION SYSTEM. DO YOU HONESTLY BELIEVE I DIDN'T KNOW ABOUT INDRA?
HEH, WHAT?
I MEAN, I GET IT. A FEW YEARS AGO, GEORGIE WOULD'VE BEEN SUPER FRAGGED... BUT SHE'S MARRIED NOW. I THINK SHE UNDERSTANDS HOW IMPORTANT A RELATIONSHIP CAN BE.
AND, YEAH, SOMETIMES WE DO STUPID THINGS JUST TO AVOID FEELING ALONE IN THE UNIVERSE.

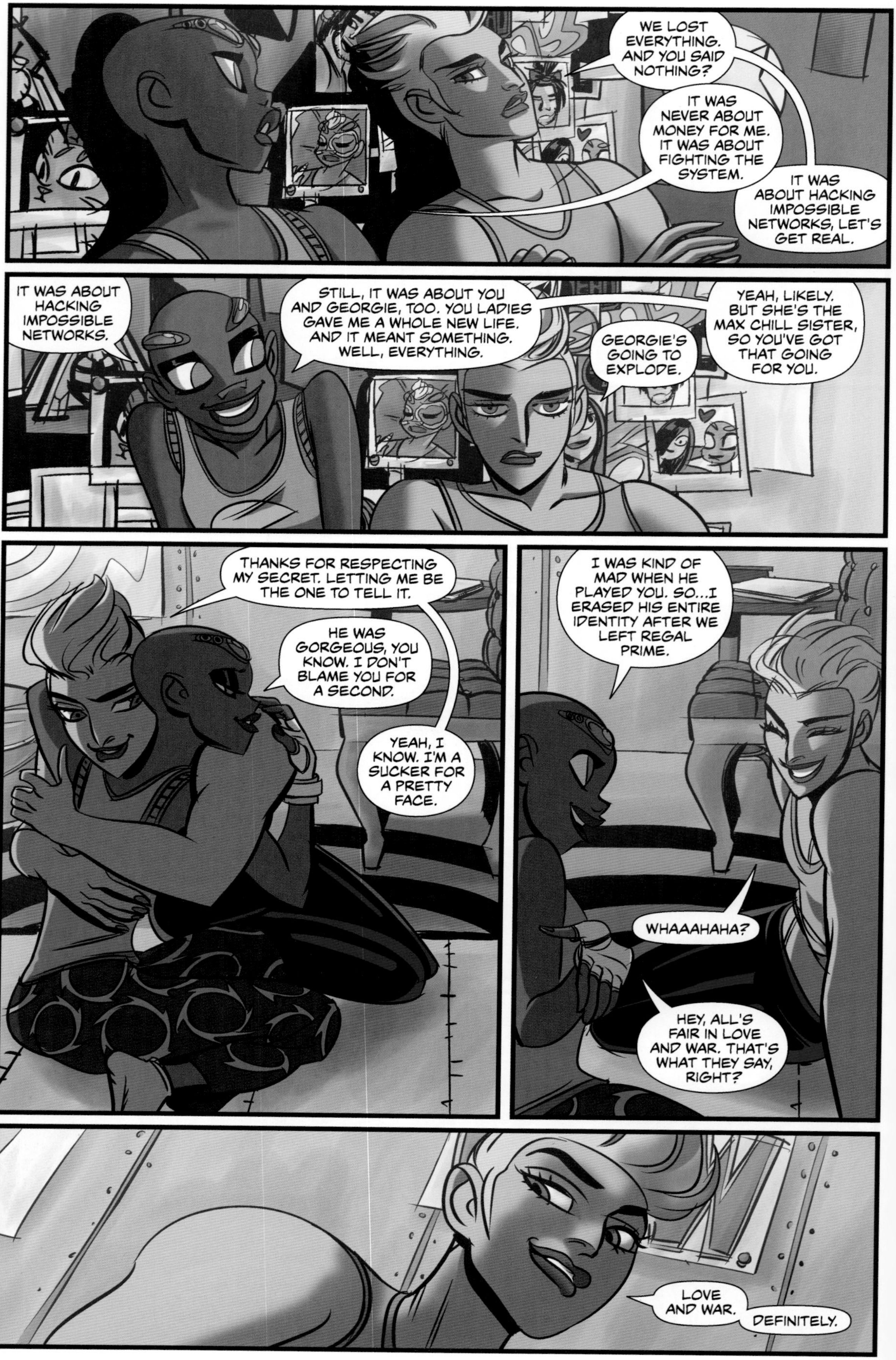

WE LOST EVERYTHING. AND YOU SAID NOTHING?
IT WAS NEVER ABOUT MONEY FOR ME. IT WAS ABOUT FIGHTING THE SYSTEM.
IT WAS ABOUT HACKING IMPOSSIBLE NETWORKS, LET'S GET REAL.
IT WAS ABOUT HACKING IMPOSSIBLE NETWORKS.
STILL, IT WAS ABOUT YOU AND GEORGIE, TOO. YOU LADIES GAVE ME A WHOLE NEW LIFE. AND IT MEANT SOMETHING. WELL, EVERYTHING.
GEORGIE'S GOING TO EXPLODE.
YEAH, LIKELY. BUT SHE'S THE MAX CHILL SISTER, SO YOU'VE GOT THAT GOING FOR YOU.
THANKS FOR RESPECTING MY SECRET. LETTING ME BE THE ONE TO TELL IT.
HE WAS GORGEOUS, YOU KNOW. I DON'T BLAME YOU FOR A SECOND.
YEAH, I KNOW. I'M A SUCKER FOR A PRETTY FACE.
I WAS KIND OF MAD WHEN HE PLAYED YOU. SO...I ERASED HIS ENTIRE IDENTITY AFTER WE LEFT REGAL PRIME.
WHAAAHAHA?
HEY, ALL'S FAIR IN LOVE AND WAR. THAT'S WHAT THEY SAY, RIGHT?
LOVE AND WAR.
DEFINITELY.

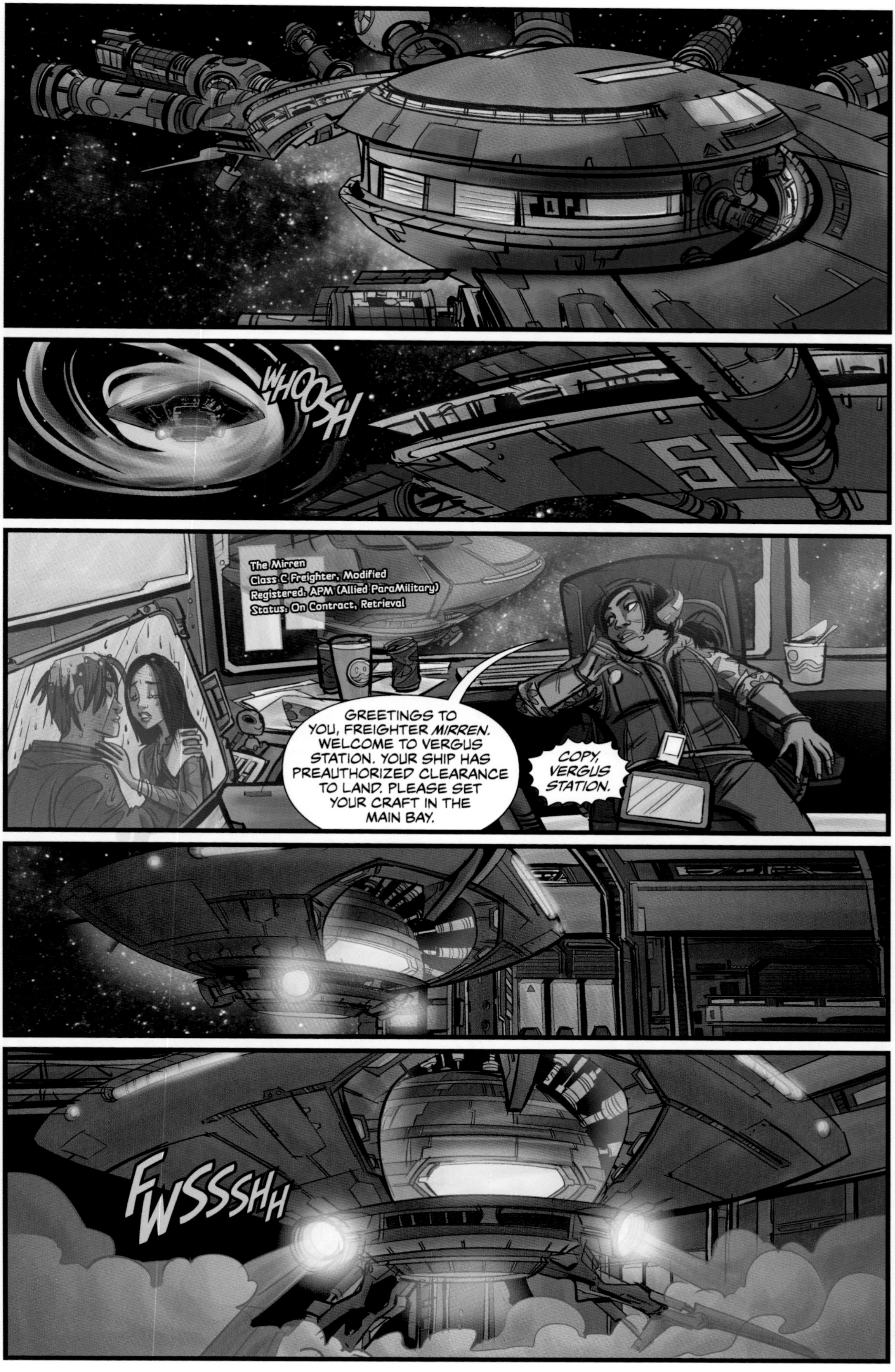
WHOOSH
The Mirren
Class C Freighter, Modified
Registered: APM (Allied ParaMilitary)
Status: On Contract, Retrieval
GREETINGS TO YOU, FREIGHTER *MIRREN*. WELCOME TO VERGUS STATION. YOUR SHIP HAS PREAUTHORIZED CLEARANCE TO LAND. PLEASE SET YOUR CRAFT IN THE MAIN BAY.
COPY, VERGUS STATION.
FWSSSHH

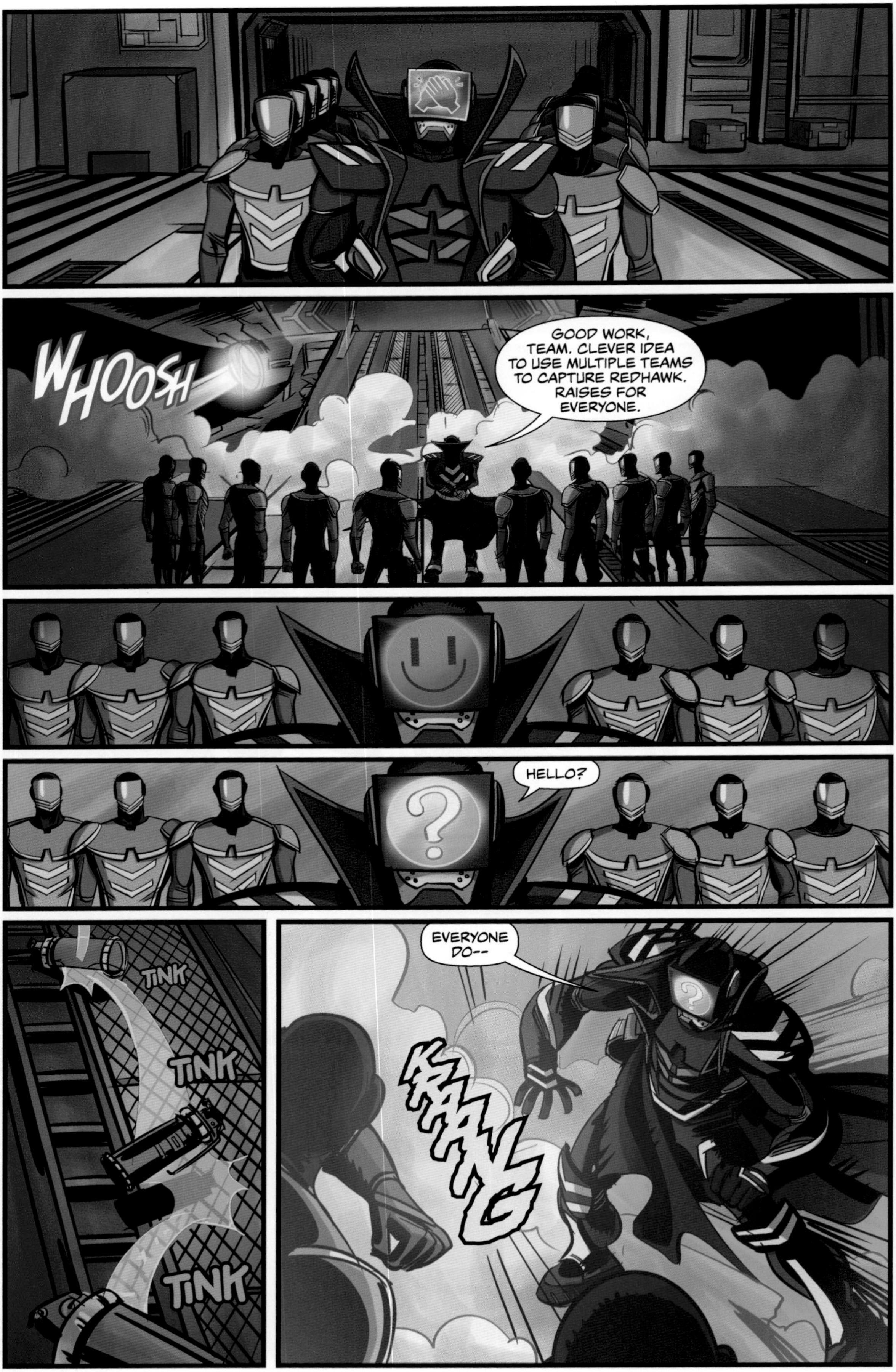
WHOOSH
GOOD WORK, TEAM. CLEVER IDEA TO USE MULTIPLE TEAMS TO CAPTURE REDHAWK. RAISES FOR EVERYONE.
HELLO?
TINK
TINK
TINK
EVERYONE DO--
KRANG

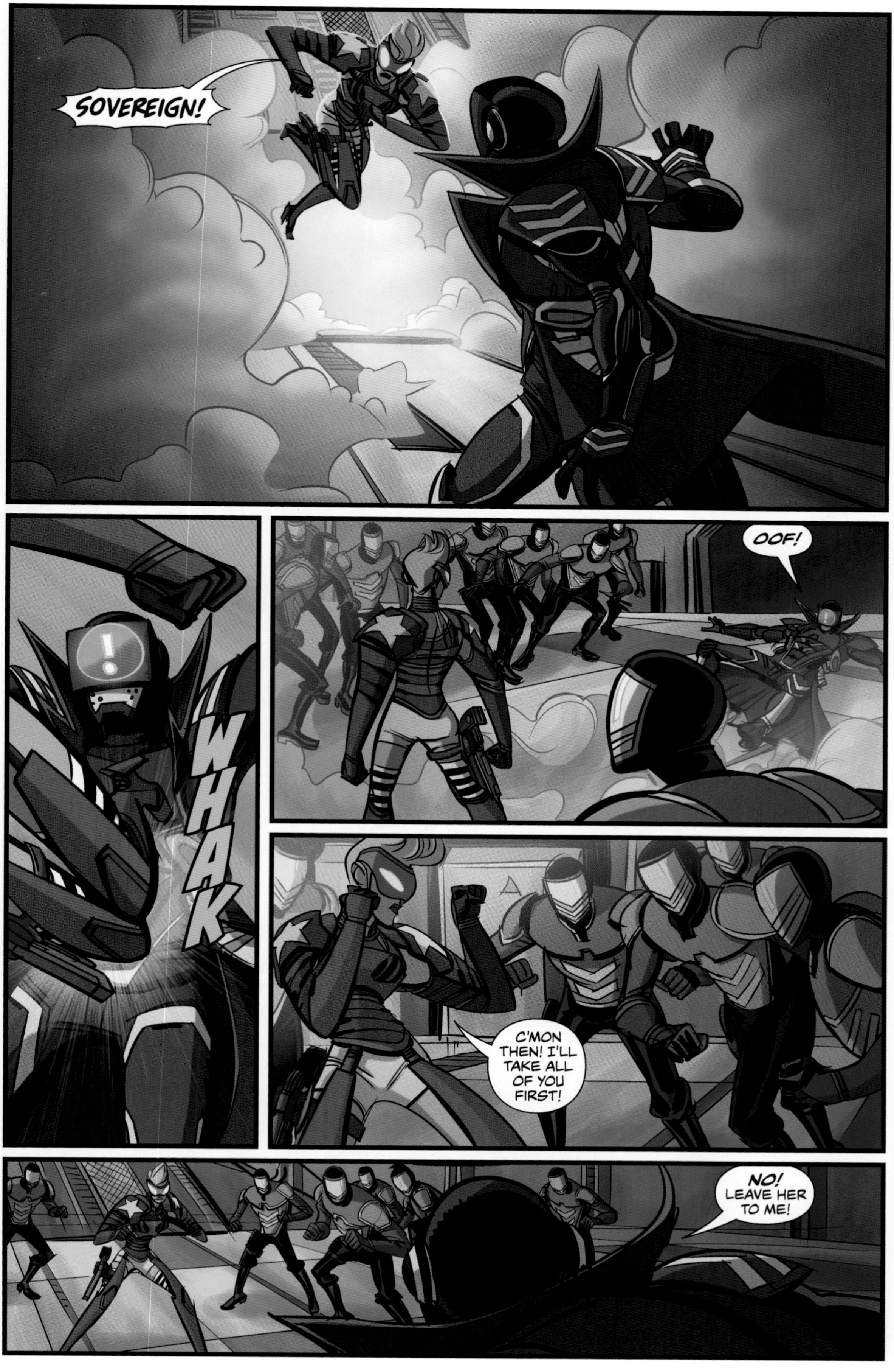
SOVEREIGN!
WHAK
OOF!
C'MON THEN! I'LL TAKE ALL OF YOU FIRST!
NO! LEAVE HER TO ME!

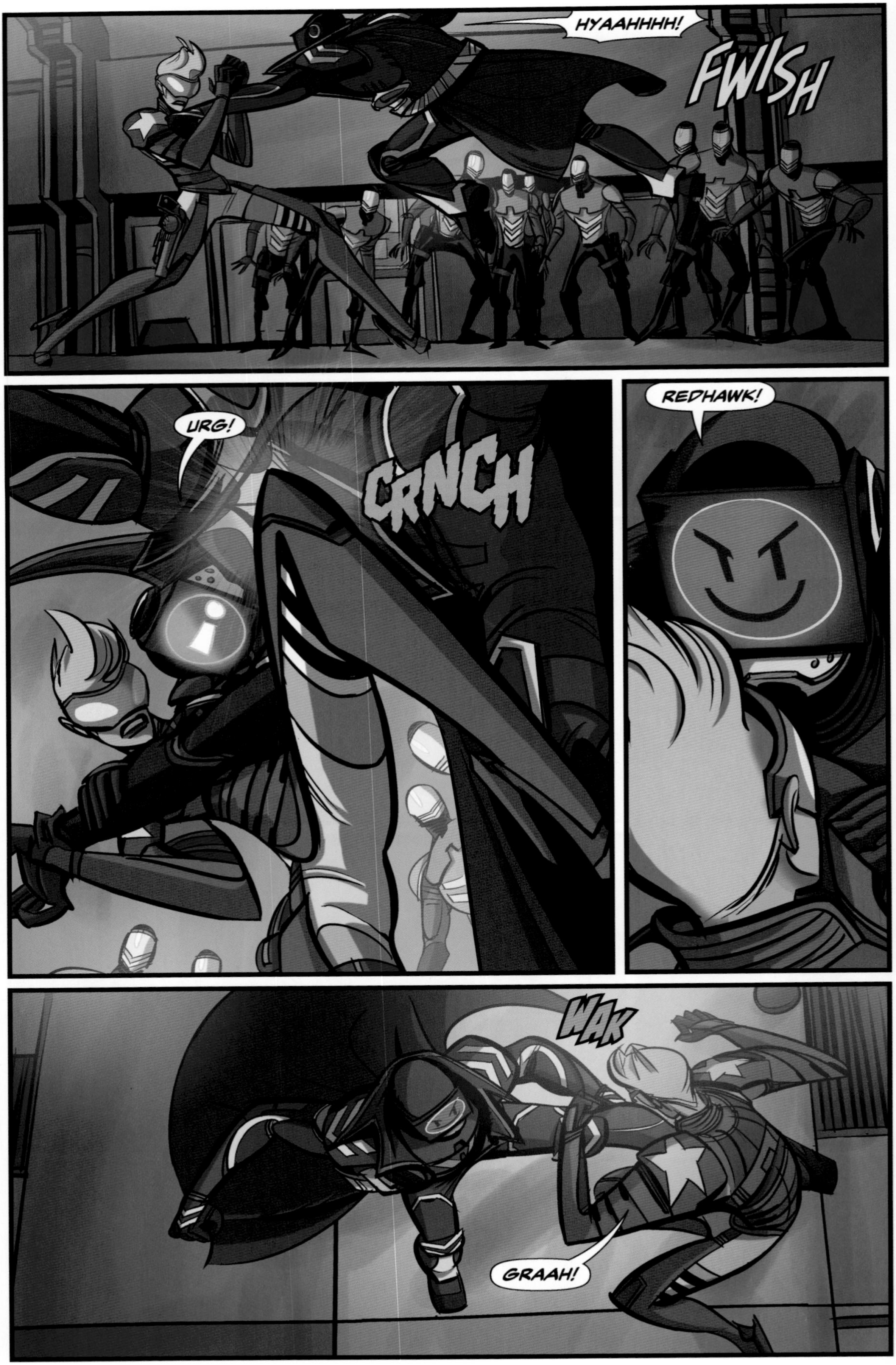
HYAAHHHH!
FWISH
URG!
CRNCH
REDHAWK!
WAK
GRAAH!

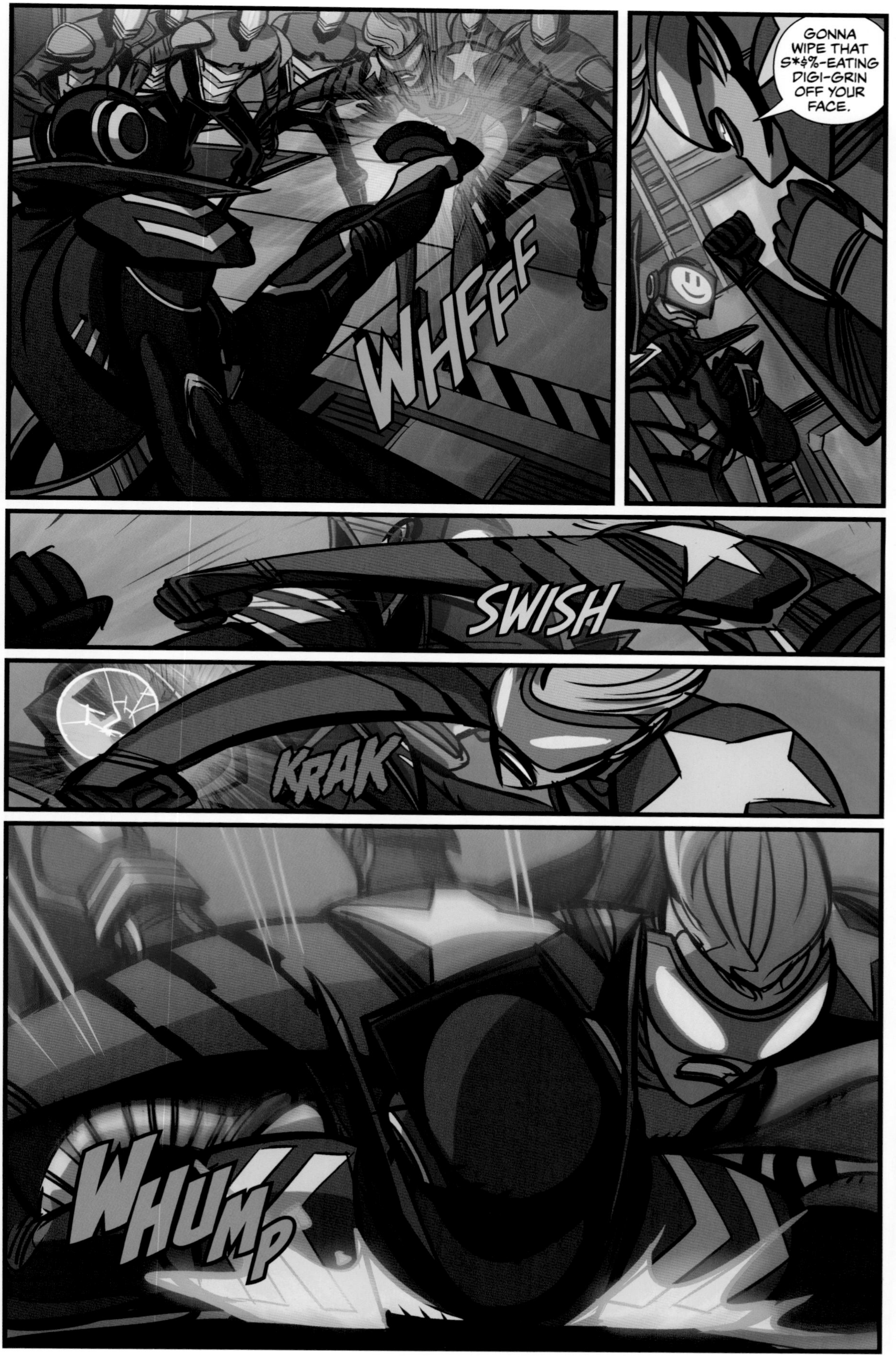
WHFFF
GONNA WIPE THAT S*$%-EATING DIGI-GRIN OFF YOUR FACE.
SWISH
KRAK
WHUMP

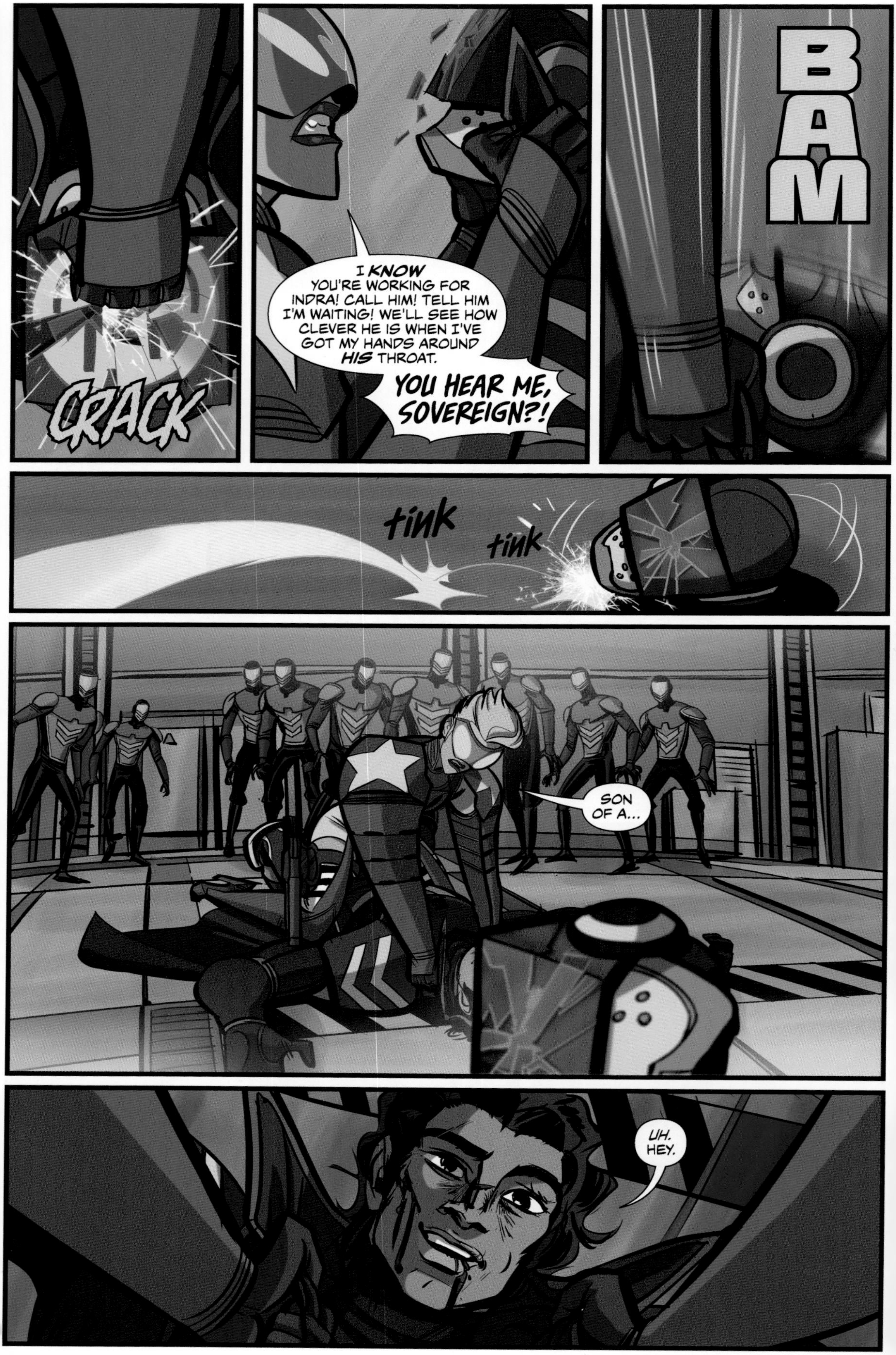
CRACK
I KNOW YOU'RE WORKING FOR INDRA! CALL HIM! TELL HIM I'M WAITING! WE'LL SEE HOW CLEVER HE IS WHEN I'VE GOT MY HANDS AROUND HIS THROAT.
YOU HEAR ME, SOVEREIGN?!
BAM
tink
tink
SON OF A...
UH. HEY.

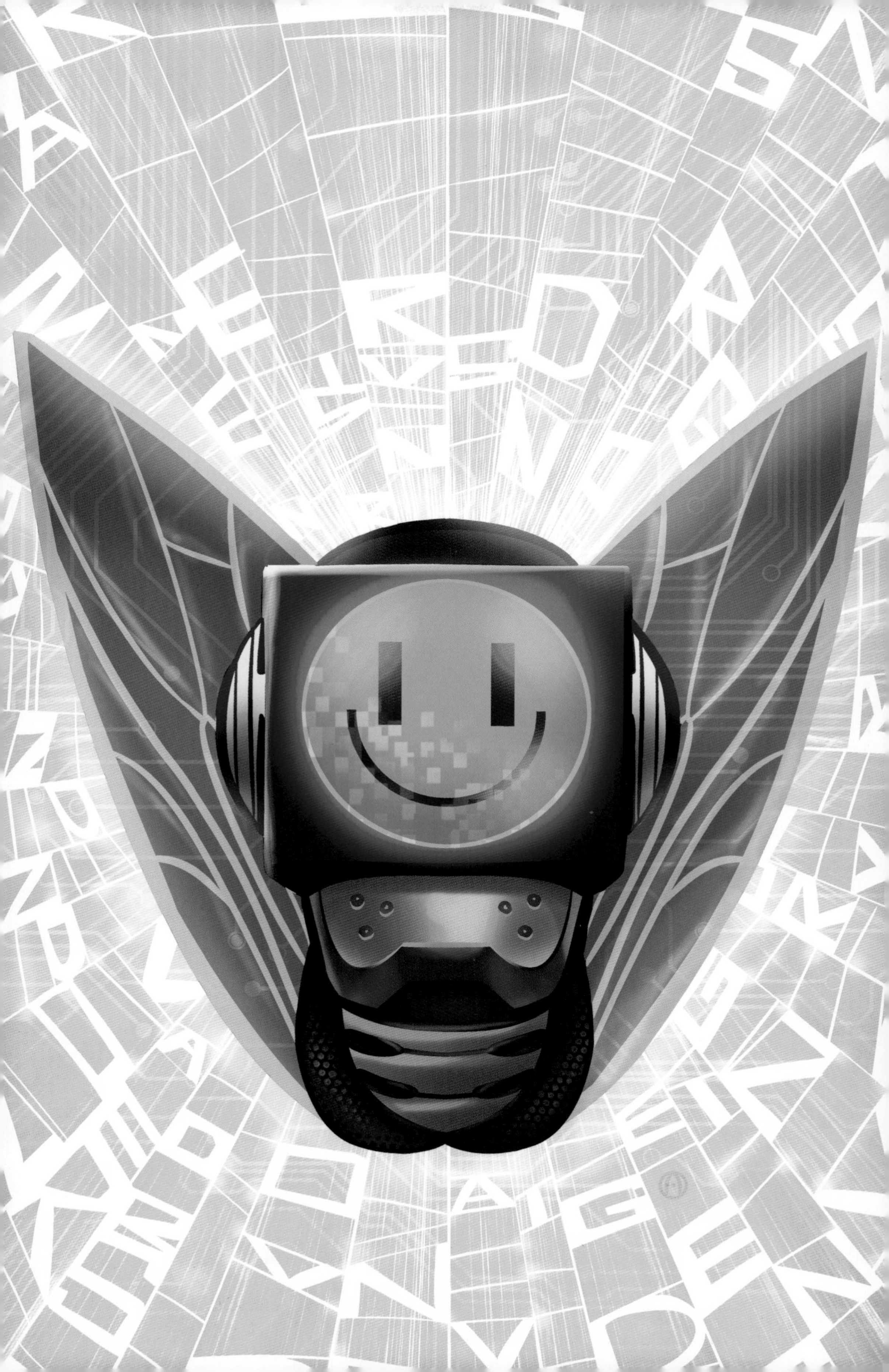

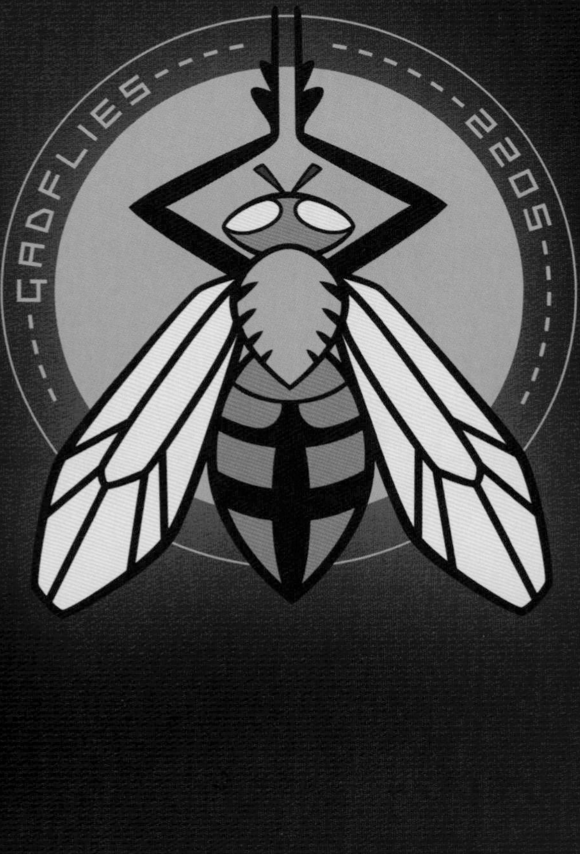
GADFLIES
2205

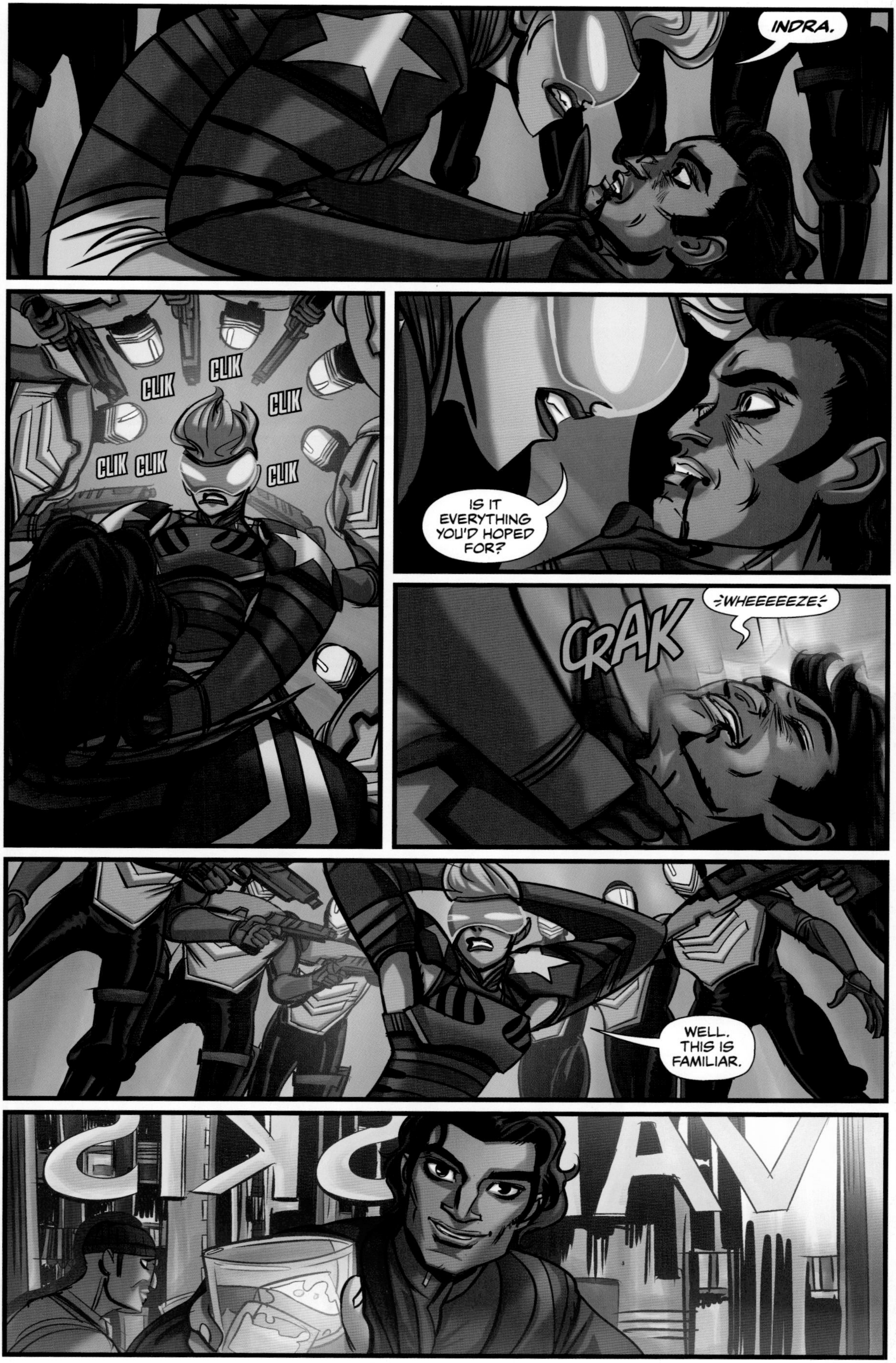
INDRA.
CLIK
CLIK
CLIK
CLIK CLIK
CLIK
IS IT EVERYTHING YOU'D HOPED FOR?
CRAK
WHEEEEEZE
WELL. THIS IS FAMILIAR.

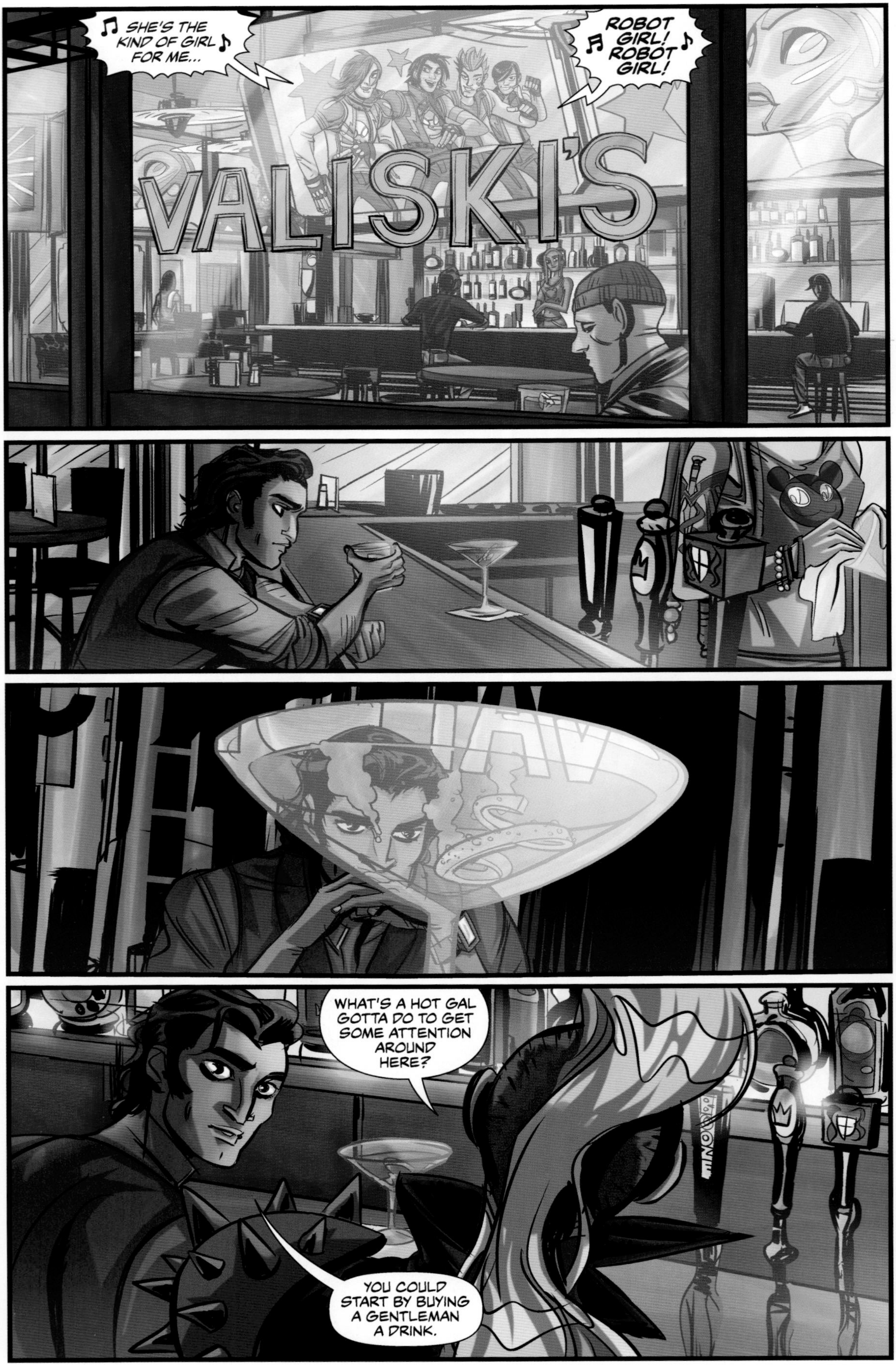
♫ SHE'S THE KIND OF GIRL FOR ME... ♪
♫ ROBOT GIRL! ROBOT GIRL! ♪
VALISKI'S
WHAT'S A HOT GAL GOTTA DO TO GET SOME ATTENTION AROUND HERE?
YOU COULD START BY BUYING A GENTLEMAN A DRINK.

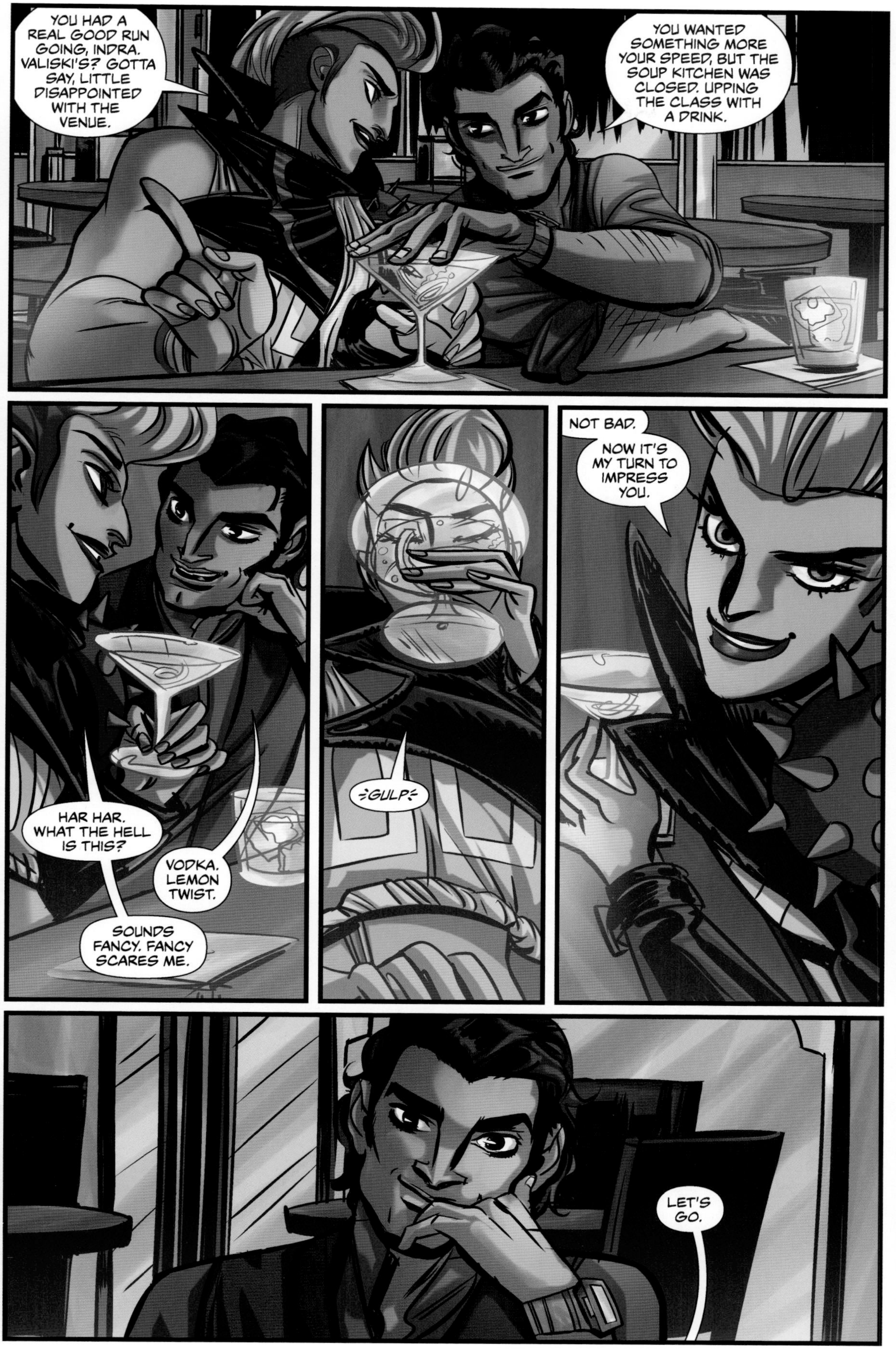
YOU HAD A REAL GOOD RUN GOING, INDRA. VALISKI'S? GOTTA SAY, LITTLE DISAPPOINTED WITH THE VENUE.
YOU WANTED SOMETHING MORE YOUR SPEED, BUT THE SOUP KITCHEN WAS CLOSED. UPPING THE CLASS WITH A DRINK.
HAR HAR. WHAT THE HELL IS THIS?
VODKA. LEMON TWIST.
SOUNDS FANCY. FANCY SCARES ME.
GULP
NOT BAD.
NOW IT'S MY TURN TO IMPRESS YOU.
LET'S GO.

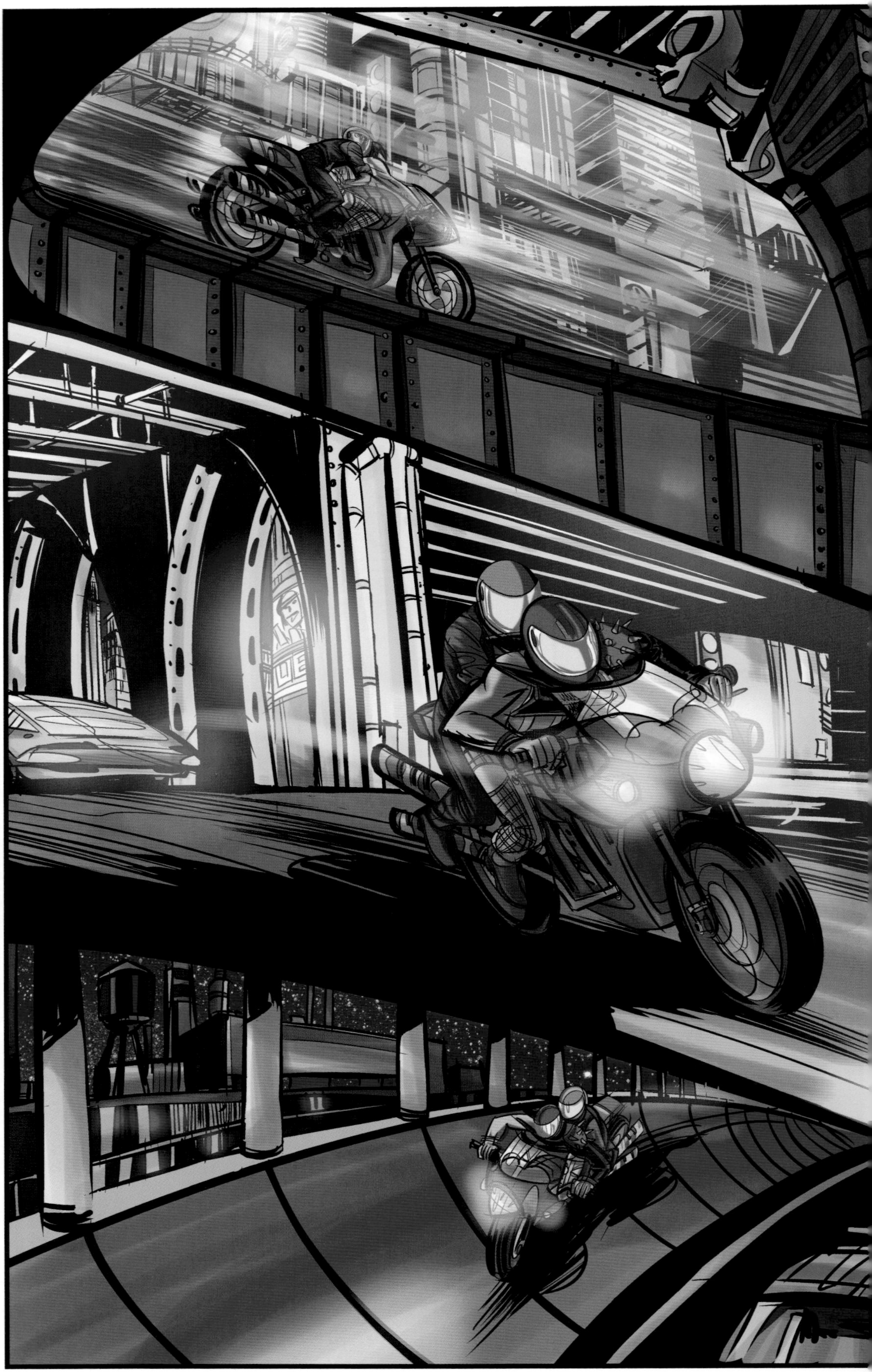

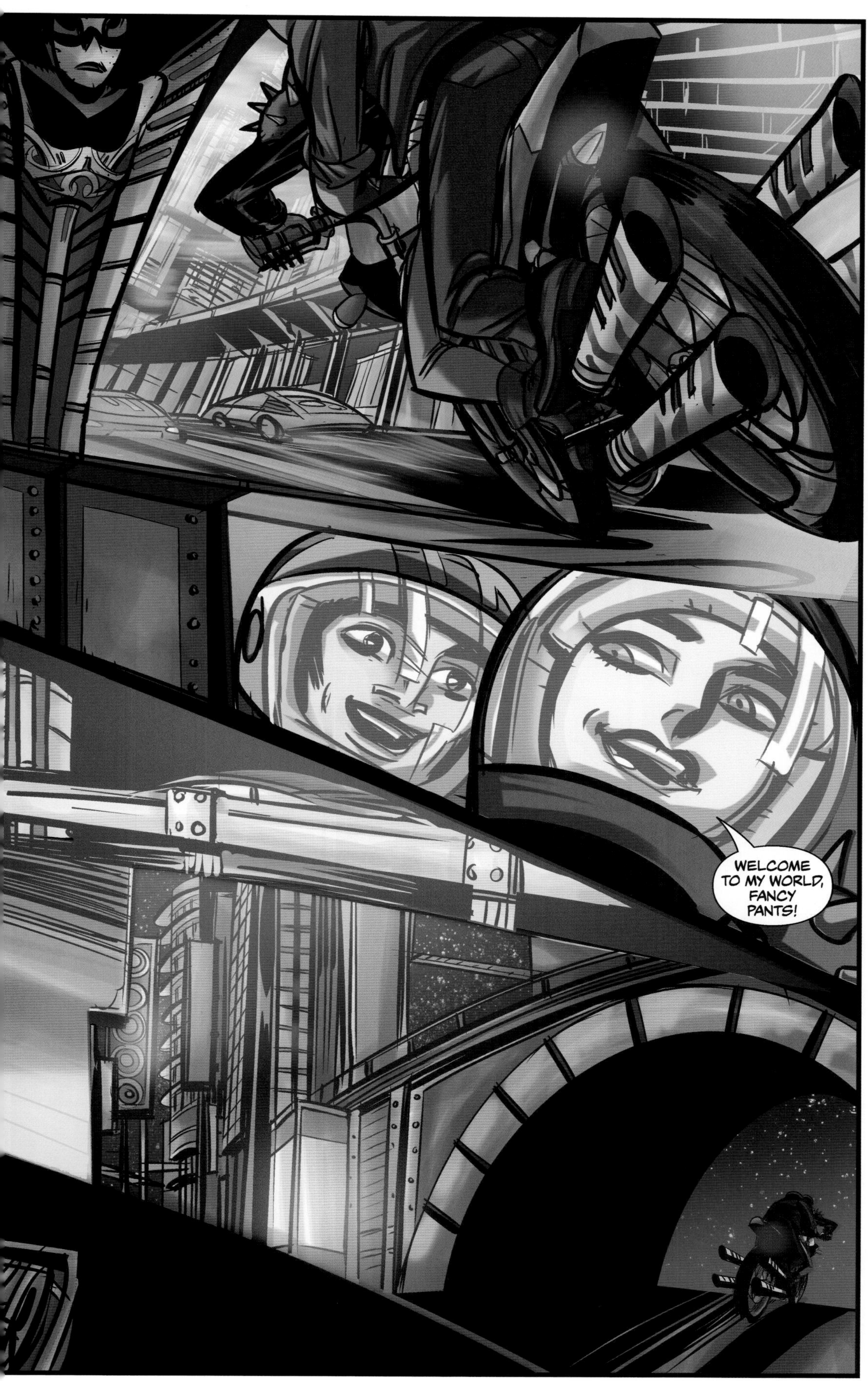
WELCOME TO MY WORLD, FANCY PANTS!

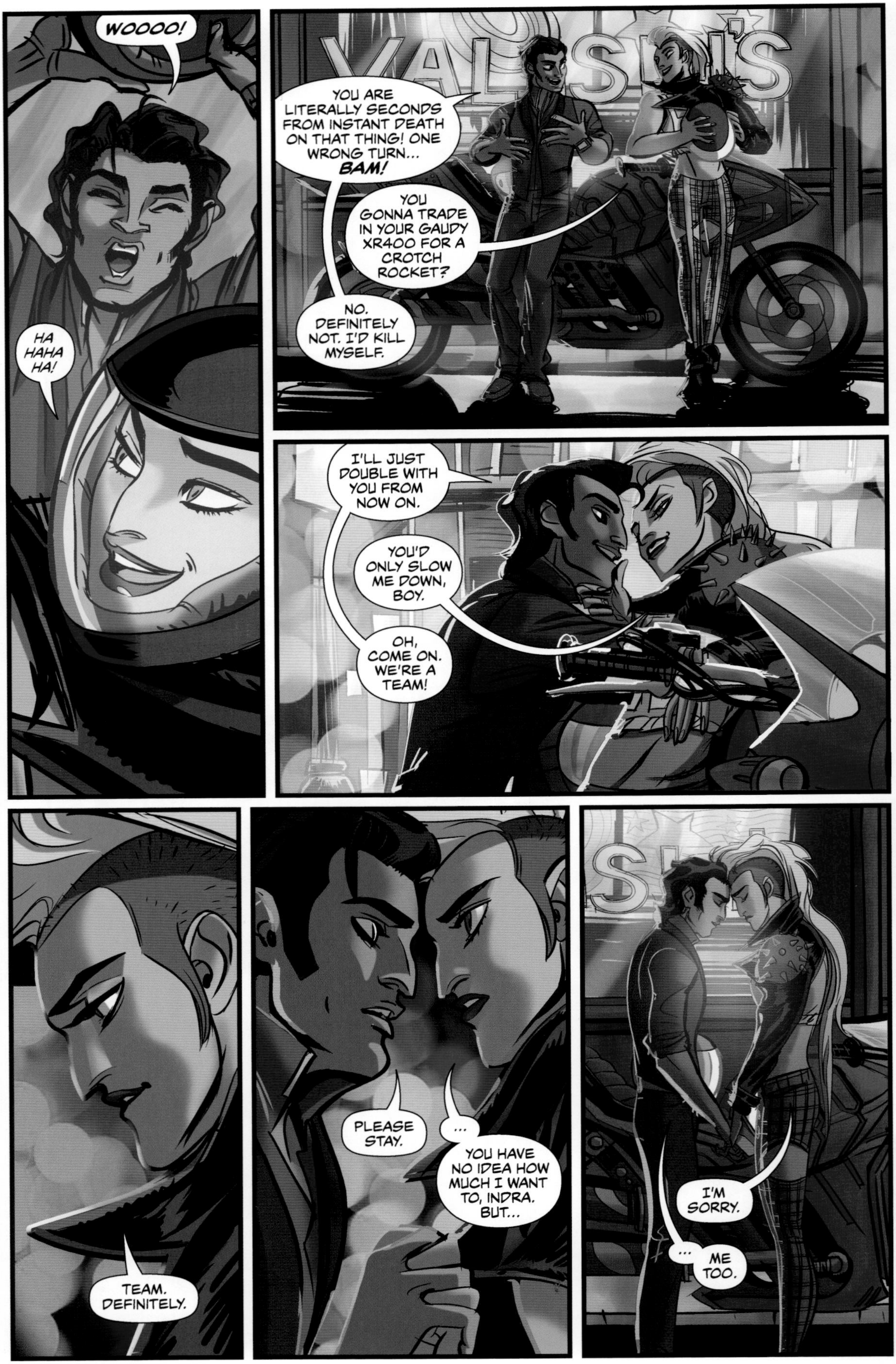
WOOOO!
HA HAHA HA!
VALSHI'S
YOU ARE LITERALLY SECONDS FROM INSTANT DEATH ON THAT THING! ONE WRONG TURN... BAM!
YOU GONNA TRADE IN YOUR GAUDY XR400 FOR A CROTCH ROCKET?
NO. DEFINITELY NOT. I'D KILL MYSELF.
I'LL JUST DOUBLE WITH YOU FROM NOW ON.
YOU'D ONLY SLOW ME DOWN, BOY.
OH, COME ON. WE'RE A TEAM!
TEAM. DEFINITELY.
PLEASE STAY.
...
YOU HAVE NO IDEA HOW MUCH I WANT TO, INDRA. BUT...
I'M SORRY.
...
ME TOO.

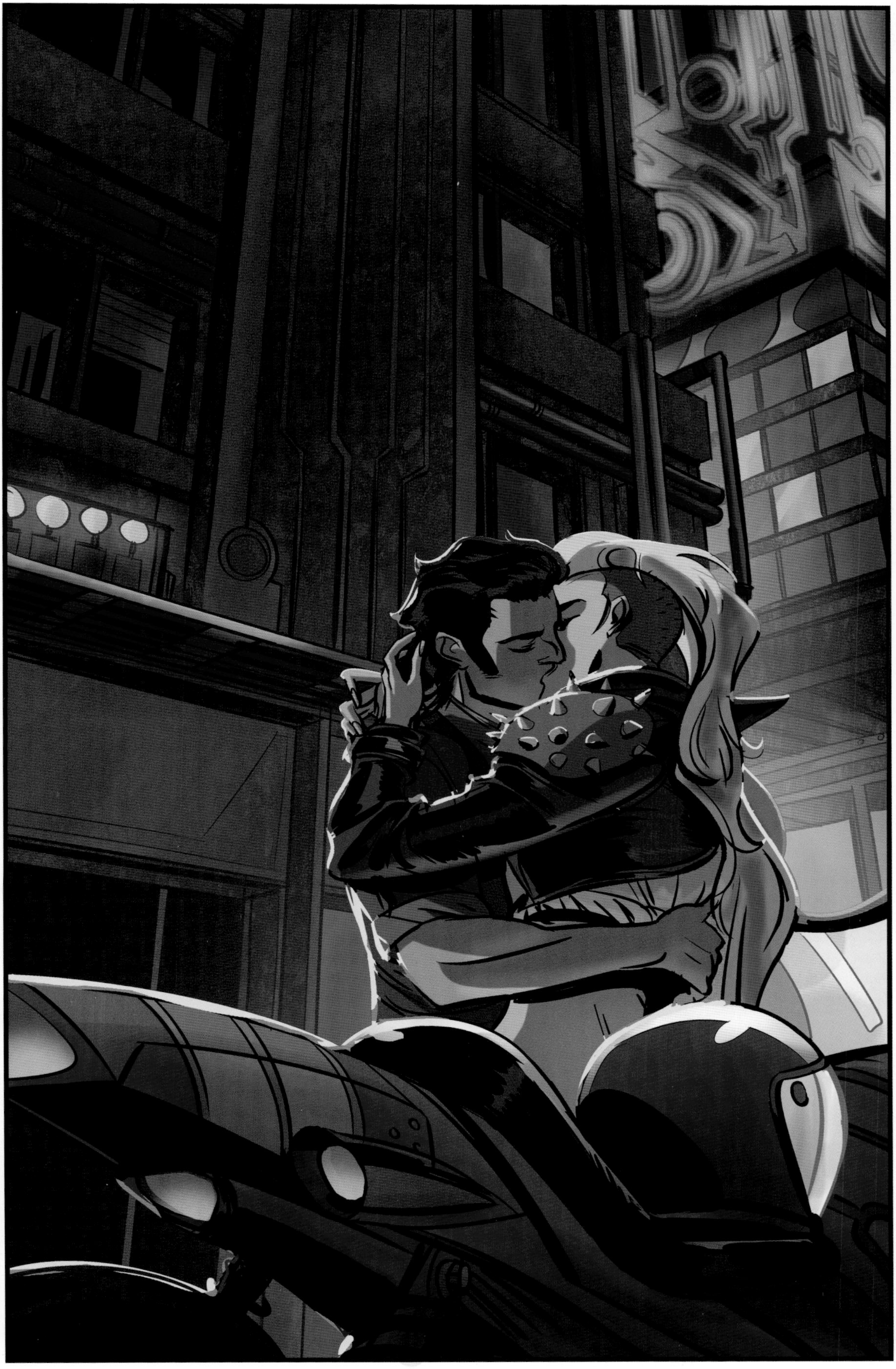

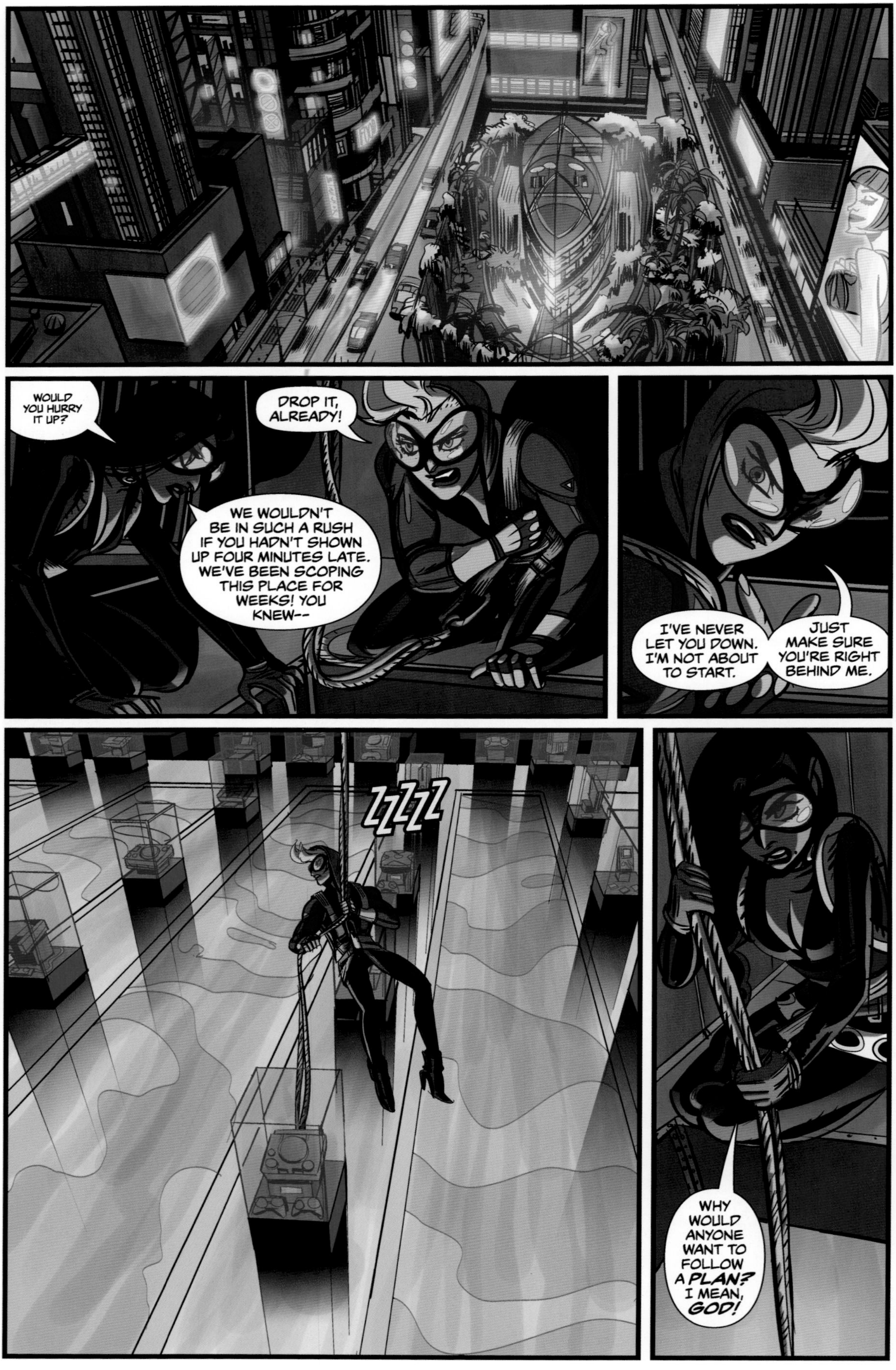
WOULD YOU HURRY IT UP?
DROP IT, ALREADY!
WE WOULDN'T BE IN SUCH A RUSH IF YOU HADN'T SHOWN UP FOUR MINUTES LATE. WE'VE BEEN SCOPING THIS PLACE FOR WEEKS! YOU KNEW--
JUST MAKE SURE YOU'RE RIGHT BEHIND ME.
I'VE NEVER LET YOU DOWN. I'M NOT ABOUT TO START.
ZZZZZ
WHY WOULD ANYONE WANT TO FOLLOW A *PLAN?* I MEAN, *GOD!*

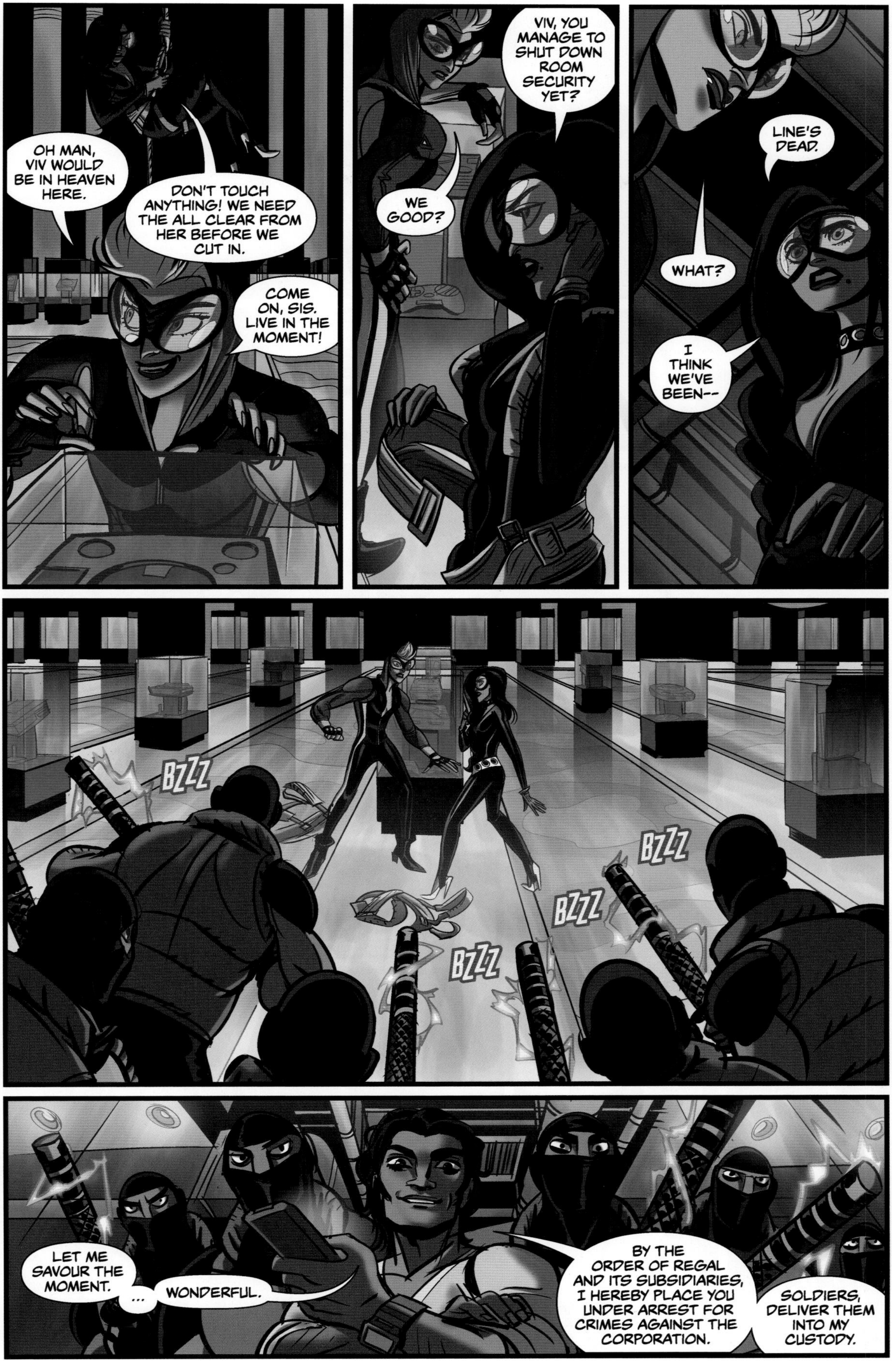
OH MAN, VIV WOULD BE IN HEAVEN HERE.
DON'T TOUCH ANYTHING! WE NEED THE ALL CLEAR FROM HER BEFORE WE CUT IN.
COME ON, SIS. LIVE IN THE MOMENT!
VIV, YOU MANAGE TO SHUT DOWN ROOM SECURITY YET?
WE GOOD?
LINE'S DEAD.
WHAT?
I THINK WE'VE BEEN--
BZZZ
BZZZ
BZZZ
BZZZ
LET ME SAVOUR THE MOMENT.
...
WONDERFUL.
BY THE ORDER OF REGAL AND ITS SUBSIDIARIES, I HEREBY PLACE YOU UNDER ARREST FOR CRIMES AGAINST THE CORPORATION.
SOLDIERS, DELIVER THEM INTO MY CUSTODY.

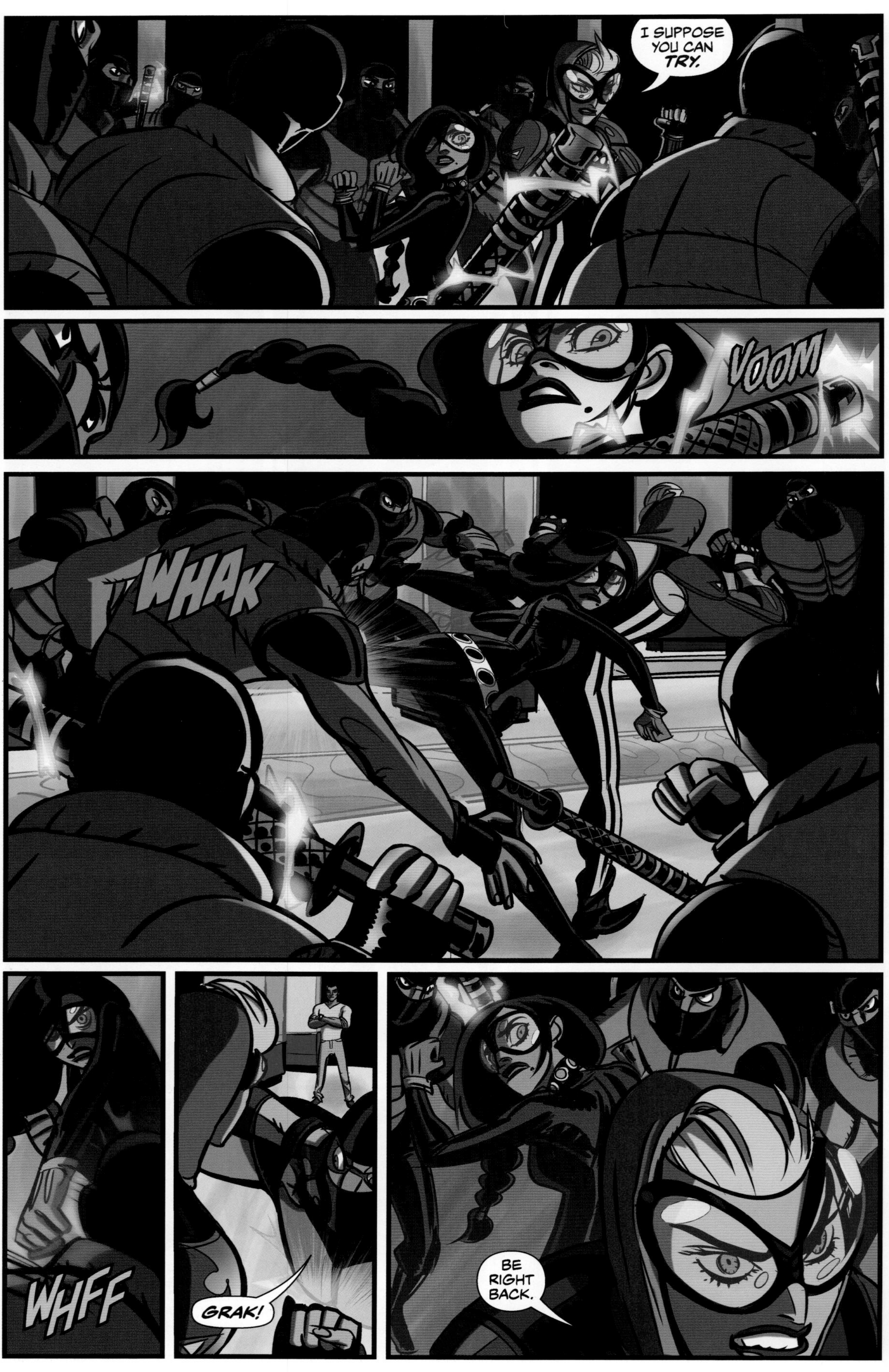
I SUPPOSE YOU CAN TRY.
VOOM
WHAK
WHFF
GRAK!
BE RIGHT BACK.

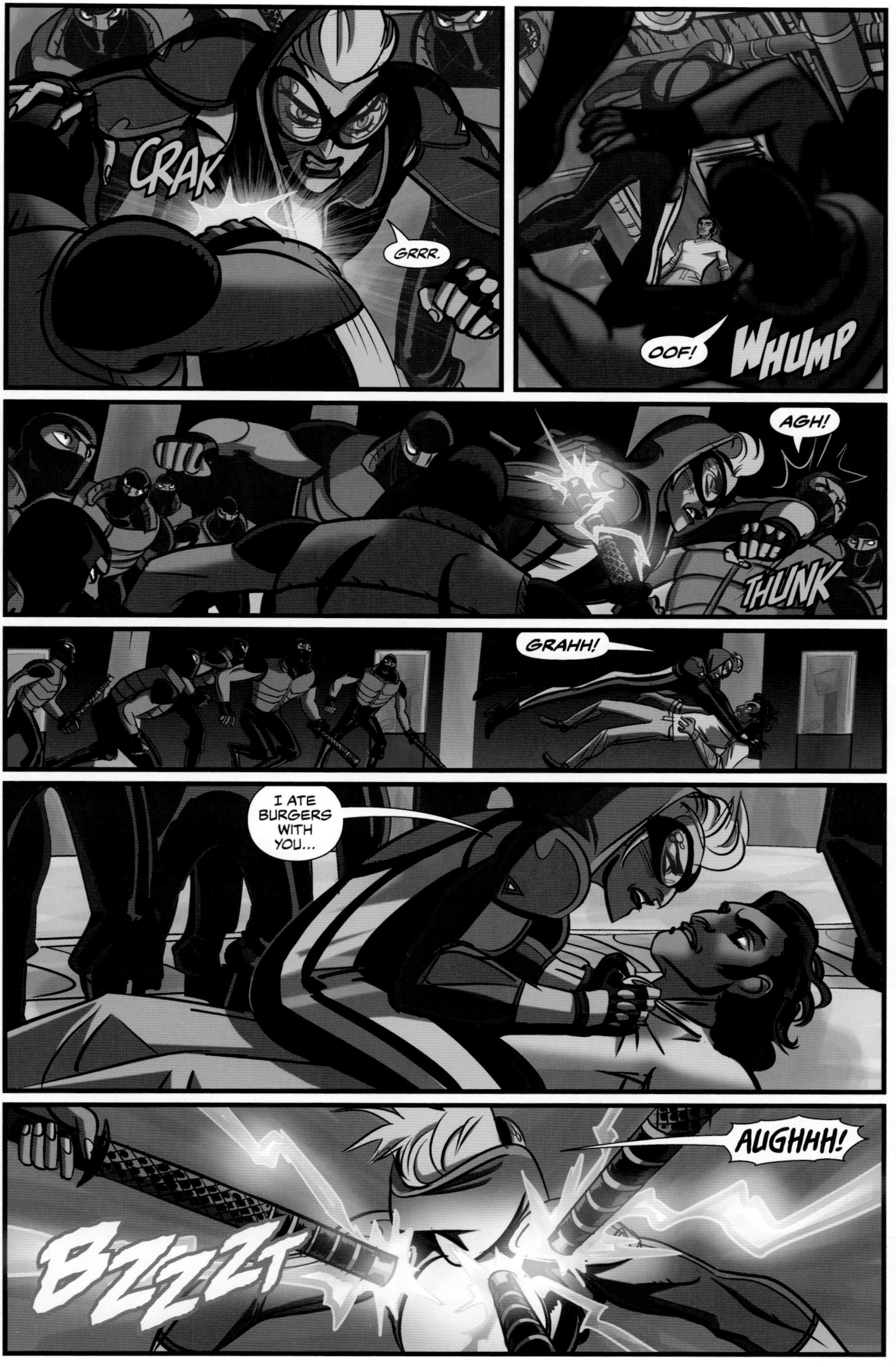
CRAK
GRRR.
OOF!
WHUMP
AGH!
THUNK
GRAHH!
I ATE BURGERS WITH YOU...
AUGHHH!
BZZZZT

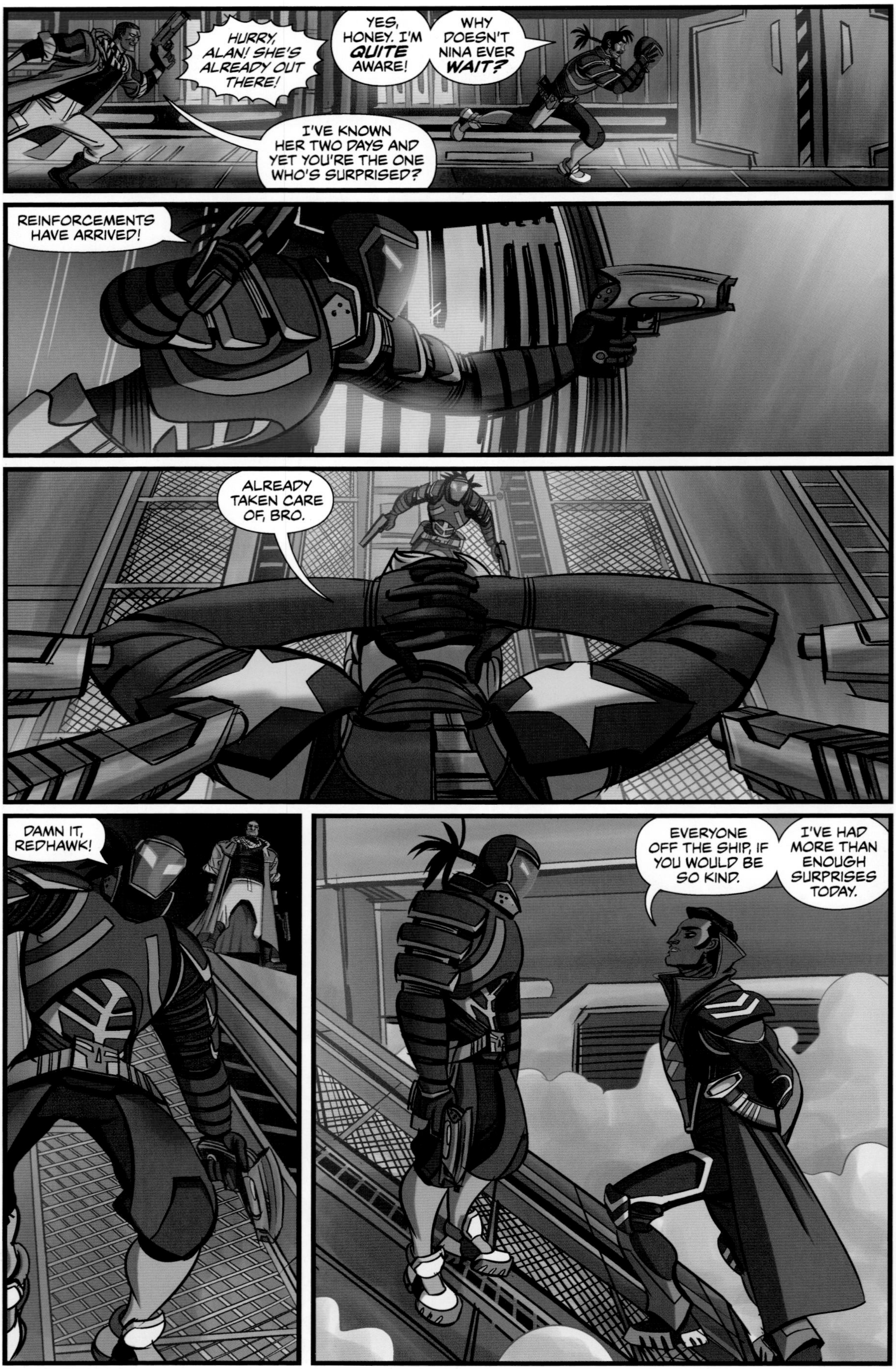
HURRY, ALAN! SHE'S ALREADY OUT THERE!
YES, HONEY. I'M QUITE AWARE!
WHY DOESN'T NINA EVER WAIT?
I'VE KNOWN HER TWO DAYS AND YET YOU'RE THE ONE WHO'S SURPRISED?
REINFORCEMENTS HAVE ARRIVED!
ALREADY TAKEN CARE OF, BRO.
DAMN IT, REDHAWK!
EVERYONE OFF THE SHIP, IF YOU WOULD BE SO KIND.
I'VE HAD MORE THAN ENOUGH SURPRISES TODAY.

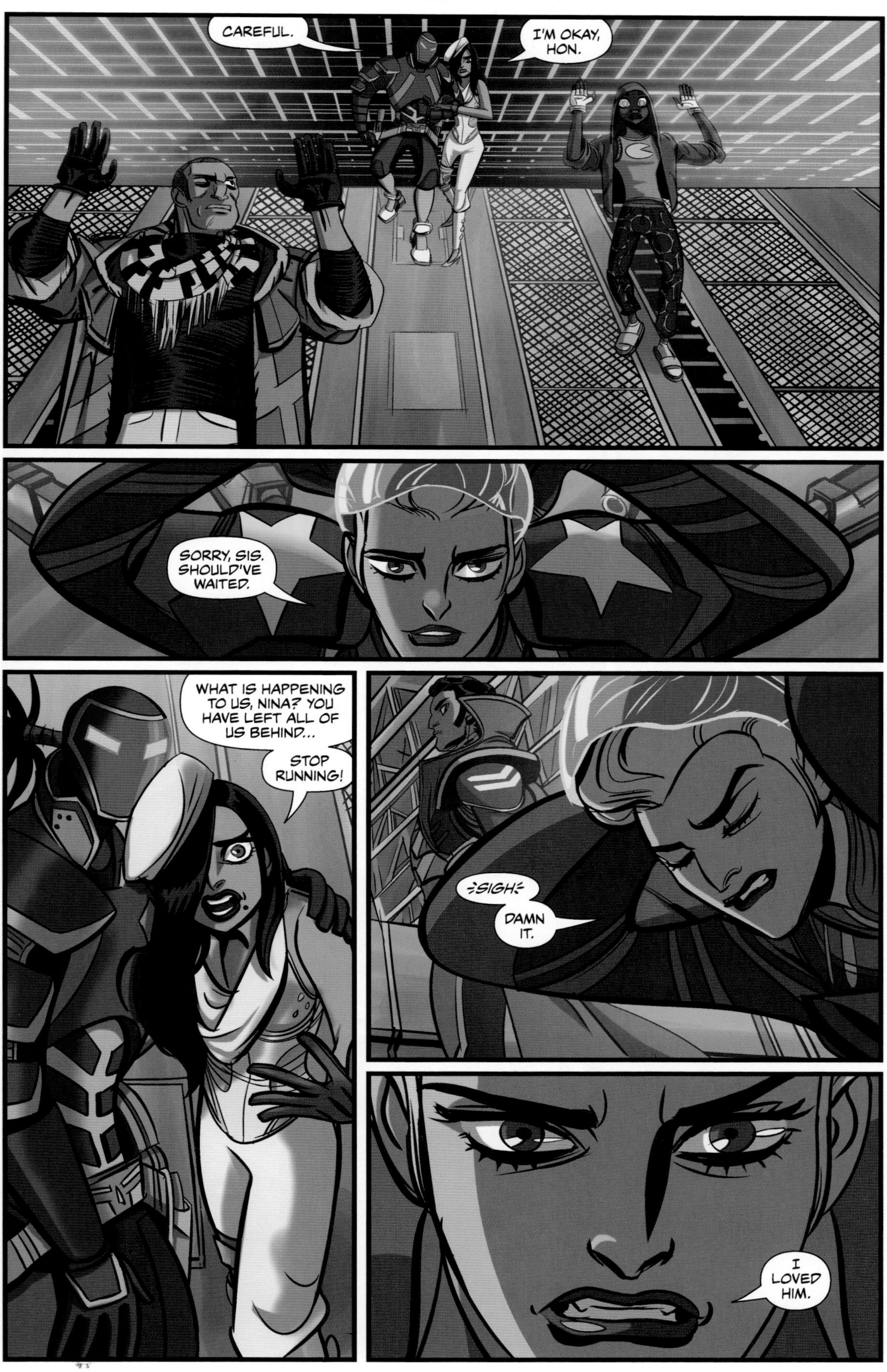
CAREFUL.
I'M OKAY, HON.
SORRY, SIS. SHOULD'VE WAITED.
WHAT IS HAPPENING TO US, NINA? YOU HAVE LEFT ALL OF US BEHIND...
STOP RUNNING!
SIGH
DAMN IT.
I LOVED HIM.

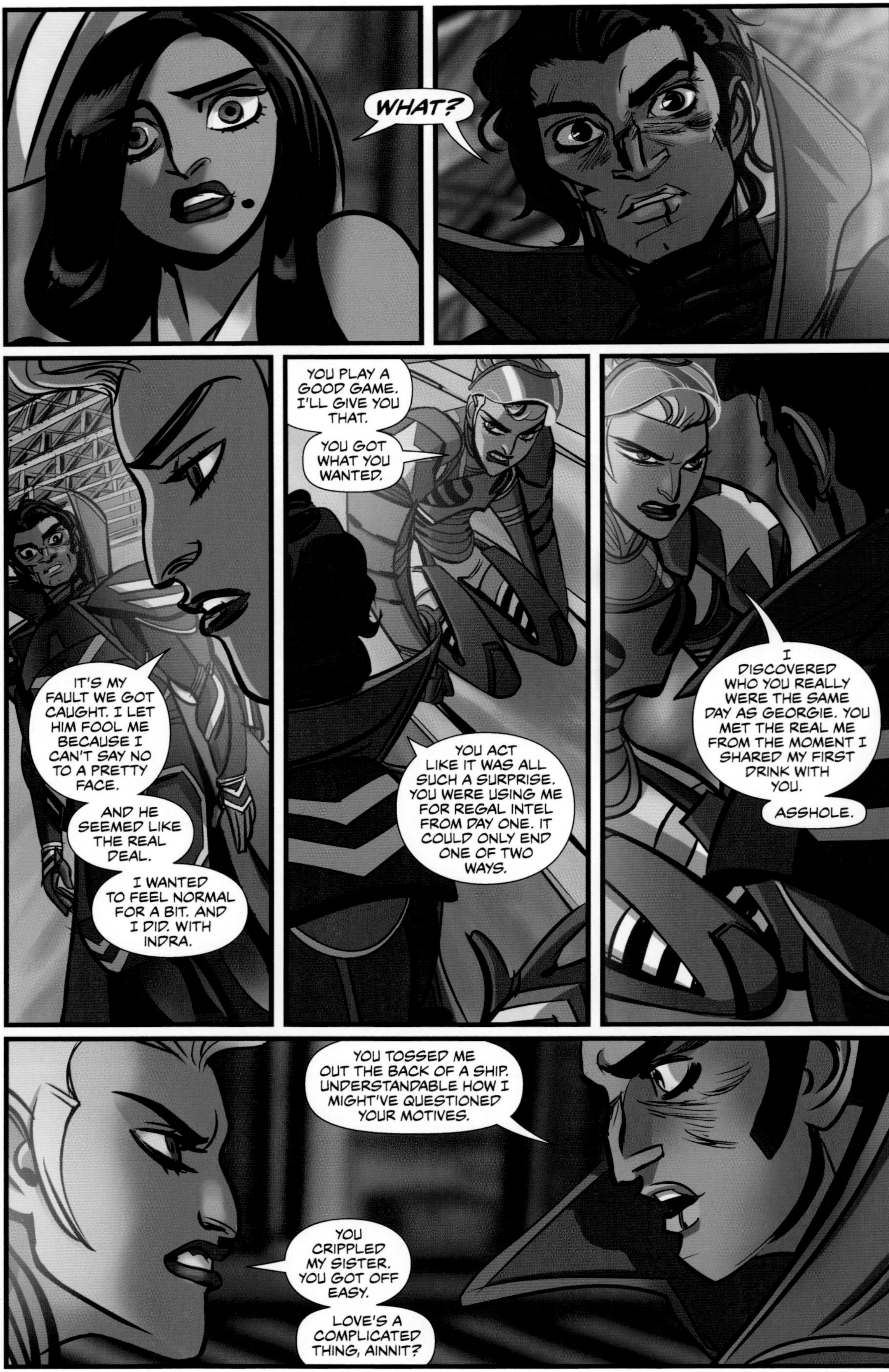
WHAT?
IT'S MY FAULT WE GOT CAUGHT. I LET HIM FOOL ME BECAUSE I CAN'T SAY NO TO A PRETTY FACE.
AND HE SEEMED LIKE THE REAL DEAL.
I WANTED TO FEEL NORMAL FOR A BIT. AND I DID. WITH INDRA.
YOU PLAY A GOOD GAME. I'LL GIVE YOU THAT.
YOU GOT WHAT YOU WANTED.
YOU ACT LIKE IT WAS ALL SUCH A SURPRISE. YOU WERE USING ME FOR REGAL INTEL FROM DAY ONE. IT COULD ONLY END ONE OF TWO WAYS.
I DISCOVERED WHO YOU REALLY WERE THE SAME DAY AS GEORGIE. YOU MET THE REAL ME FROM THE MOMENT I SHARED MY FIRST DRINK WITH YOU.
ASSHOLE.
YOU TOSSED ME OUT THE BACK OF A SHIP. UNDERSTANDABLE HOW I MIGHT'VE QUESTIONED YOUR MOTIVES.
YOU CRIPPLED MY SISTER. YOU GOT OFF EASY.
LOVE'S A COMPLICATED THING, AINNIT?

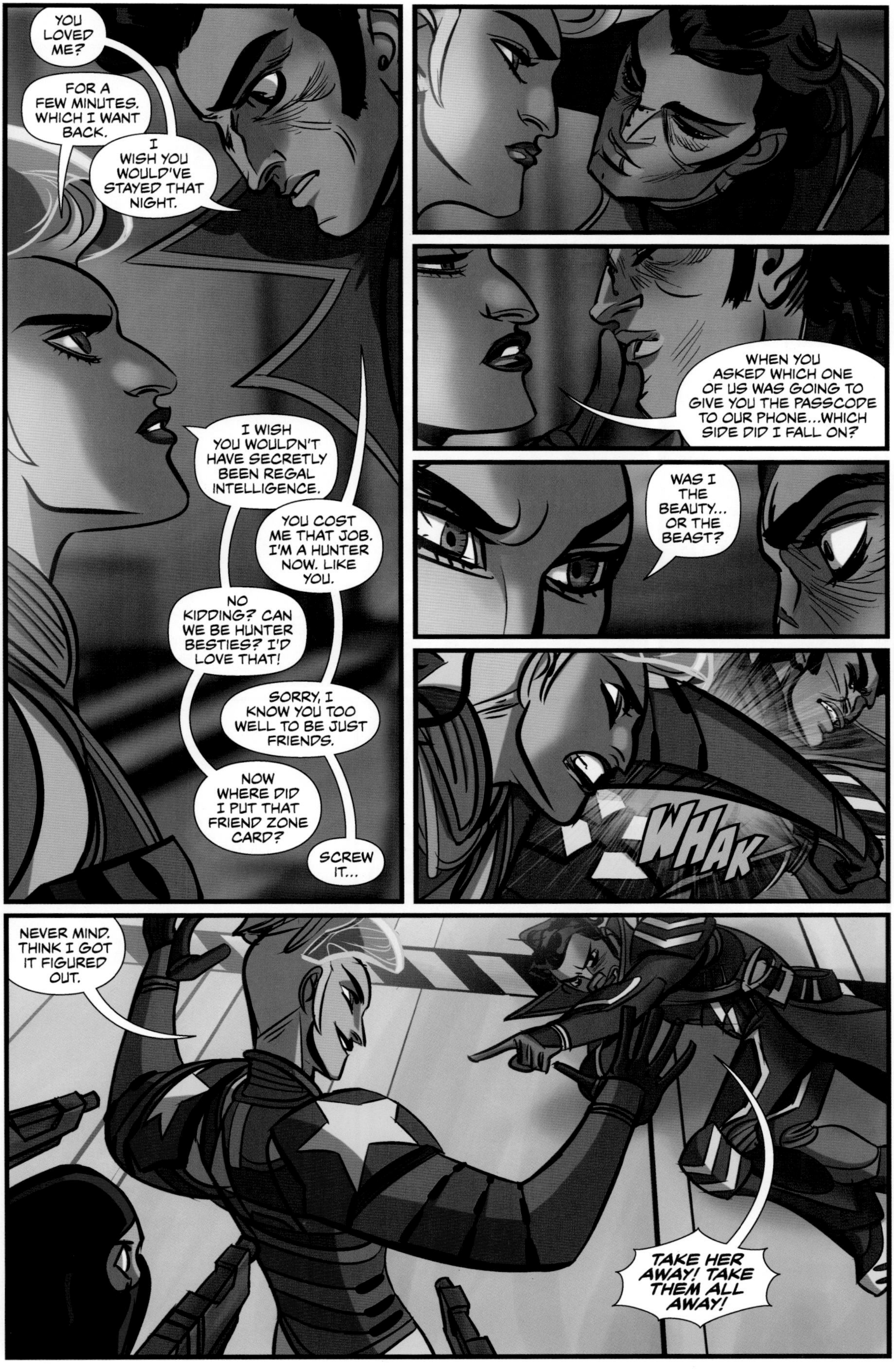
YOU LOVED ME?
FOR A FEW MINUTES. WHICH I WANT BACK.
I WISH YOU WOULD'VE STAYED THAT NIGHT.
I WISH YOU WOULDN'T HAVE SECRETLY BEEN REGAL INTELLIGENCE.
YOU COST ME THAT JOB. I'M A HUNTER NOW. LIKE YOU.
NO KIDDING? CAN WE BE HUNTER BESTIES? I'D LOVE THAT!
SORRY, I KNOW YOU TOO WELL TO BE JUST FRIENDS.
NOW WHERE DID I PUT THAT FRIEND ZONE CARD?
SCREW IT...
WHEN YOU ASKED WHICH ONE OF US WAS GOING TO GIVE YOU THE PASSCODE TO OUR PHONE...WHICH SIDE DID I FALL ON?
WAS I THE BEAUTY... OR THE BEAST?
WHAK
NEVER MIND. THINK I GOT IT FIGURED OUT.
TAKE HER AWAY! TAKE THEM ALL AWAY!

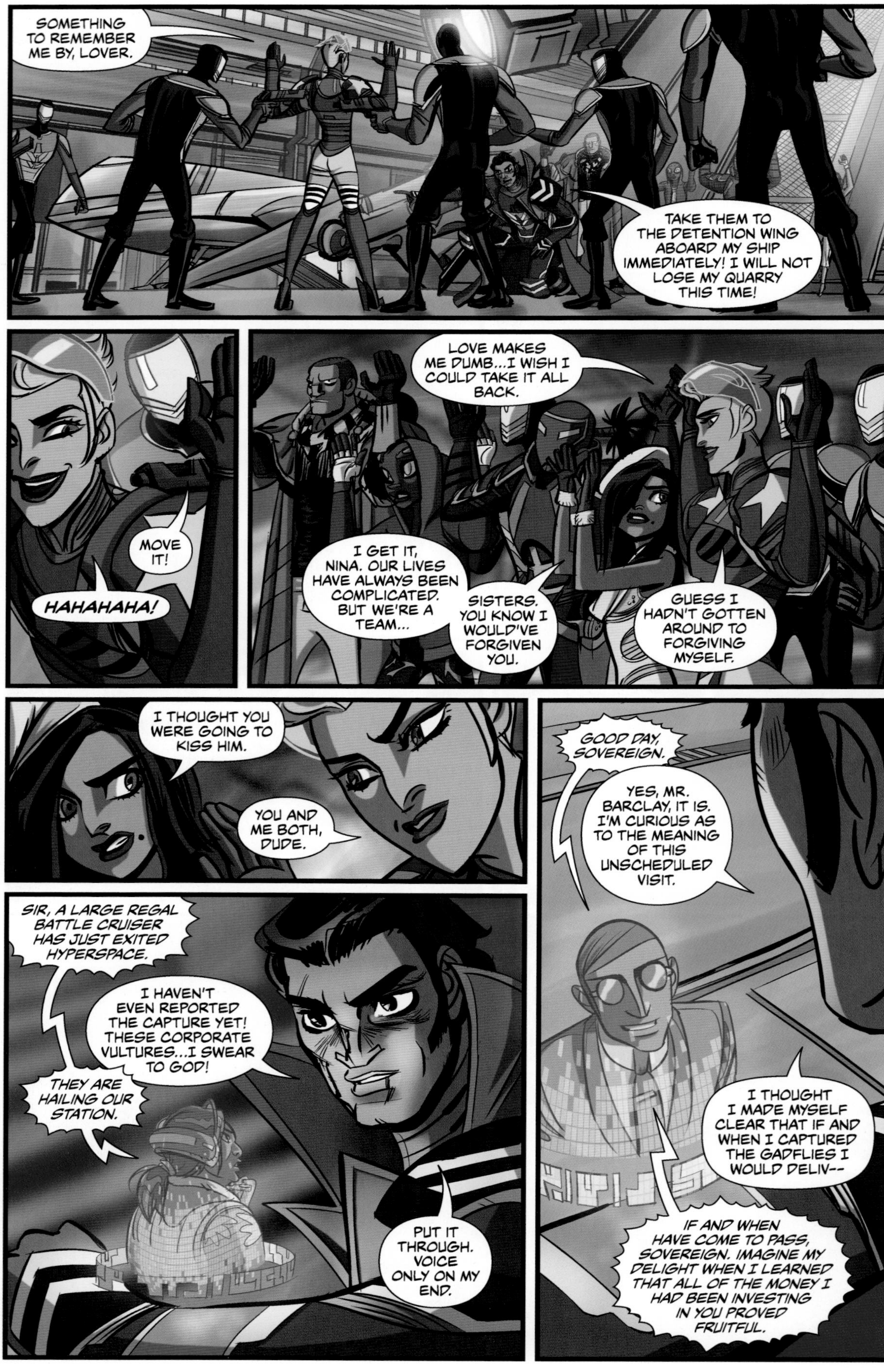
SOMETHING TO REMEMBER ME BY, LOVER.
TAKE THEM TO THE DETENTION WING ABOARD MY SHIP IMMEDIATELY! I WILL NOT LOSE MY QUARRY THIS TIME!
MOVE IT!
HAHAHAHA!
LOVE MAKES ME DUMB...I WISH I COULD TAKE IT ALL BACK.
I GET IT, NINA. OUR LIVES HAVE ALWAYS BEEN COMPLICATED. BUT WE'RE A TEAM...
SISTERS. YOU KNOW I WOULD'VE FORGIVEN YOU.
GUESS I HADN'T GOTTEN AROUND TO FORGIVING MYSELF.
I THOUGHT YOU WERE GOING TO KISS HIM.
YOU AND ME BOTH, DUDE.
SIR, A LARGE REGAL BATTLE CRUISER HAS JUST EXITED HYPERSPACE.
I HAVEN'T EVEN REPORTED THE CAPTURE YET! THESE CORPORATE VULTURES...I SWEAR TO GOD!
THEY ARE HAILING OUR STATION.
PUT IT THROUGH. VOICE ONLY ON MY END.
GOOD DAY, SOVEREIGN.
YES, MR. BARCLAY, IT IS. I'M CURIOUS AS TO THE MEANING OF THIS UNSCHEDULED VISIT.
I THOUGHT I MADE MYSELF CLEAR THAT IF AND WHEN I CAPTURED THE GADFLIES I WOULD DELIV--
IF AND WHEN HAVE COME TO PASS, SOVEREIGN. IMAGINE MY DELIGHT WHEN I LEARNED THAT ALL OF THE MONEY I HAD BEEN INVESTING IN YOU PROVED FRUITFUL.

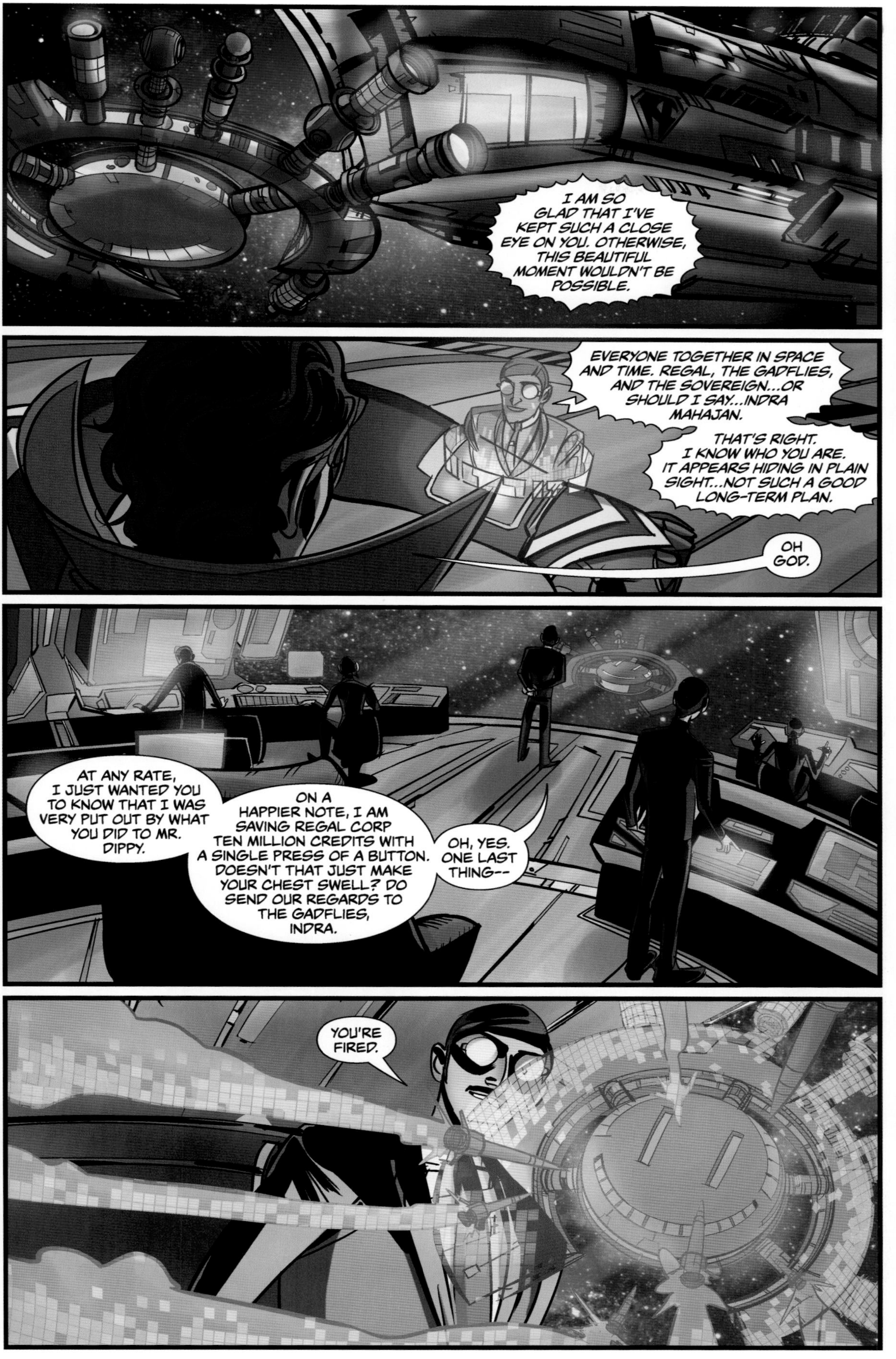
I AM SO GLAD THAT I'VE KEPT SUCH A CLOSE EYE ON YOU. OTHERWISE, THIS BEAUTIFUL MOMENT WOULDN'T BE POSSIBLE.
EVERYONE TOGETHER IN SPACE AND TIME. REGAL, THE GADFLIES, AND THE SOVEREIGN...OR SHOULD I SAY...INDRA MAHAJAN.
THAT'S RIGHT. I KNOW WHO YOU ARE. IT APPEARS HIDING IN PLAIN SIGHT...NOT SUCH A GOOD LONG-TERM PLAN.
OH GOD.
AT ANY RATE, I JUST WANTED YOU TO KNOW THAT I WAS VERY PUT OUT BY WHAT YOU DID TO MR. DIPPY.
ON A HAPPIER NOTE, I AM SAVING REGAL CORP TEN MILLION CREDITS WITH A SINGLE PRESS OF A BUTTON. DOESN'T THAT JUST MAKE YOUR CHEST SWELL? DO SEND OUR REGARDS TO THE GADFLIES, INDRA.
OH, YES. ONE LAST THING--
YOU'RE FIRED.

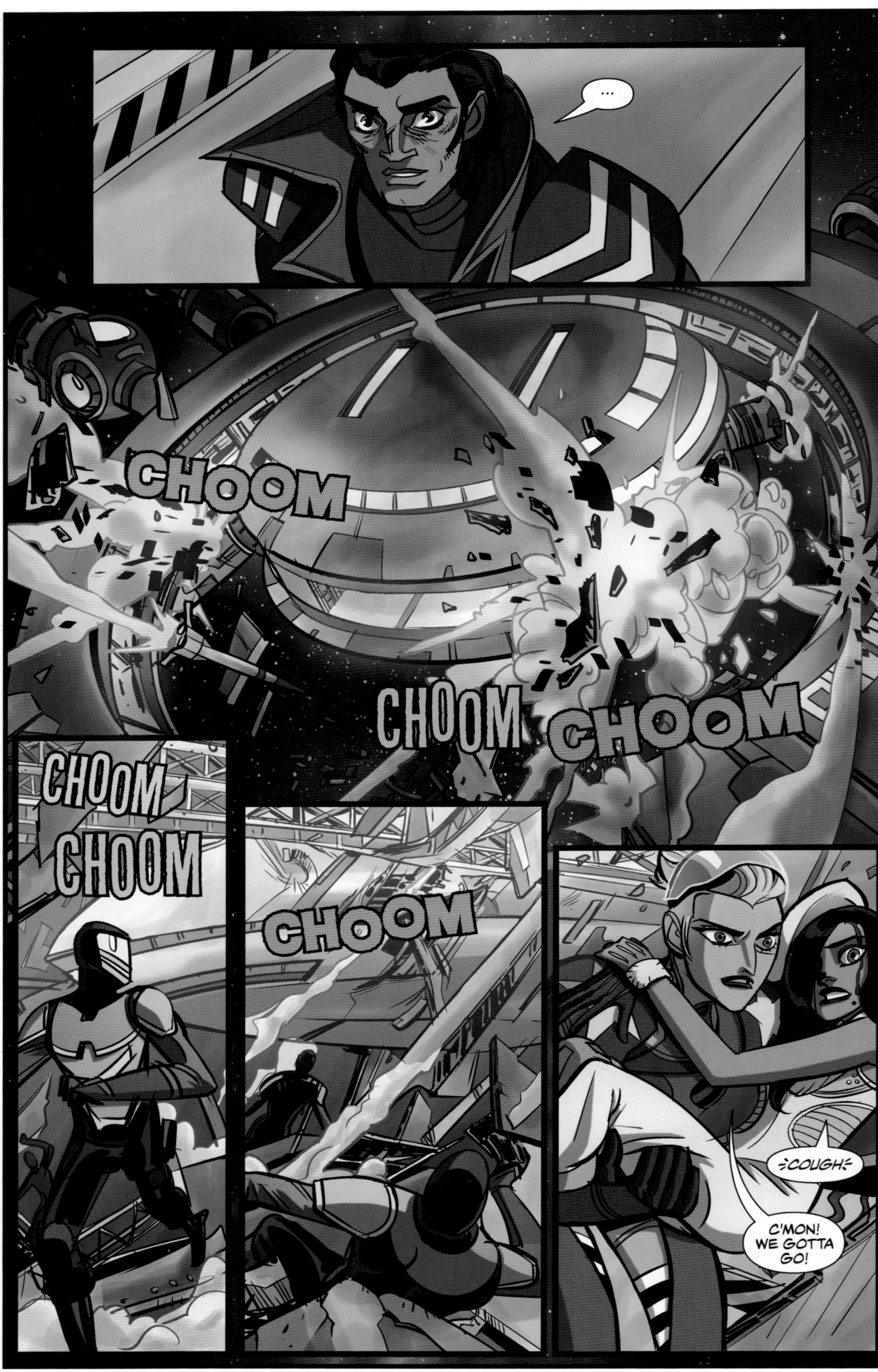
...
CHOOM
CHOOM
CHOOM
CHOOM
CHOOM
CHOOM
COUGH
C'MON! WE GOTTA GO!

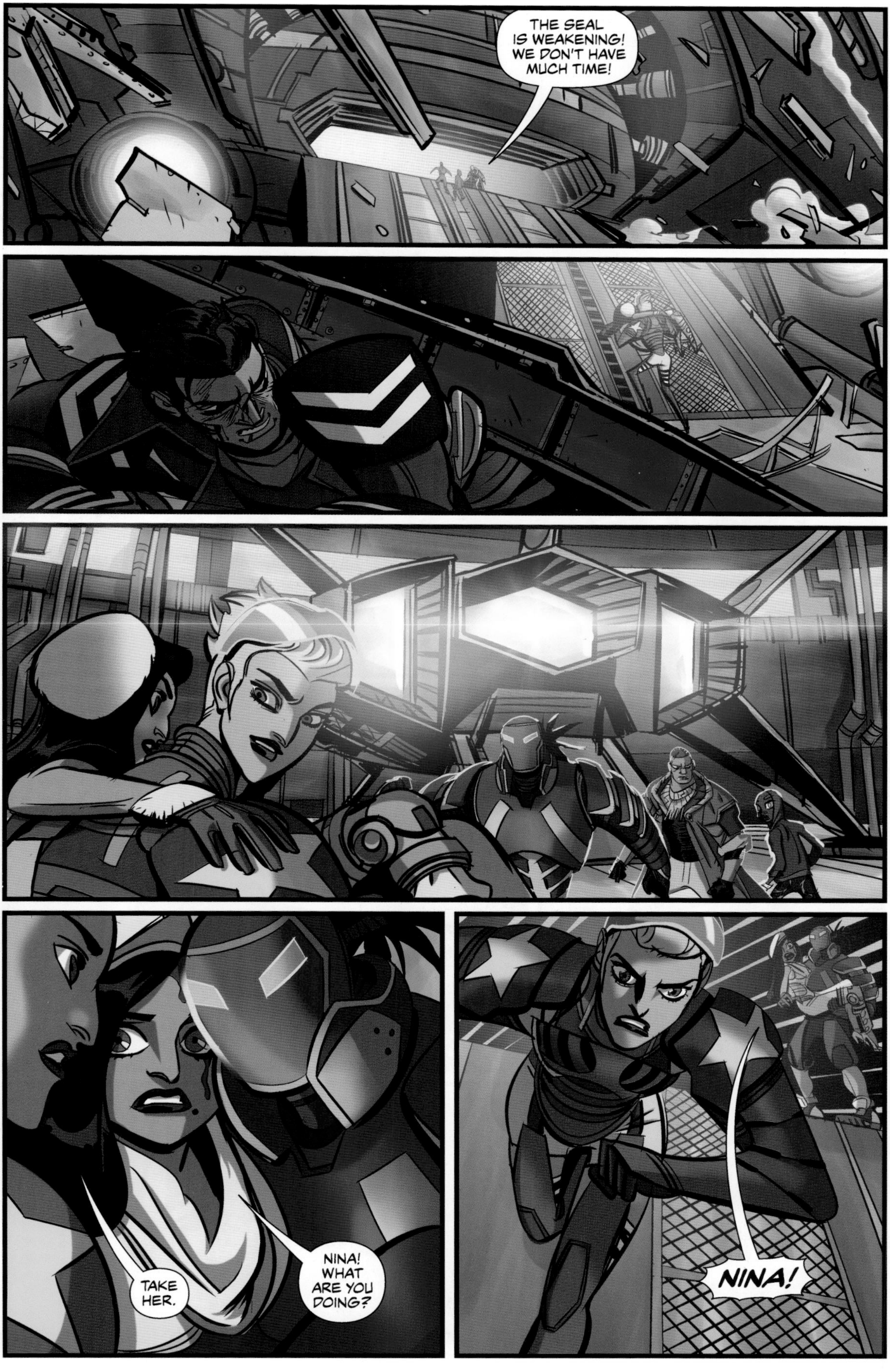
THE SEAL IS WEAKENING! WE DON'T HAVE MUCH TIME!
TAKE HER.
NINA! WHAT ARE YOU DOING?
NINA!

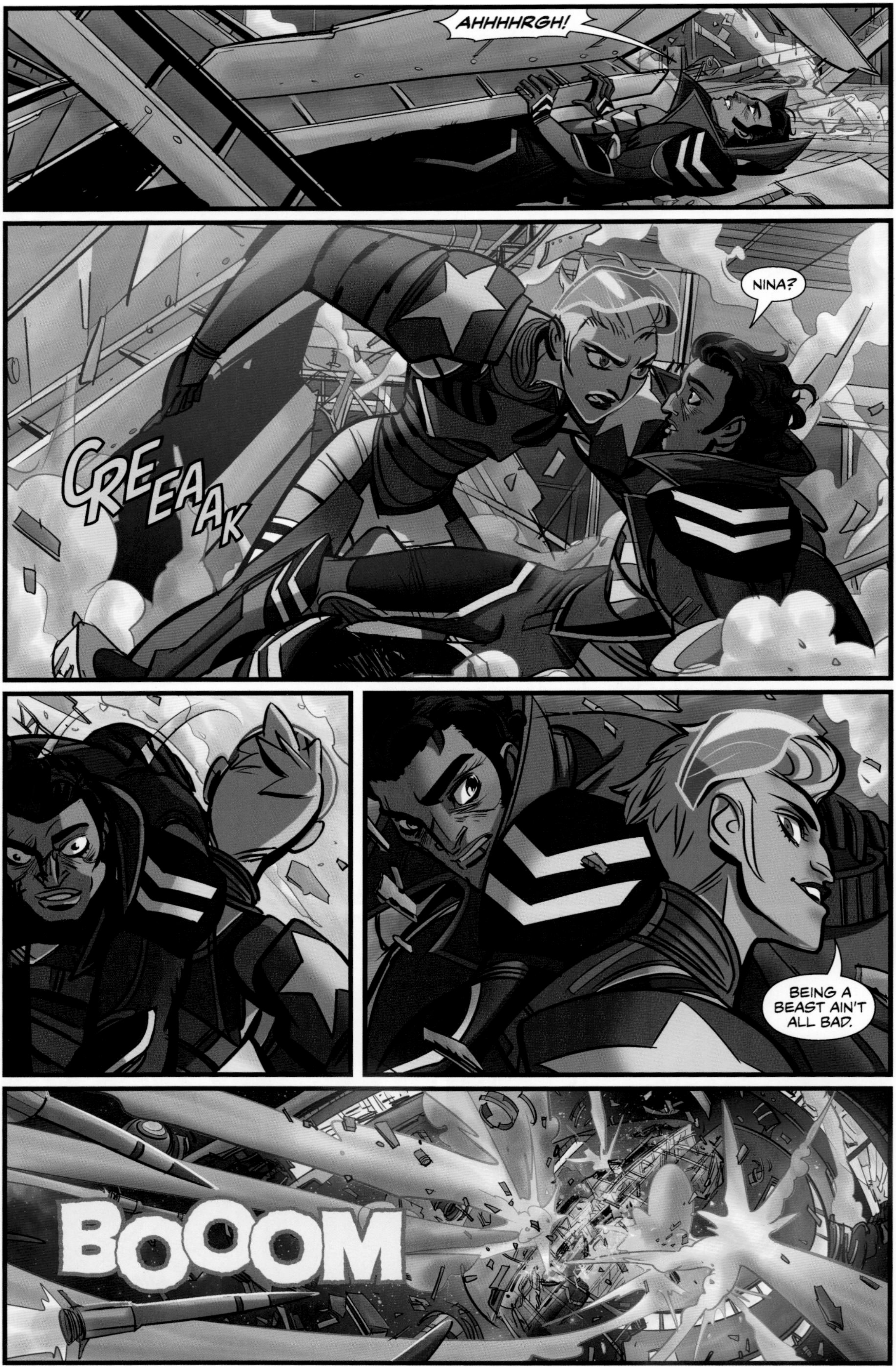
AHHHHRGH!
NINA?
CREEAAK
BEING A BEAST AIN'T ALL BAD.
BOOOOM

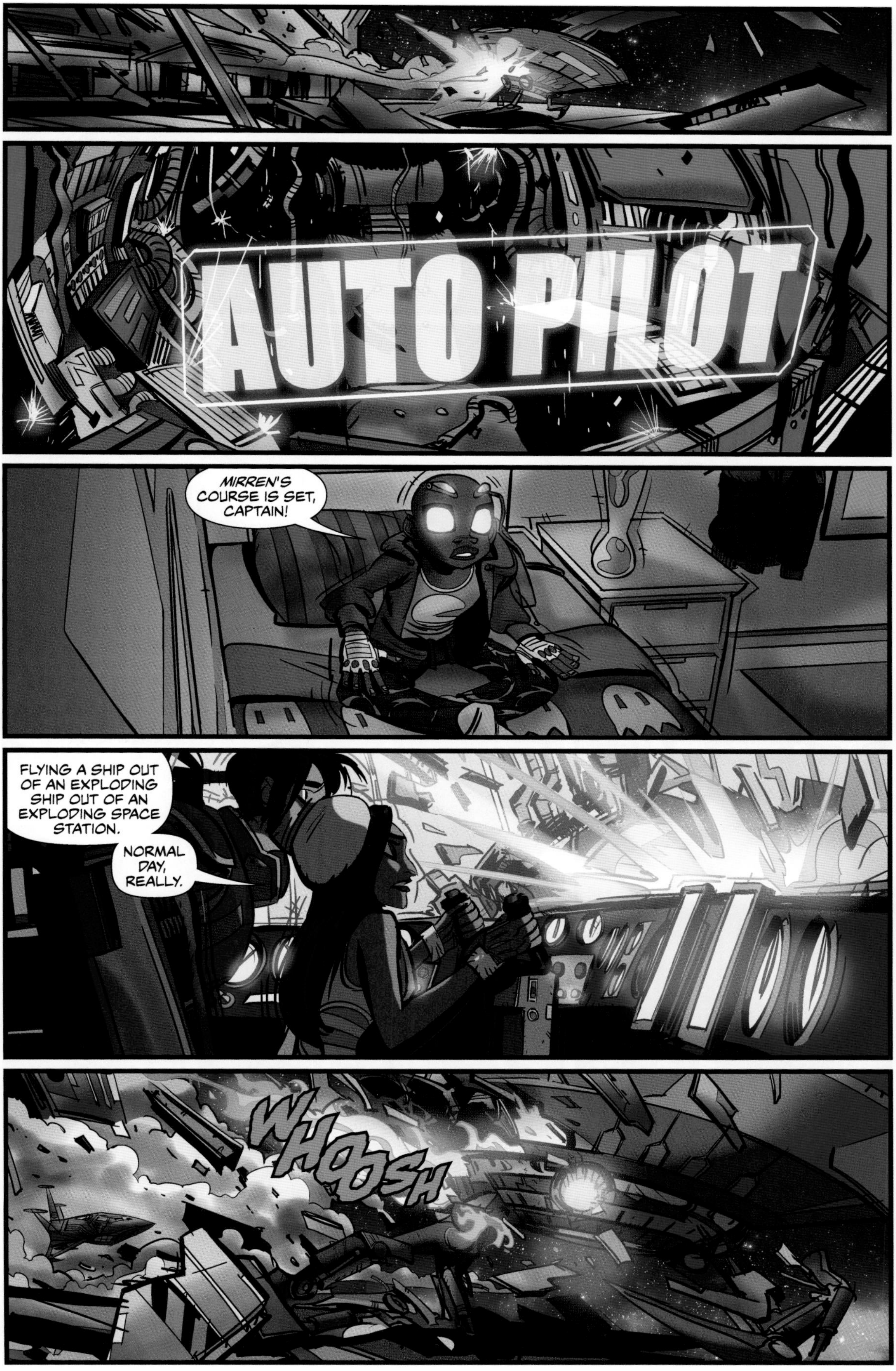
AUTO PILOT
MIRREN'S COURSE IS SET, CAPTAIN!
FLYING A SHIP OUT OF AN EXPLODING SHIP OUT OF AN EXPLODING SPACE STATION.
NORMAL DAY, REALLY.
WHOOSH

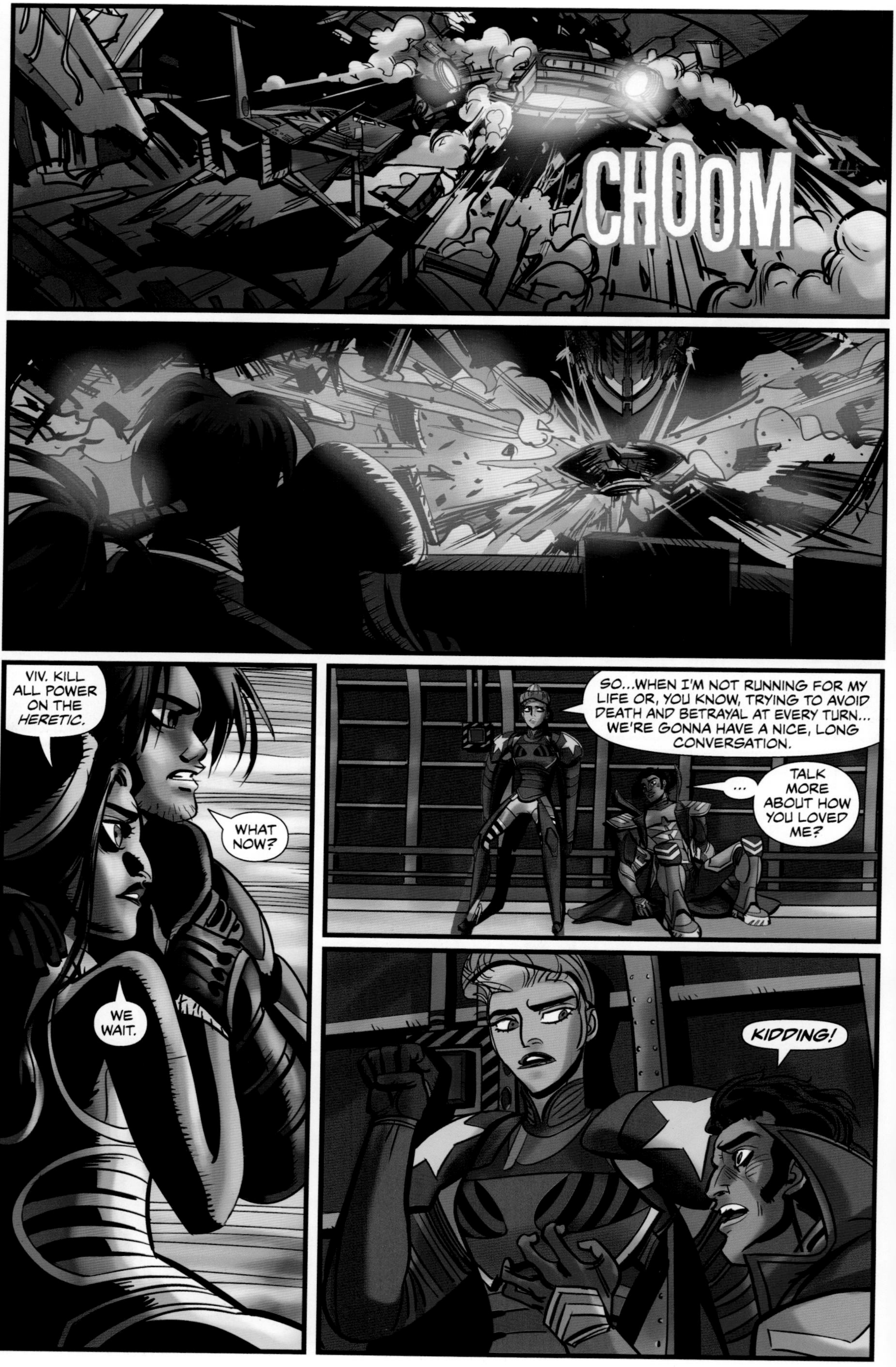
CHOOM
VIV. KILL ALL POWER ON THE *HERETIC.*
WHAT NOW?
WE WAIT.
SO...WHEN I'M NOT RUNNING FOR MY LIFE OR, YOU KNOW, TRYING TO AVOID DEATH AND BETRAYAL AT EVERY TURN... WE'RE GONNA HAVE A NICE, LONG CONVERSATION.
...
TALK MORE ABOUT HOW YOU LOVED ME?
KIDDING!

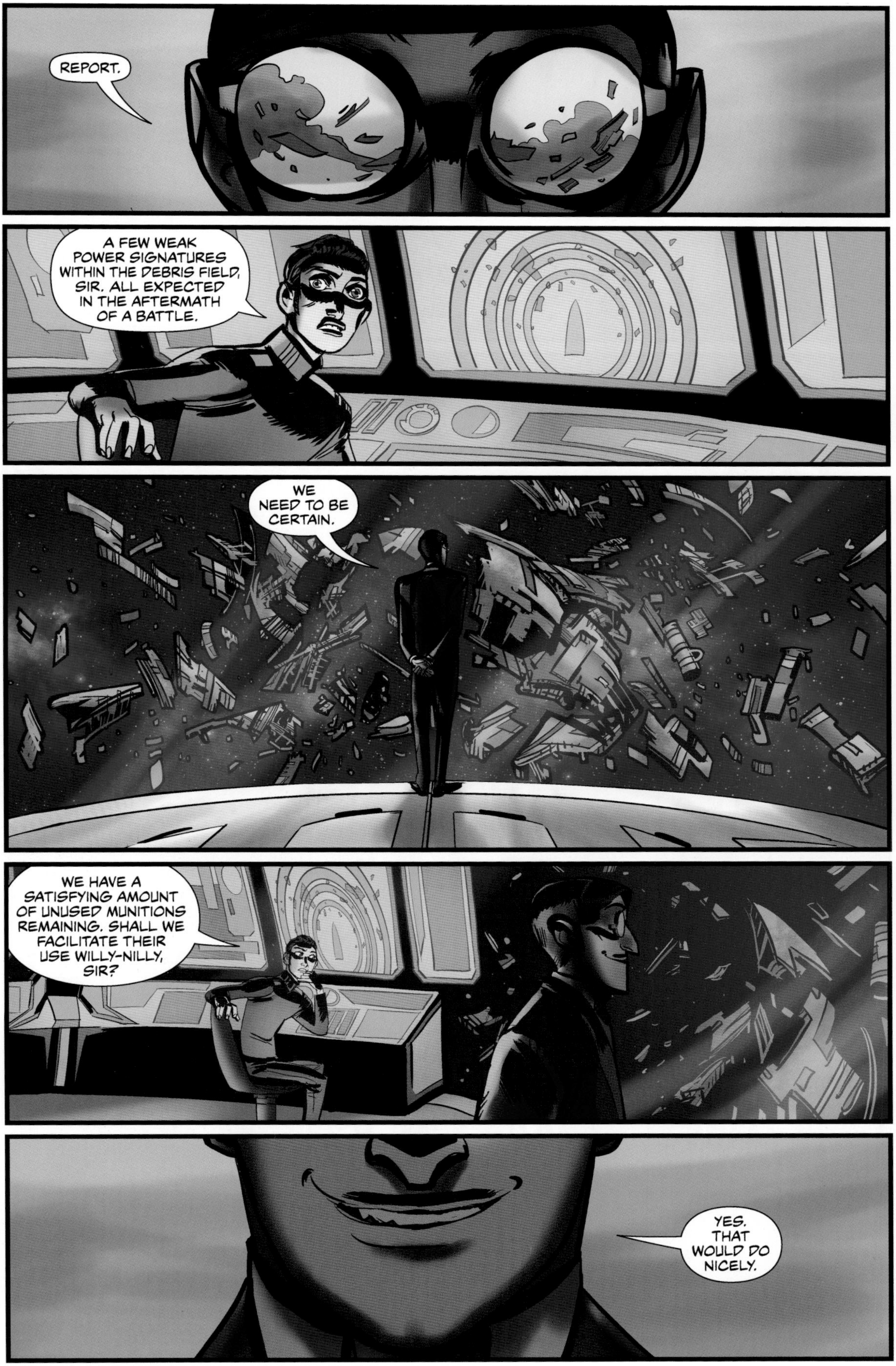
REPORT.
A FEW WEAK POWER SIGNATURES WITHIN THE DEBRIS FIELD, SIR. ALL EXPECTED IN THE AFTERMATH OF A BATTLE.
WE NEED TO BE CERTAIN.
WE HAVE A SATISFYING AMOUNT OF UNUSED MUNITIONS REMAINING. SHALL WE FACILITATE THEIR USE WILLY-NILLY, SIR?
YES. THAT WOULD DO NICELY.

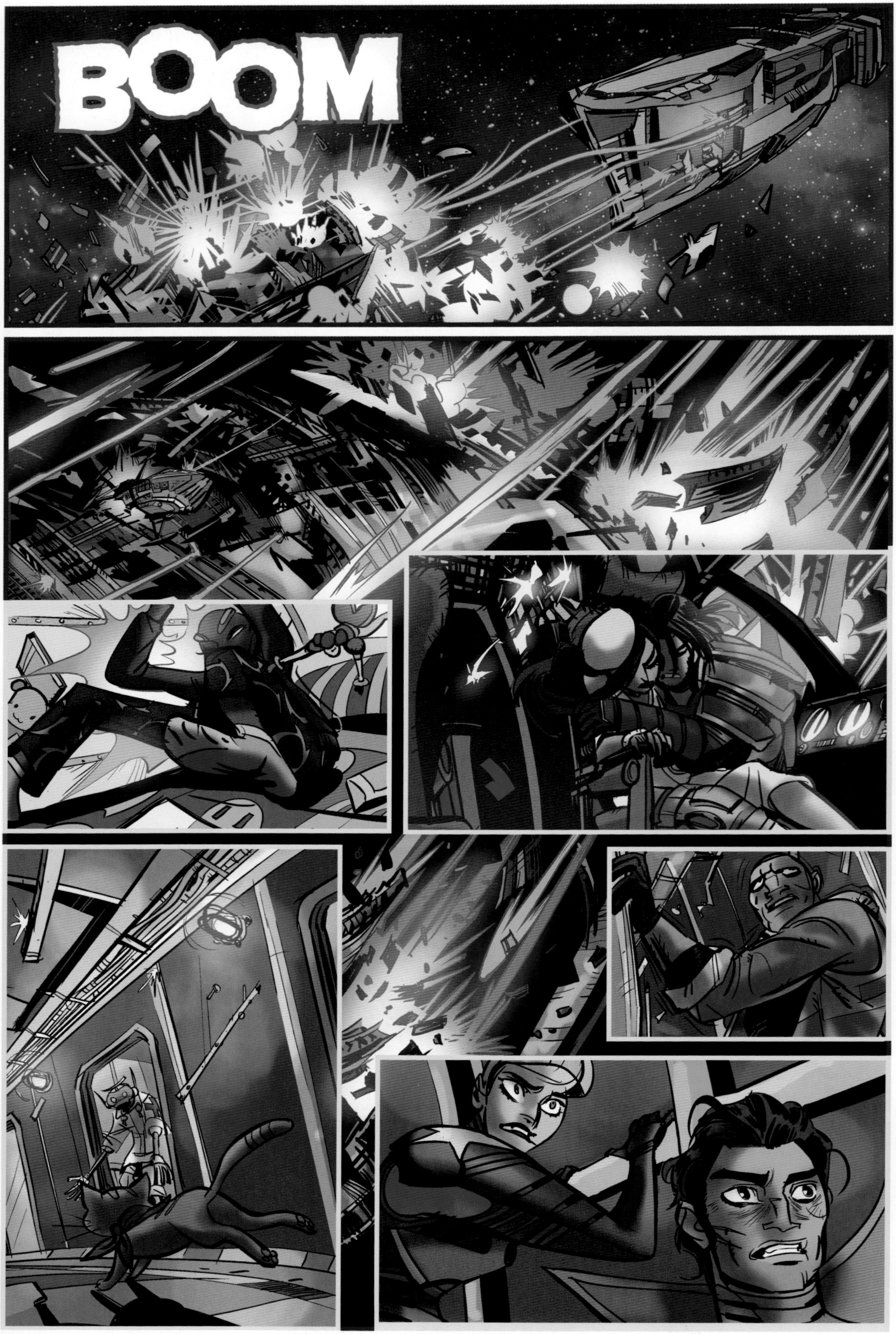
BOOM

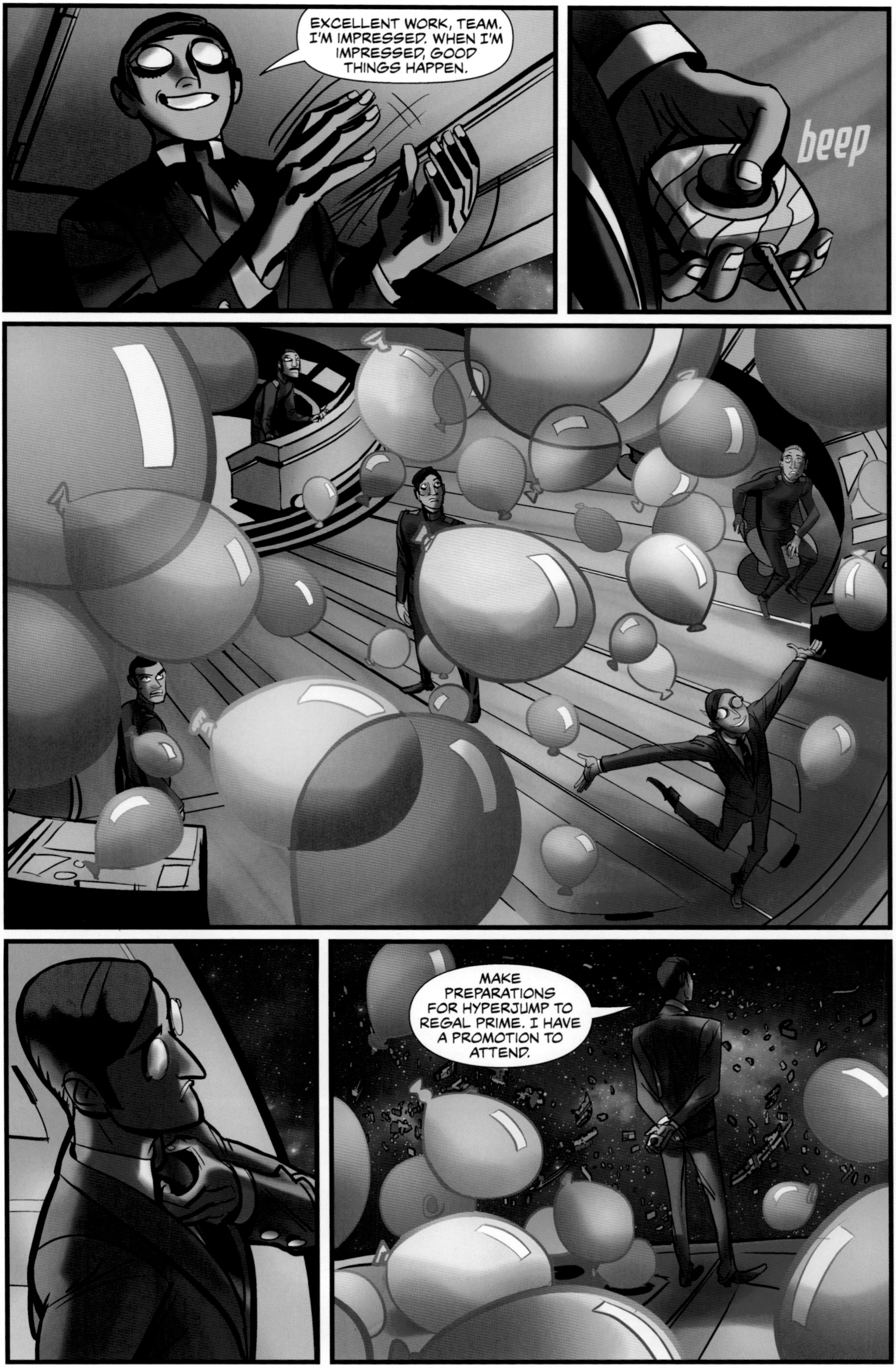
EXCELLENT WORK, TEAM. I'M IMPRESSED. WHEN I'M IMPRESSED, GOOD THINGS HAPPEN.
beep
MAKE PREPARATIONS FOR HYPERJUMP TO REGAL PRIME. I HAVE A PROMOTION TO ATTEND.

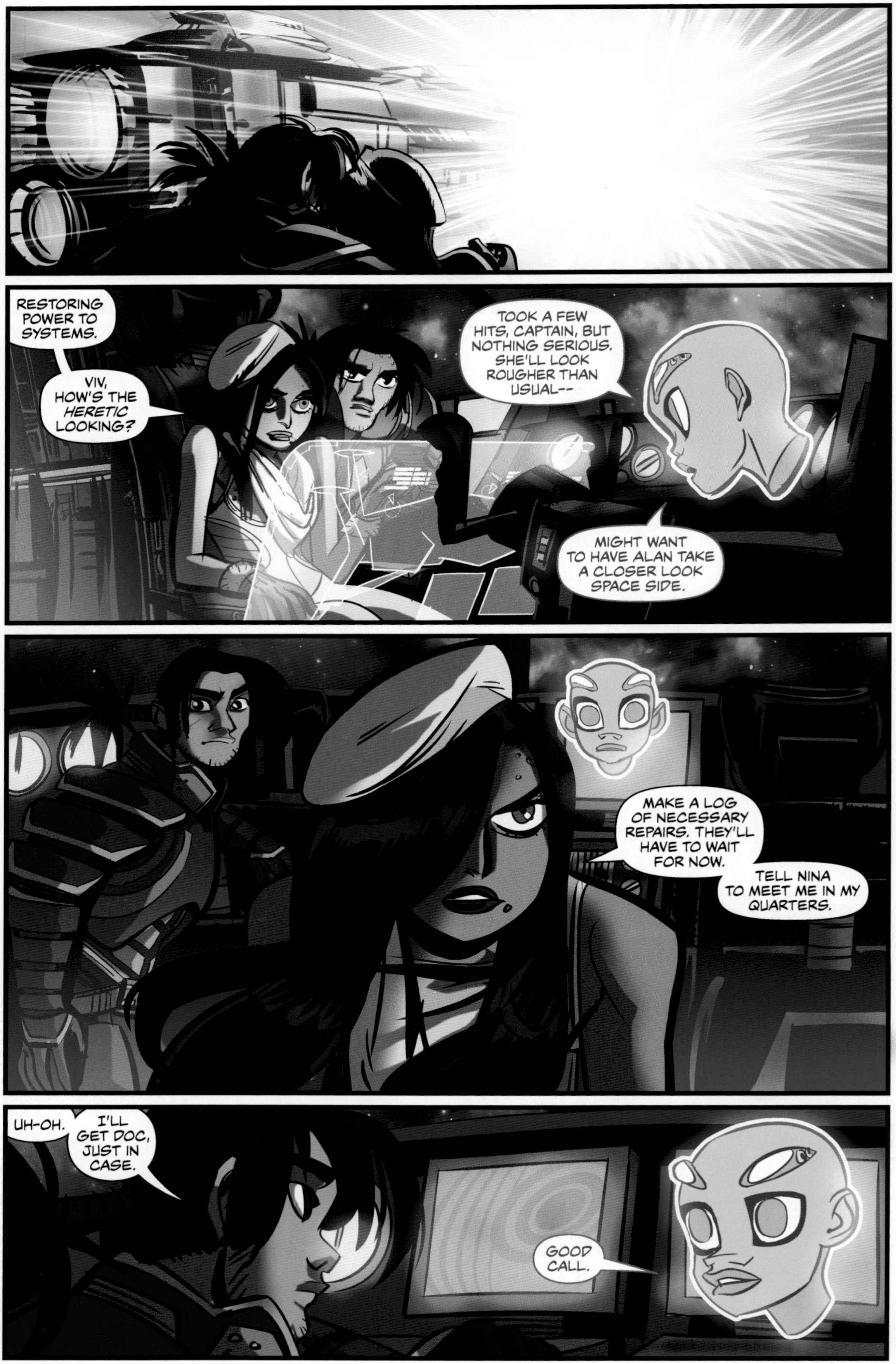
RESTORING POWER TO SYSTEMS.
VIV, HOW'S THE *HERETIC* LOOKING?
TOOK A FEW HITS, CAPTAIN, BUT NOTHING SERIOUS. SHE'LL LOOK ROUGHER THAN USUAL--
MIGHT WANT TO HAVE ALAN TAKE A CLOSER LOOK SPACE SIDE.
MAKE A LOG OF NECESSARY REPAIRS. THEY'LL HAVE TO WAIT FOR NOW.
TELL NINA TO MEET ME IN MY QUARTERS.
UH-OH.
I'LL GET DOC, JUST IN CASE.
GOOD CALL.

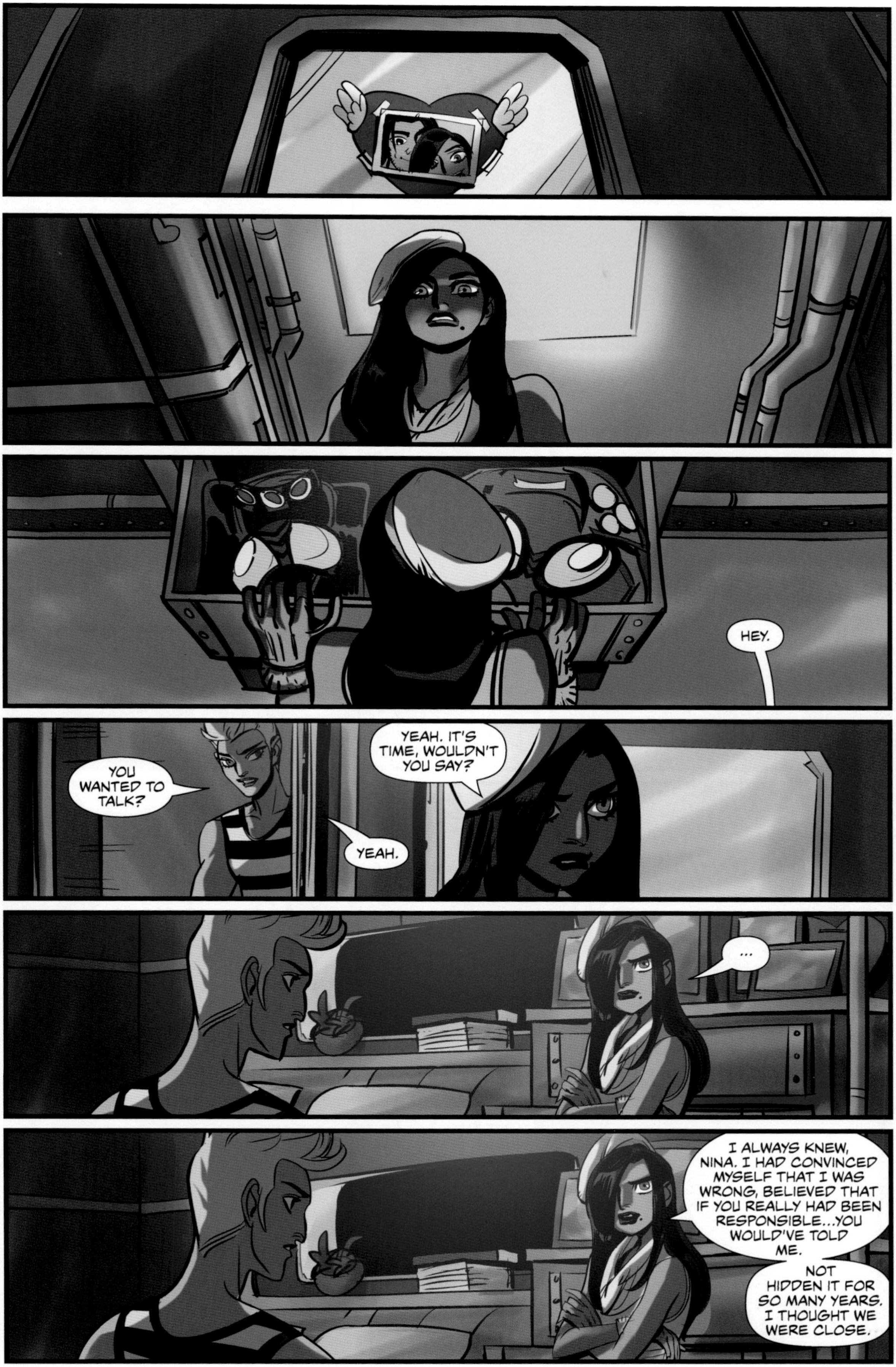
HEY.
YOU WANTED TO TALK?
YEAH.
YEAH. IT'S TIME, WOULDN'T YOU SAY?
...
I ALWAYS KNEW, NINA. I HAD CONVINCED MYSELF THAT I WAS WRONG, BELIEVED THAT IF YOU REALLY HAD BEEN RESPONSIBLE...YOU WOULD'VE TOLD ME.
NOT HIDDEN IT FOR SO MANY YEARS. I THOUGHT WE WERE CLOSE.

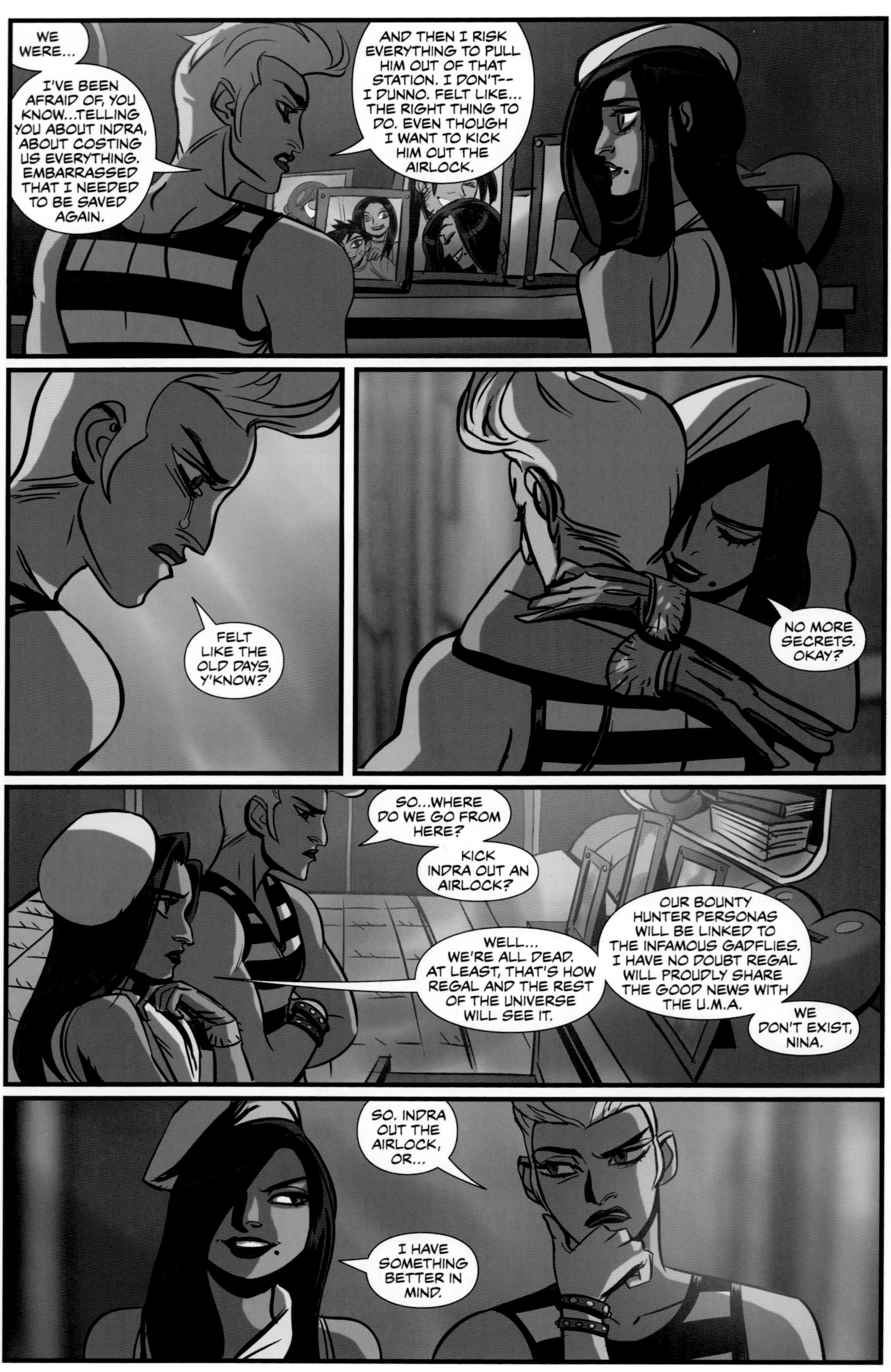
WE WERE...
I'VE BEEN AFRAID OF, YOU KNOW...TELLING YOU ABOUT INDRA, ABOUT COSTING US EVERYTHING. EMBARRASSED THAT I NEEDED TO BE SAVED AGAIN.
AND THEN I RISK EVERYTHING TO PULL HIM OUT OF THAT STATION. I DON'T-- I DUNNO. FELT LIKE... THE RIGHT THING TO DO. EVEN THOUGH I WANT TO KICK HIM OUT THE AIRLOCK.
FELT LIKE THE OLD DAYS, Y'KNOW?
NO MORE SECRETS. OKAY?
SO...WHERE DO WE GO FROM HERE?
KICK INDRA OUT AN AIRLOCK?
WELL... WE'RE ALL DEAD. AT LEAST, THAT'S HOW REGAL AND THE REST OF THE UNIVERSE WILL SEE IT.
OUR BOUNTY HUNTER PERSONAS WILL BE LINKED TO THE INFAMOUS GADFLIES. I HAVE NO DOUBT REGAL WILL PROUDLY SHARE THE GOOD NEWS WITH THE U.M.A.
WE DON'T EXIST, NINA.
SO. INDRA OUT THE AIRLOCK, OR...
I HAVE SOMETHING BETTER IN MIND.

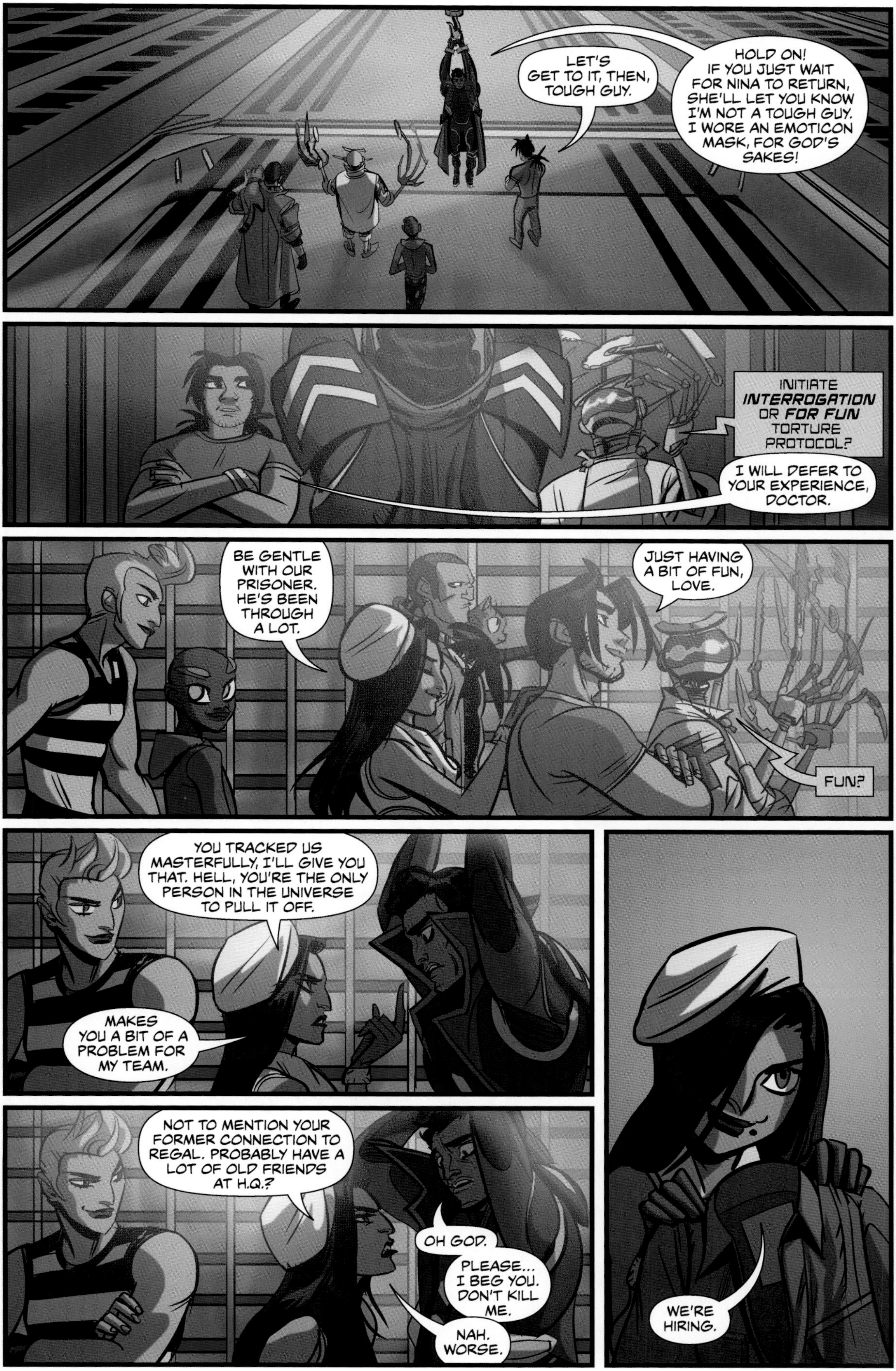
LET'S GET TO IT, THEN, TOUGH GUY.
HOLD ON! IF YOU JUST WAIT FOR NINA TO RETURN, SHE'LL LET YOU KNOW I'M NOT A TOUGH GUY. I WORE AN EMOTICON MASK, FOR GOD'S SAKES!
INITIATE INTERROGATION OR FOR FUN TORTURE PROTOCOL?
I WILL DEFER TO YOUR EXPERIENCE, DOCTOR.
BE GENTLE WITH OUR PRISONER. HE'S BEEN THROUGH A LOT.
JUST HAVING A BIT OF FUN, LOVE.
FUN?
YOU TRACKED US MASTERFULLY, I'LL GIVE YOU THAT. HELL, YOU'RE THE ONLY PERSON IN THE UNIVERSE TO PULL IT OFF.
MAKES YOU A BIT OF A PROBLEM FOR MY TEAM.
NOT TO MENTION YOUR FORMER CONNECTION TO REGAL. PROBABLY HAVE A LOT OF OLD FRIENDS AT H.Q.?
OH GOD.
PLEASE... I BEG YOU. DON'T KILL ME.
NAH. WORSE.
WE'RE HIRING.

MONTHS LATER.

DON'T DO IT, CAT!

FRIENDS DON'T TREAT EACH OTHER THAT WAY! I MAY BE AN EMOTIONLESS ROBOT BUT I STILL HAVE--

CRASH

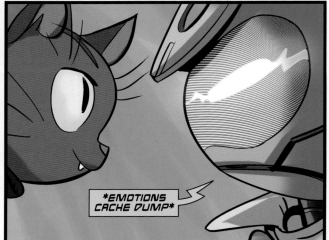

EMOTIONS CACHE DUMP

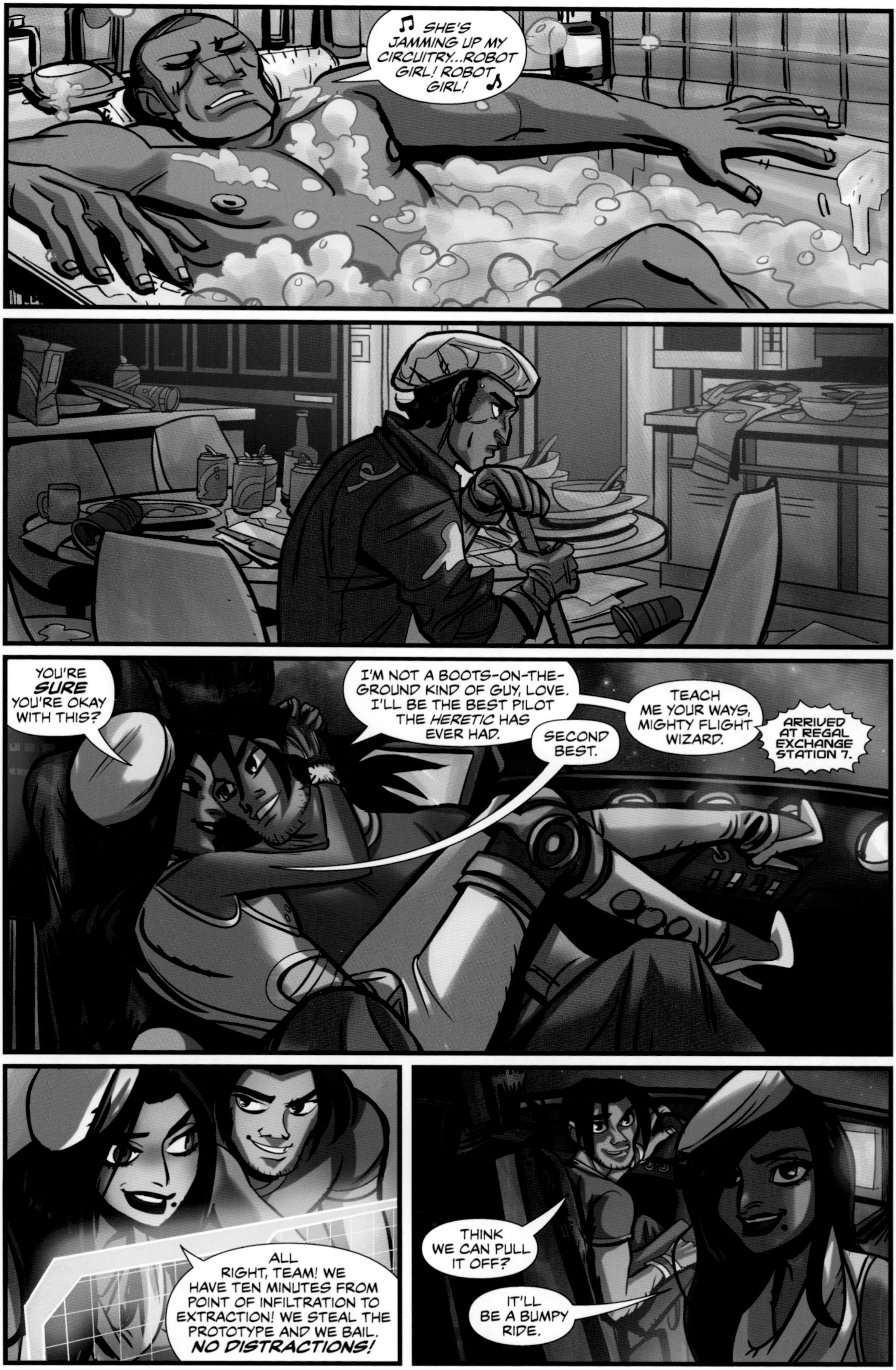
♫ SHE'S JAMMING UP MY CIRCUITRY...ROBOT GIRL! ROBOT GIRL! ♪
YOU'RE *SURE* YOU'RE OKAY WITH THIS?
I'M NOT A BOOTS-ON-THE-GROUND KIND OF GUY, LOVE. I'LL BE THE BEST PILOT THE *HERETIC* HAS EVER HAD.
SECOND BEST.
TEACH ME YOUR WAYS, MIGHTY FLIGHT WIZARD.
ARRIVED AT REGAL EXCHANGE STATION 7.
ALL RIGHT, TEAM! WE HAVE TEN MINUTES FROM POINT OF INFILTRATION TO EXTRACTION! WE STEAL THE PROTOTYPE AND WE BAIL. **NO DISTRACTIONS!**
THINK WE CAN PULL IT OFF?
IT'LL BE A BUMPY RIDE.

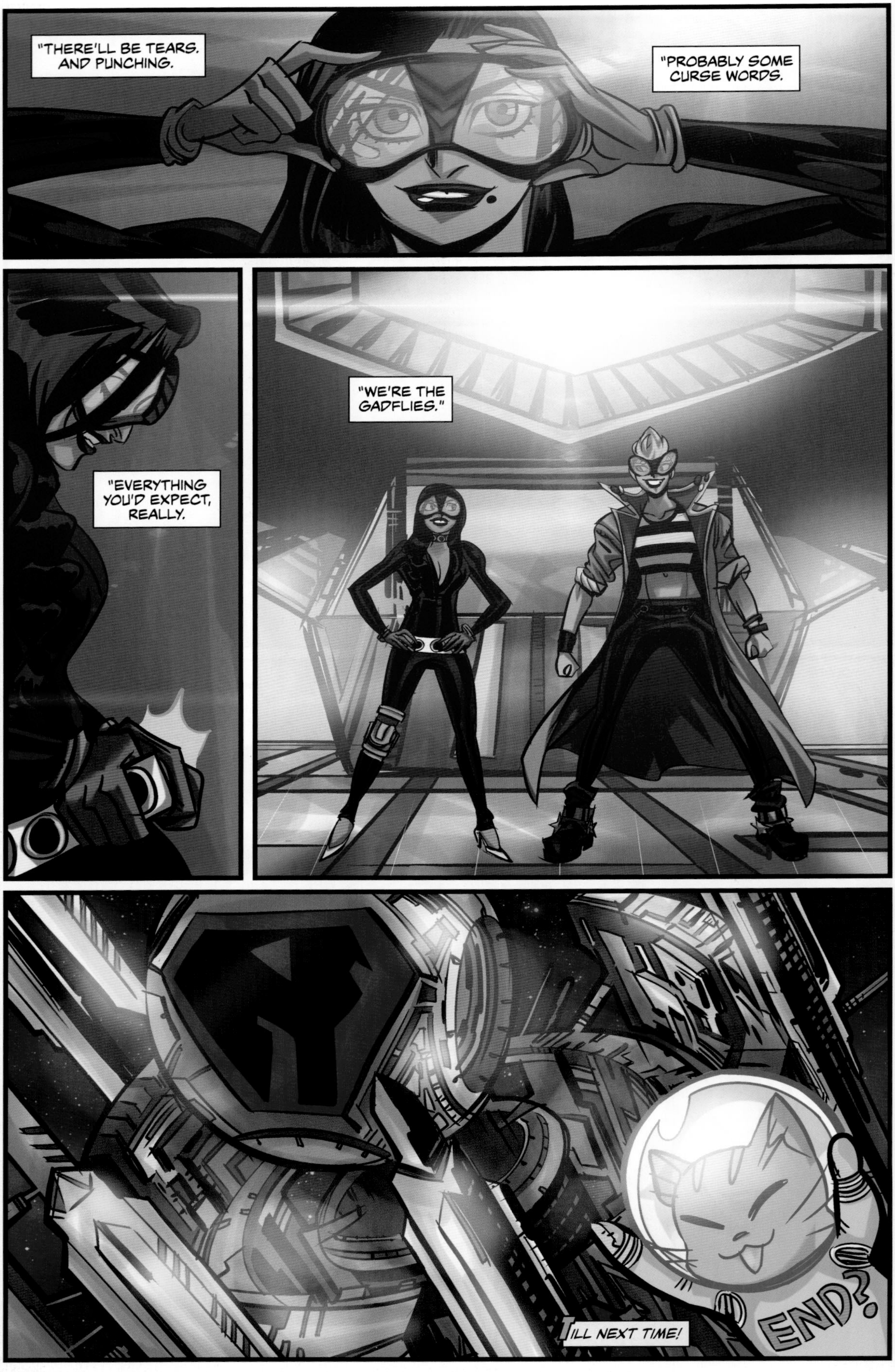
"THERE'LL BE TEARS. AND PUNCHING.
"PROBABLY SOME CURSE WORDS.
"EVERYTHING YOU'D EXPECT, REALLY.
"WE'RE THE GADFLIES."
END?
TILL NEXT TIME!

BEHIND THE SCENES: CHARACTER DESIGN

AN INTERVIEW WITH ARTIST MINDY LEE, THE WOMAN BEHIND THE STYLE OF *BOUNTY*

What is the process for designing a character's look?

Finding a look really depends on the personality and background. For *Bounty*, I worked closely with the writer, Kurtis, to get a detailed understanding of each character and their role. Kurtis was also very specific in his desire for the characters to have different ethnic backgrounds. I did research and numerous sketches to get acquainted with the characteristics he desired. Finding a look that I was happy with and then a streamlined approach to make them easy to draw from all angles over and over was quite the challenge.

What were the first sketches of Nina and Georgie like?

Nina and Georgie are polar opposites. Nina is tall and muscular, while Georgie is petite and curvy. The unique part of their design process was that they had to be designed at the same time. One defined the other. The more muscular and tall Nina's design became, the smaller Georgie got. The more rounded the facial features of Georgie, the sharper the facial features of Nina. To show they are sisters, I gave them both the family nose.

What has been the biggest change in a *Bounty* character design from first concept to final character model?

Alan's armor was quite hard to nail down. I knew I wanted him to have a street-fashion feel and a spiked ponytail, but it was really hard to find a look that could stand toe to toe with Nina's. I decided to add a gunslinger feel to his armor by adding the double-holster belt in issue #2. I also have an entire sketchbook of Nina's numerous mech armor designs. They were all great in their own right, but her current armor fits her frame the best.

Where do you find inspiration or influence for your costume designs?

I looked to many sources for inspiration: fashion magazines, samurai armor, iconic video game character designs, anime mech armor designs, and elements from my personal life. For Nina, her attitude and fashion were in part inspired by a friend of mine. I have a few colorful pairs of pajama bottoms that probably informed Vivian's.

What are some of your favorite character designs from other comics?

I was greatly influenced by some of the more stylized comic artists: Eric Canete, Paul Pope, Toby Cypress, Jamie Hewlett, and Robert Valley. I also have some anime influences, like Gainax studios, *Ghost in the Shell*, and Yoh Yoshinari.

BEHIND THE SCENES: THE *BOUNTY* LOGO

AN INTERVIEW WITH JIMMY PRESLER, THE MAN BEHIND THE *BOUNTY* LOGO

What is your position at Dark Horse?
I'm a designer. I work on projects like designing trade paperbacks, laying out art books, and creating logos for new comics.

What books have you worked on or are you currently working on?
Besides *Bounty*, I'm currently working on the second volume of *Lady Killer*, *The Art of The Venture Bros.*, and several other unannounced projects. I recently wrapped up the *Past Aways* trade paperback and *The Art of Broken Age*. Some of my older work includes *Archie vs. Predator*, *Catalyst Comix*, and *The Art of He-Man and the Masters of the Universe*.

What were the influences that you brought to this logo?
Some of Kurtis's early direction pointed me toward 1990s anime, and I grew up watching some of that on Toonami and Adult Swim and renting anything that looked cool. So I tried to tap into that era of Japanese and American animation: shows with a lot of bright color and kinetic energy that just looked exciting, like *Gundam*, *Cowboy Bebop*, *Power Puff Girls*, and other shows from that era.

What other logos have you designed at Dark Horse?
Some of the logos I've worked on include *The Steam Man*, *Polar*, *Mystery Girl*, various *Star Wars* titles, and a few of the logos for Alex de Campi's *Grindhouse* series (*Slay Ride*, *Blood Lagoon*, and *Lady Danger*).

What are some of your current favorite comic logos?
There is a lot of great work being done here at Dark Horse and across the industry. All of the Mignolaverse titles, like *Lobster Johnson* and *B.P.R.D. Hell on Earth*, feature great logo work by Amy Arendts, Rick DeLucco, and Cindy Cacerez-Sprague. Image has a lot of very striking logos, including *Paper Girls*, *Black Science*, *Revival*, and *Zero*. Design is becoming more integrated into comics these days, and it's a pretty exciting time to be part of the industry.

BOUNTY
BOUNTY
BOUNTY
バウンティー

WOULD YOU LIKE TO KNOW MORE? YOU MIGHT ALSO ENJOY THE FOLLOWING . . .

THE BEGINNING OF . . .

BOUNTY

What follows this page is the *Bounty* story that Kurtis Wiebe and Mindy Lee used to pitch the project to Dark Horse Comics. You'll notice some big design changes were made to the characters before they became their final versions, but we thought this would be fun to include as bonus content. Enjoy!

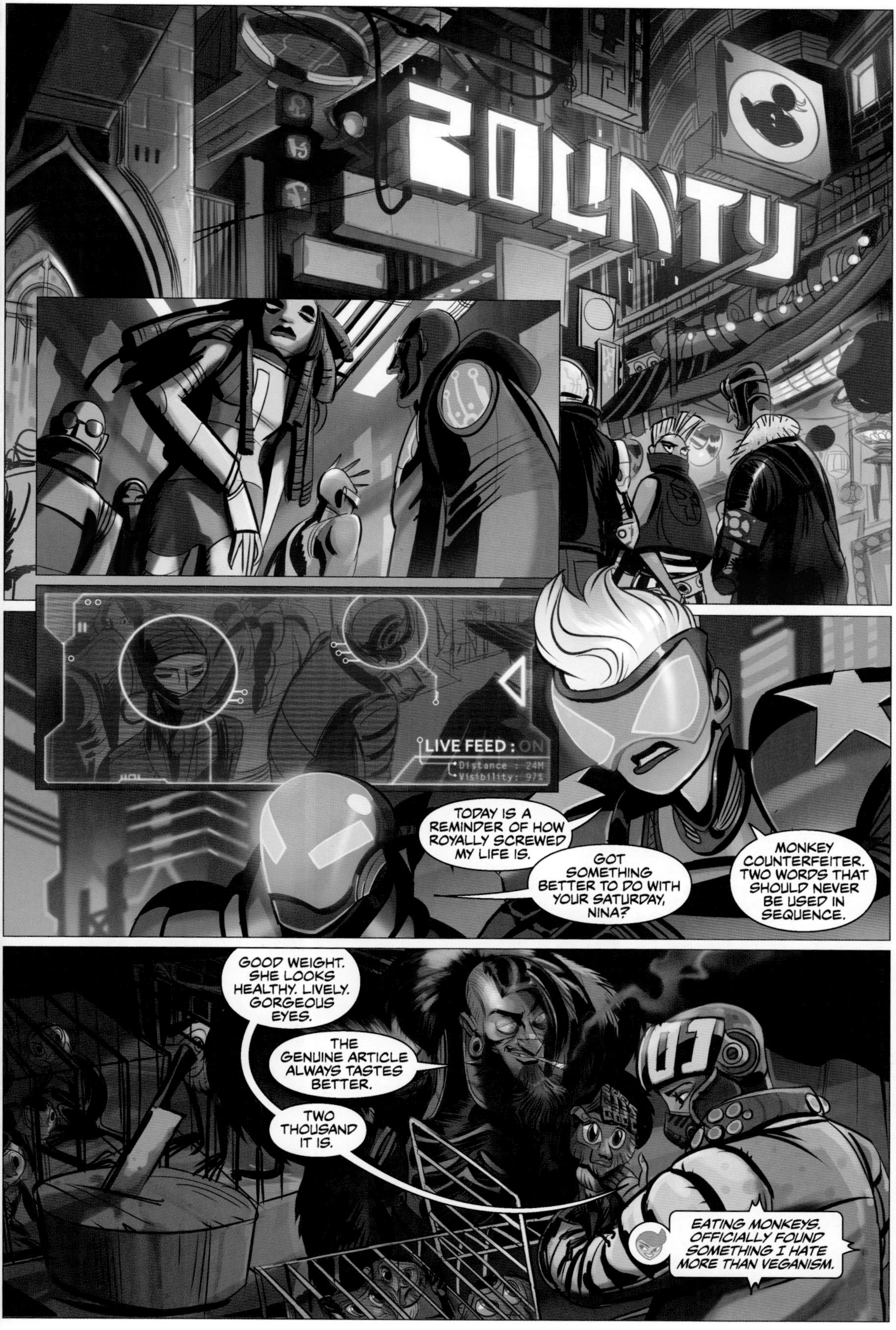

BOUNTY
LIVE FEED : ON
Distance : 24M
Visibility: 97%
TODAY IS A REMINDER OF HOW ROYALLY SCREWED MY LIFE IS.
GOT SOMETHING BETTER TO DO WITH YOUR SATURDAY, NINA?
MONKEY COUNTERFEITER. TWO WORDS THAT SHOULD NEVER BE USED IN SEQUENCE.
GOOD WEIGHT. SHE LOOKS HEALTHY. LIVELY. GORGEOUS EYES.
THE GENUINE ARTICLE ALWAYS TASTES BETTER.
TWO THOUSAND IT IS.
EATING MONKEYS. OFFICIALLY FOUND SOMETHING I HATE MORE THAN VEGANISM.

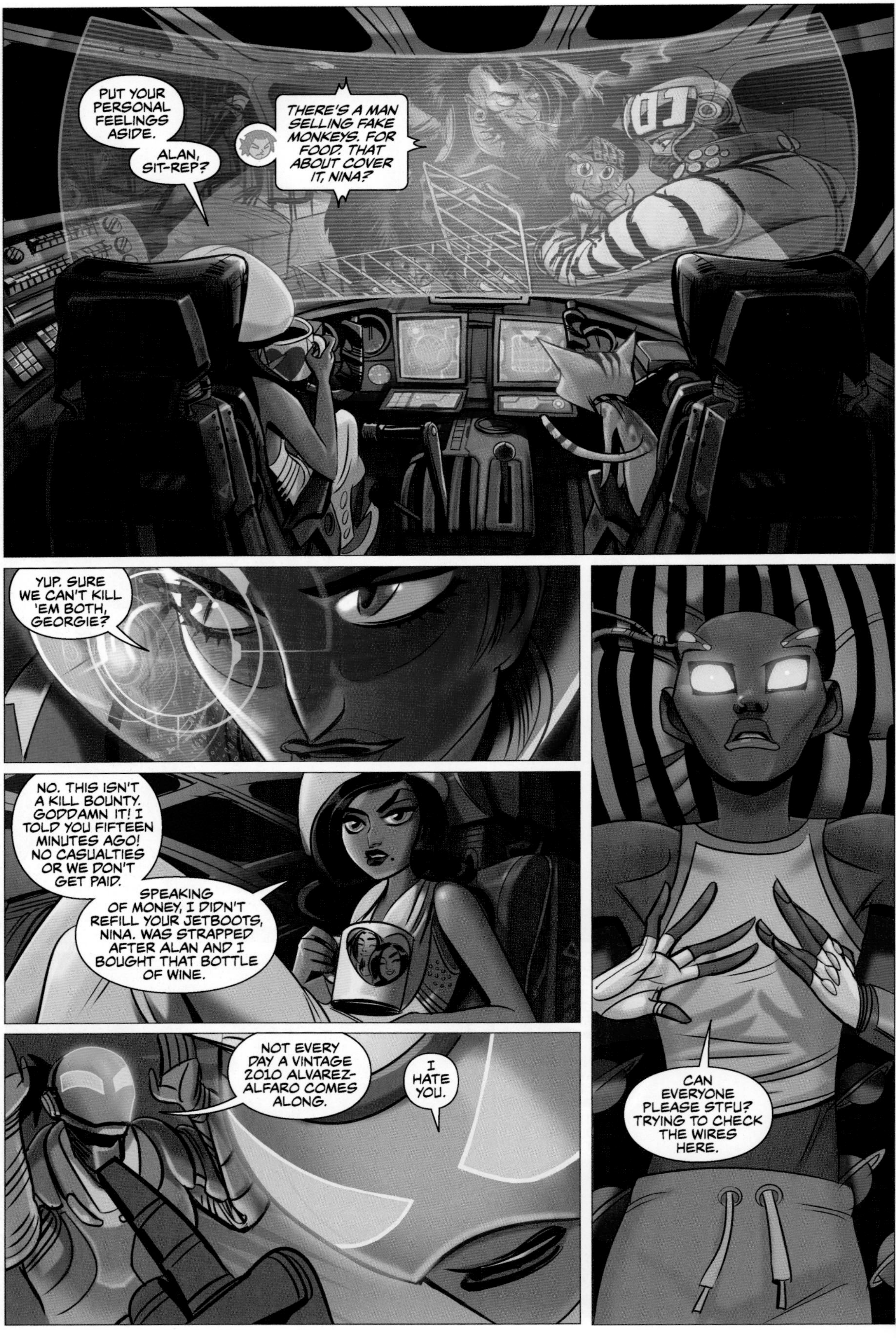

PUT YOUR PERSONAL FEELINGS ASIDE.
ALAN, SIT-REP?
THERE'S A MAN SELLING FAKE MONKEYS. FOR FOOD. THAT ABOUT COVER IT, NINA?
YUP. SURE WE CAN'T KILL 'EM BOTH, GEORGIE?
NO. THIS ISN'T A KILL BOUNTY. GODDAMN IT! I TOLD YOU FIFTEEN MINUTES AGO! NO CASUALTIES OR WE DON'T GET PAID.
SPEAKING OF MONEY, I DIDN'T REFILL YOUR JETBOOTS, NINA. WAS STRAPPED AFTER ALAN AND I BOUGHT THAT BOTTLE OF WINE.
NOT EVERY DAY A VINTAGE 2010 ALVAREZ-ALFARO COMES ALONG.
I HATE YOU.
CAN EVERYONE PLEASE STFU? TRYING TO CHECK THE WIRES HERE.

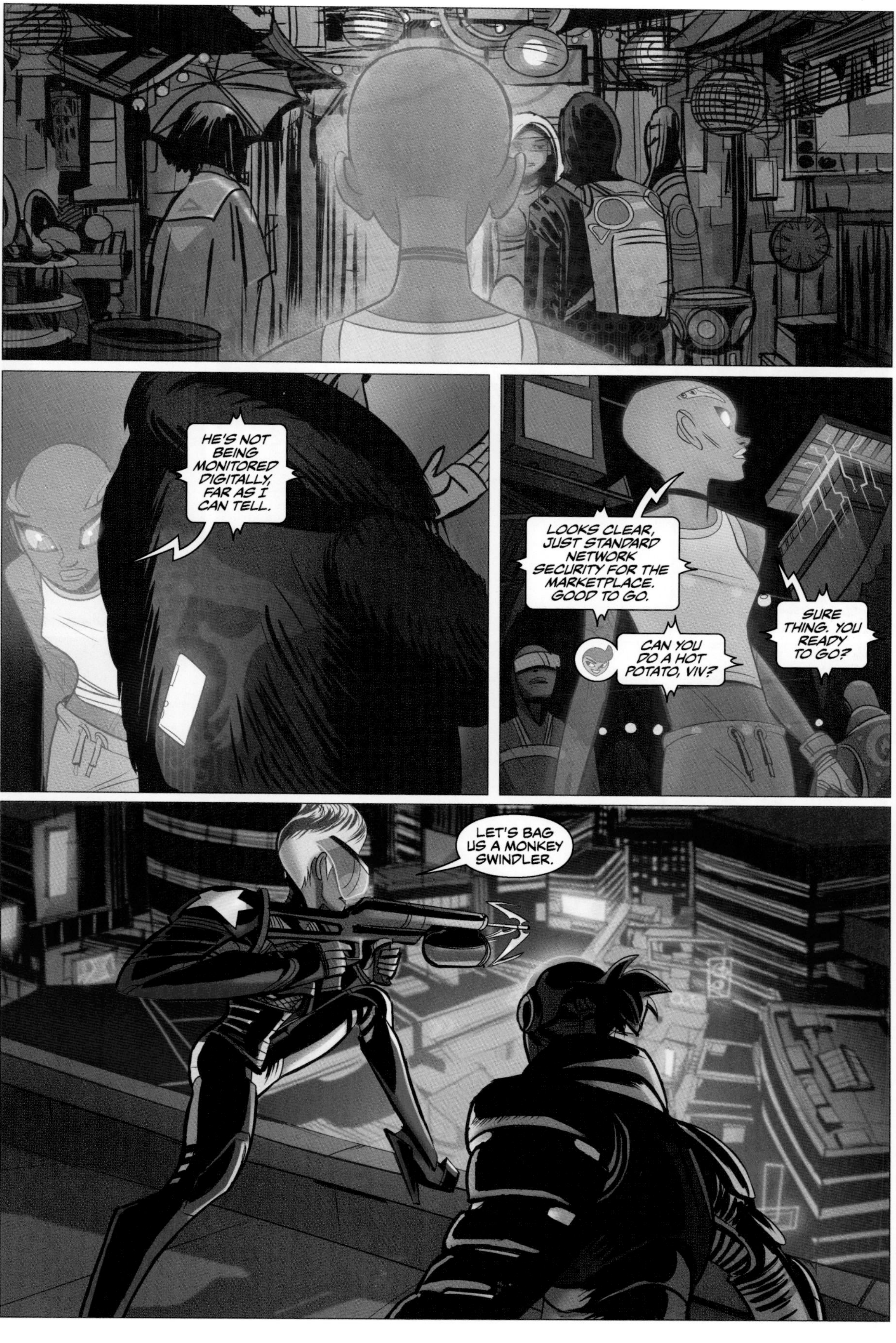
HE'S NOT BEING MONITORED DIGITALLY, FAR AS I CAN TELL.
LOOKS CLEAR, JUST STANDARD NETWORK SECURITY FOR THE MARKETPLACE. GOOD TO GO.
CAN YOU DO A HOT POTATO, VIV?
SURE THING. YOU READY TO GO?
LET'S BAG US A MONKEY SWINDLER.

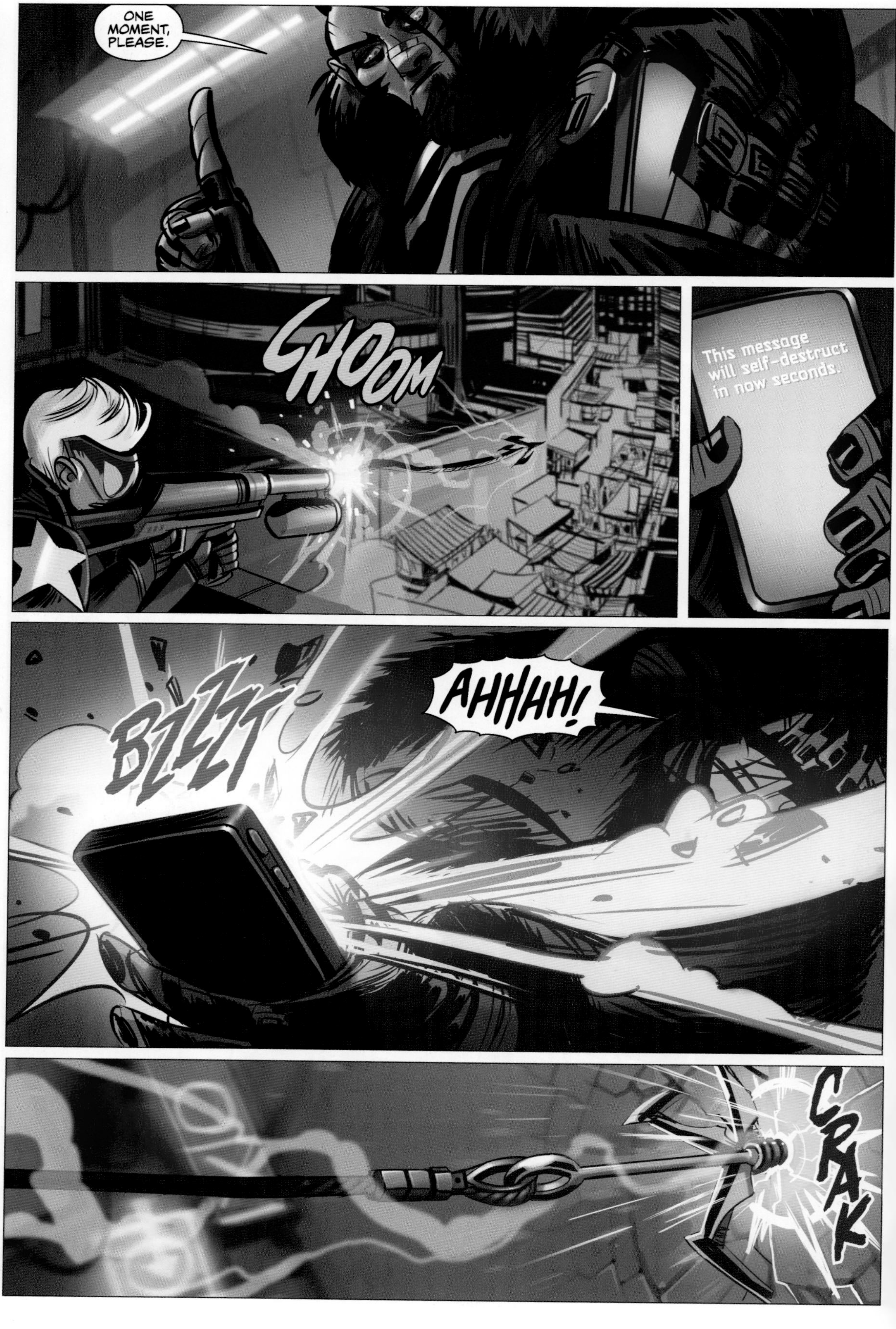
ONE MOMENT, PLEASE.
CHOOM
This message will self-destruct in now seconds.
BZZZT
AHHHH!
CRAK

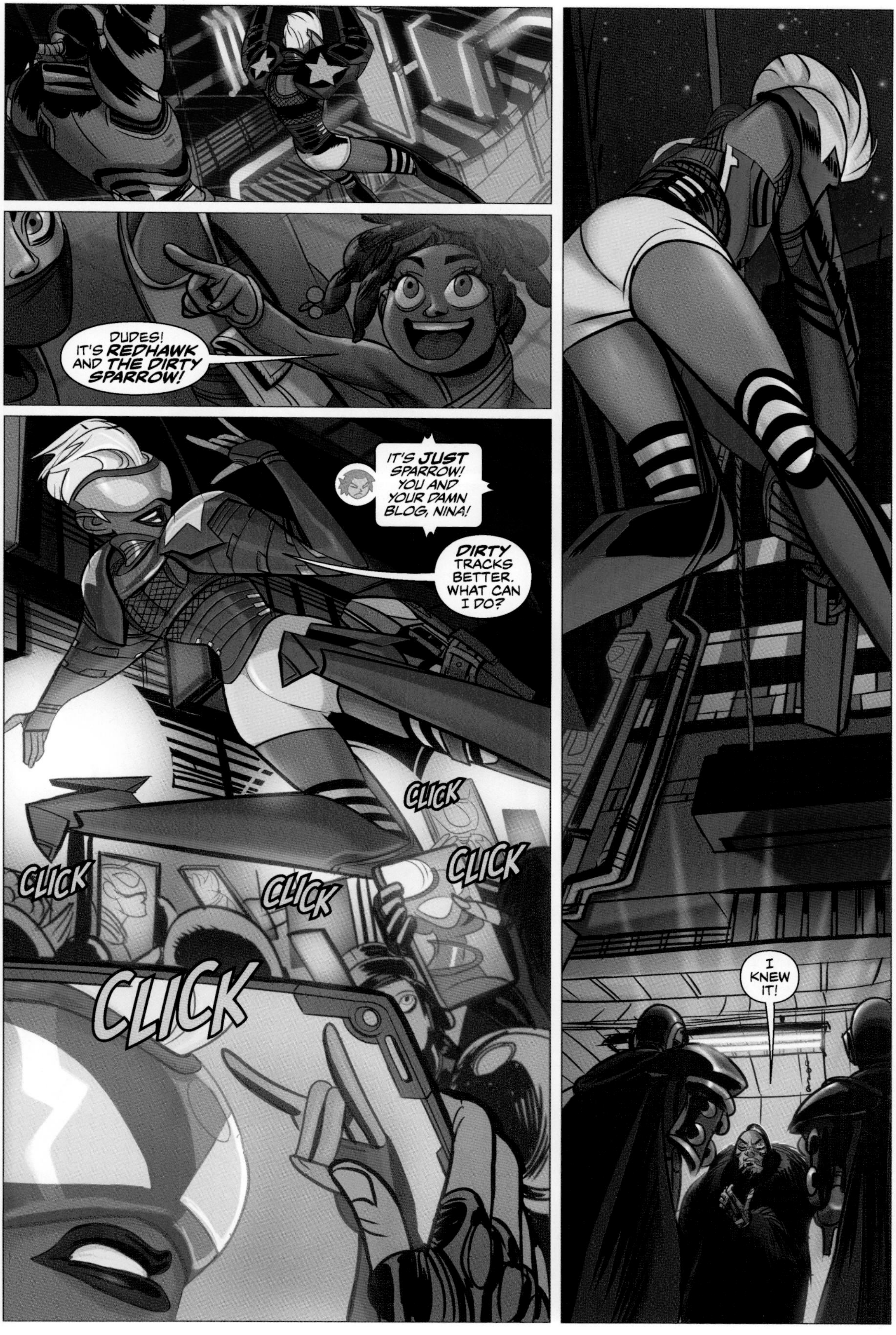
DUDES! IT'S REDHAWK AND THE DIRTY SPARROW!
IT'S JUST SPARROW! YOU AND YOUR DAMN BLOG, NINA!
DIRTY TRACKS BETTER. WHAT CAN I DO?
CLICK
CLICK
CLICK
CLICK
CLICK
I KNEW IT!

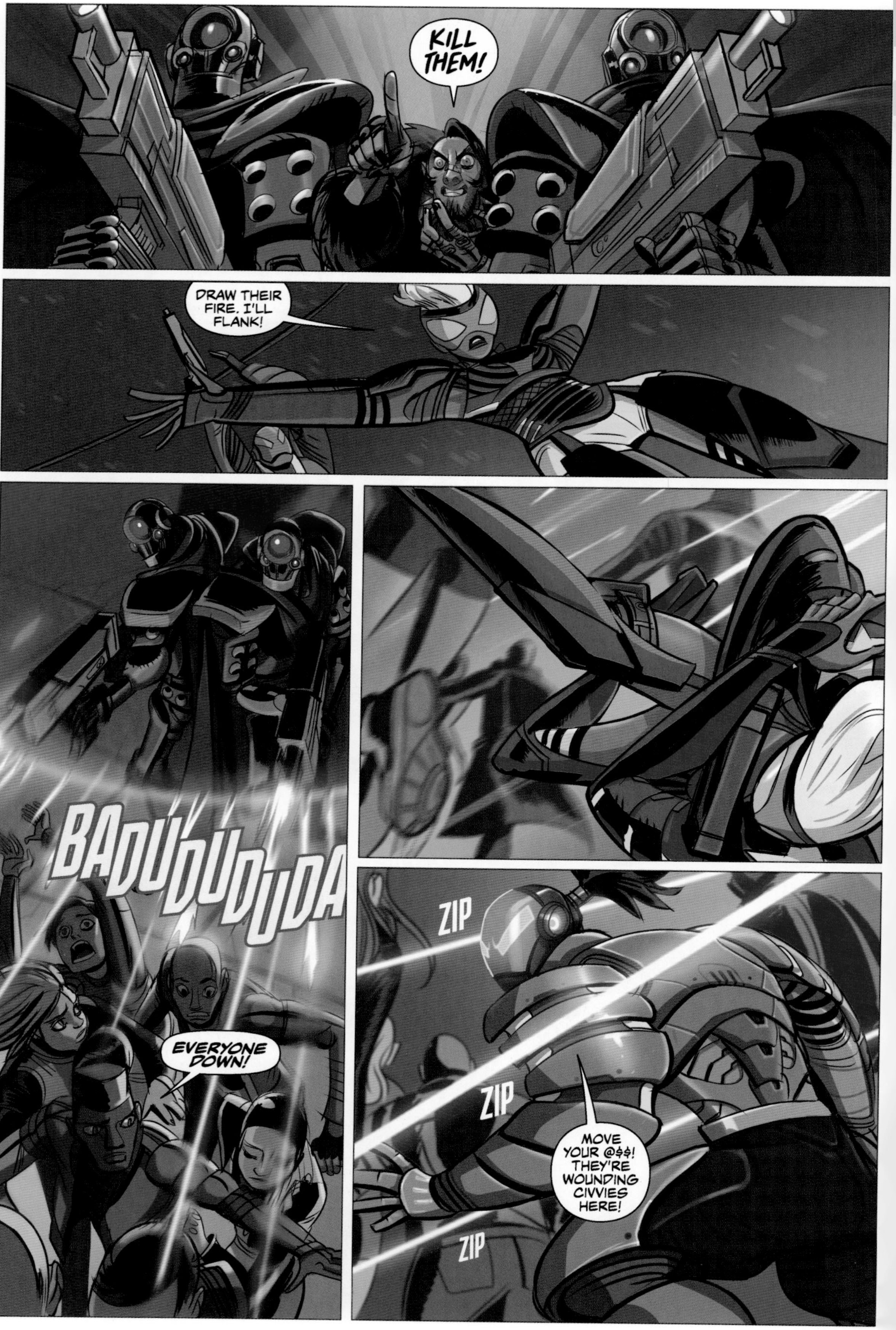
KILL THEM!
DRAW THEIR FIRE. I'LL FLANK!
BADUDUDUDUDA
EVERYONE DOWN!
ZIP
ZIP
ZIP
MOVE YOUR @$$! THEY'RE WOUNDING CIVVIES HERE!